Psychoanalytic Insights into Social, Political, and Organizational Dynamics

T0309263

This fascinating interdisciplinary work explores U.S. politics since 2015 and offers psychodynamic insights into the unconscious undercurrents of contemporary culture and politics in the United States.

Allcorn and Stein expertly lead readers up the steep learning curve of understanding the Trump era by exploring seven key elements of recent political dynamics. Using the complementary psychodynamic models of object relations, Group Relations, and Karen Horney's tripartite theory, this book makes sense of the Age of Trump and its chaotic world of alternate facts, conspiracy theories, reality TV politics, hoax pandemics, and the sweeping chaos of life in the United States. This sense-making relies on two triangulations. The first represents the complex systemic political scene. The second uses three psychoanalytic theories to understand social, political, and organizational dynamics. This book is a key resource for helping readers know and understand ourselves, our fellow citizens, colleagues, family, friends, and what Trump and his followers call "them" such as liberals and foreign immigrants, as well as both the larger polarized social and political context in the United States today. The book also provides concrete examples of how these discoveries can be operationalized both in organizations and at the level of national government and leadership.

This book is an essential reading for students in organizational behavior including leadership and how governments operate, as well as behavioral health professionals consulting or offering therapy to organizations.

Seth Allcorn is the former Vice President for Business and Finance at the University of New England in Biddeford, Maine. Dr. Allcorn has more than 20 years of experience working with physicians, hospitals and academic medical centers, and organizational consultant specializing in the management of change, strategic planning, and organizational restructuring. He is a founding member of the International Society for the Psychoanalytic Study of Organization.

Howard F. Stein is an organizational, applied, psychoanalytic, and medical anthropologist, psychohistorian, organizational consultant, and poet. He is Professor Emeritus of Family and Preventive Medicine at the University of Oklahoma Health Sciences Center in Oklahoma City, Oklahoma, where he taught for nearly 35 years. He facilitated the American Indian Diabetes Prevention Center's meetings from 2012 to 2017. He is a long-time member of the International Psychohistorical Association.

Psychoanalytic Insights into Social, Political, and Organizational Dynamics

Understanding the Age of Trump

Seth Allcorn and Howard F. Stein

Routledge
Taylor & Francis Group

NEW YORK AND LONDON

First published 2022
by Routledge
605 Third Avenue, New York, NY 10158

and by Routledge
2 Park Square, Milton Park, Abingdon, Oxon, OX14 4RN

Routledge is an imprint of the Taylor & Francis Group, an informa business

Library of Congress Cataloging-in-Publication Data
Names: Allcorn, Seth, author. | Stein, Howard F., author.
Title: Psychoanalytic insights into social, political, and
organizational dynamics : understanding the age of Trump / Seth
Allcorn and Howard F. Stein.
Description: New York, NY : Routledge, 2021. | Includes
bibliographical references and index. |
Identifiers: LCCN 2021006547 (print) | LCCN 2021006548
(ebook) | ISBN 9781032008479 (hbk) | ISBN 9781032005393 (pbk) |
ISBN 9781003176084 (ebk)
Subjects: LCSH: United States–Politics and government–21st
century. | Political culture–United States–History–21st century. |
Conspiracy theories–United States–History–21st century. | Trump,
Donald, 1946- | Fake news–United States–History–21st century.
Classification: LCC JK275 .A344 2021 (print) | LCC JK275
(ebook) | DDC 973.933–dc23
LC record available at https://lccn.loc.gov/2021006547
LC ebook record available at https://lccn.loc.gov/2021006548

ISBN: 978-1-032-00847-9 (hbk)
ISBN: 978-1-032-00539-3 (pbk)
ISBN: 978-1-003-17608-4 (ebk)

Typeset in Bembo
by KnowledgeWorks Global Ltd.

Contents

Figure

Foreword

This book was written at the close of the era of Trump. What we have been witnessing in the United States over the past four years cries out for understanding and explanation. Despite the fact that the Age of Trump didn't exist until 2016, there has been a huge amount written describing and at times explaining this phenomenon we are experiencing. Allcorn and Stein review much of this material in the course of presenting their account of the era of Trump with its many components and complexities.

Seth Allcorn and Howard Stein have been at this project for a while. Starting in the spring of 2017 and continuing through the summer of 2020, Seth and Howard, or Seth by himself, have published six separate papers in the *Journal of Psychohistory* seeking to understand and explore various aspects of the presidency of Donald Trump. They have used this material, along with a good deal of new material, to give us the most comprehensive account of the psychological, psychosocial, and psychohistorical aspects of the Trump era that has been written. The book is divided into three sections – Trump, his character, and his behavior; the relation between Trump the charismatic leader and his enthralled followers; and the ideologies they have expressed and have acted on. The aim of this book is to understand these three aspects of the Trump era and how they interact to produce what we are witnessing. There are clearly irrational processes at play in this situation. Psychoanalysis and psychoanalytic psychohistory are excellent tools to use for trying to understand what is transpiring in these strange times.

To aid in this task they make use of psychoanalytic theory. They use concepts and principles from three different psychoanalytic points of view with the goal of providing an orderly way of understanding the motives and processes of Trump and his followers. They use the work of Wilfred Bion and his understanding of group functioning; object relations theory chiefly based on the work of Melanie Klein and those who have followed her; and Karen Horney's work on the three defensive styles employed by individuals and groups to ward off or manage anxiety.

Both Allcorn and Stein have done a great deal of work as consultants to a variety of organizations and have written extensively about the psychological aspects of the behavior of organizations and those in them. They apply some of the insights they have developed in their consulting work to understanding the organizational psychological principles operative in the Trump regime and in his followers.

The authors start the book with an examination of Trump and his personality, chiefly the narcissistic aspects which so many who have written about him have drawn attention to. They then review some of the literature on autocracy as a form of government and authoritarianism as a style of leadership, and then discuss Trump's traits and behavior which can be characterized as manifestations of authoritarian methods of governing.

There follows an examination of the cult of Trump: the complex relationship between the leader and his followers. Making use of what is known about leadership in organizations they identify Trump as having a charismatic and paranoid leadership style. His closest followers are described as sycophants. Allcorn and Stein refer to Trump's leadership style as paranoid because he engages in the classic technique of paranoid leadership, first stoking fear – of Muslim terrorists, Mexican and Central American rapists, and drug dealers, Antifa, raging African American members of the Black Lives Matter movement, and of course, China. There are many enemies out there who wish to do us harm. Trump then presents himself as the protector and savior who will rescue his loyal followers from the many perils they are convinced are all around them. He strongly supports the Second Amendment, as he can be seen on the side of owning guns which are thought to be in the service of keeping people safe from the menaces that surround them.

The charismatic component of his leadership style is what makes him into a cult leader whose devoted followers adore him, believe everything he says, and are willing to do his bidding – as we saw at the nation's capitol on January 6, 2021, where the violent mob seemed to be under the influence of the hypnotic commands of their leader. What is perhaps most frightening is the apparently huge number of people who are in thrall to him. Sometimes referred to as Trump's army, they number perhaps as many as 30 or 40 million, a significant portion of the 74 million who voted for him in the 2020 election. These are the core members of what is usually called his base. Whatever their precise numbers, there are more than enough of them to form voting majorities in many states and to elect candidates who are pledged to remain loyal to their leader. More than by a specific set of beliefs or policy positions, they are united as a tribe – and what unites them into this tribe is their faith in their leader. They are his people.

Perhaps the strangest aspect of this cultic enactment is the reality testing issue. So many of the assertions and beliefs that form the common core that Trump and his followers adhere to are either factually incorrect and/ or frankly delusional – as in firmly believing, believing strongly enough to take action based on these beliefs in things that are not true, as well as not believing things that are. This has been the case throughout Trump's regime, from being convinced that we are being overwhelmed by Sharia Law-bringing Muslims, that Central American rapists are coming to get us, that the coronavirus doesn't exist, or it's not serious, or that the number of deaths due to COVID-19 are vastly inflated because doctors make more money doing so, to the final and certainly one of the most delusional, that Trump won the November 2020 election. These are some of the specific beliefs that exist along with the more general conviction that the world is controlled and run by powerful people and organizations that, unlike their belief about Trump, they think do not care about what happens to them, the real Americans.

It would not be unreasonable to label this as a mass psychosis. Not being able to distinguish between what is real and what isn't, along with holding delusional beliefs that are impervious to being changed no matter how much contradictory evidence may exist, are the two major cognitive attributes of psychotic behavior.

Allcorn and Stein present the case for seeing much of the acts and processes that characterize the Age of Trump as created by the melding of the leader and his followers, each influencing and reinforcing the other. They point out that in many ways Trump is an empty vessel which gets filled by the wishes and fears of his followers. He becomes their spokesperson. They then identify with him. He becomes the embodiment of all that they value and wish for. What he says is what they believe, a manifestation of their own wishes that they have projected onto and placed within him.

This is followed by an analysis of the role that right-wing ideologies have played in the Age of Trump. Trump has at best allowed, and at worst promoted, several right-wing tropes that have been present in this country long before Trump appeared on the scene and will remain when he's gone. White supremacy, xenophobia, and paranoid fear and hatred of those enemy others – the deep state, George Soros, Bill Gates, the elites, and the swamp dwellers will remain. These enemy others have replaced and serve the same function as the communist menace did throughout the Cold War for the same cohort of right-wingers, such as the members of the John Birch Society, and the supporters of McCarthyism and the Vietnam War, who were engaged in battling the forces of godless communism, both foreign and domestic.

The final section of the book focuses on Trump's loyal followers, their beliefs, and their embracing the creation of and adherence to a culture of grievance, racism, and white supremacy, and a frankly paranoid view of the world as filled with others who wish to do them harm.

The ferocity of right-wing violence-prone elements of the American populace is not something new in the history of this country. We have had the Civil War, a violent insurrection fought for the cause of white supremacy, the open Klan marches and violence inflicted on African Americans, the lynchings, the violent racist riots, that have occurred in this country. Trump and his army are just the latest iteration. But it does remind us that despite all our rhetoric about democracy, we are certainly capable of coming under the influence of a homegrown fascism.

The project that Allcorn and Stein are engaged in here is vital. To understand what is happening in this extremely polarized, tribal political climate is essential if we are to have any hope of dealing effectively with our current situation in the immediate aftermath of the Trump presidency. It is also a project that may yield knowledge that might help to prevent there being another Trump-like regime in our future.

David Lotto
Psychoanalyst in practice in Pittsfield, Massachusetts;
Editor of the Journal of Psychohistory

Preface

Writing a book about the Age of Trump in 2020 may give the appearance of polishing the brass on the *Titanic* where dramatic events unfolded rapidly because of poor judgment by the captain and crew. But the band plays on. There is a sense of writer anxiety writing about the present that immediately becomes the past juxtaposed to the daily chaos of what is about to come. There was mentioned in the media for 9/11 and the twin towers that there was a "failure of imagination" that left a "hole in the sky." Writing this book has been evolving since 2017 one paper at a time and from one topic at a time that pried its way into our consciousness. Our lived experience is captured in this book and perhaps yours.

These papers and others scattered across the years became the framework of this book. The past that the papers represent remains very present today and will reverberate for many years to come. The dynamics of what some may say is the former Republican Party may lead to it being "born again." The Lincoln Project and similar conservative groups hope to destroy Trumpism, sweep out the elected "Republican" sycophants and plant new seed with new thoughts and approaches for engaging the lives of Americans. With these appreciations in mind, we believe the chapters in this book contribute to a collective *learning curve* of the psychosocial nature of the Age of Trump. Although we have updated the book for the November 2020 election results, the significance of the age the Age of Trump and accompanying chaos, will assuredly be a presence for many years to come. We also wish to acknowledge, as we prepare to submit this manuscript, the January 6, 2021 MAGA invasion of the capitol that has broken America again in the eyes of the world. This event is an outcome of the many interrelationships discussed in this book and will no doubt become the subject of many books to come.

Our use of a "Learning Curve" speaks to *two* aspects of our work overtime that, when taken together, became the inspiration for this book. Together they contribute to a reconstructed memory and an analysis of our shared lived experience of often toxic events, changes, and moments in our recent history but also spanning many decades.

The first aspect of our learning curve speaks to how over time our work on the papers revealed themes, patterns, and an overall coherent psycho-dynamically informed cultural and historical image. Our perspective in this book may be visualized as a person standing in a crop field surrounded by the plants. There is much detail to behold. At the same time, if we were in an airplane flying over the field, we might see that it is a large rectangle or perhaps a crop circle. This imagery illustrates that the learning process metaphorically has one foot in the field and one foot in the airplane. To make as much sense as possible of what our lived experience of the Age of Trump is, we must wisely examine recent times in a detailed manner but also from a much larger historical and cultural perspective.

Learning curves represent a virtuous, upward spiral that arises from learning-from-experience. Over time more is observed, analyzed, processed, and made sense of creating learning, insight, and understanding. Our learning curve amounts to a longitudinal sense making of the chaos that is the Age of Trump. The chapters of this book link together time and psychosocial awareness of events that initially attracted our attention to write the papers.

This book also links together much of the writing of the authors across decades. There is in a larger sense a continuum of exploring, learning, and sense making dating back for us to the 1980s. There has been an evolution in our attention to events, our thoughts about what we observed and our sense making of these observations. We gradually learned to make better sense of our observations and experience.

This book builds forward from what has been learned by raising for inspection the harmful downward spiral that, at the present, seems to consume most of the political national culture. Rigid adherence to ideology drives what seems to be a void absent of a learning curve. Ideologies such as small government and individual freedoms, low taxes, and deregulation are often solutions that compound the problems the United States and other nations and societies face. A failure of national leadership that adhered to the small-government ideology has made the SARS-CoV-2 pandemic in the United States a "terminal" event for hundreds of thousands of people.

These ideologies often become the problem creating a failure-to-learn from experience, as symbolized by the mythic snake Ouroboros, that folds back upon itself where the solution creates problems and the solution is the problem, but the solution is also the ideology. This dynamic may be visualizable as an unreflective repetition that creates a downward and destructive spiral. Ideological solutions both compound "the problem" and become the problem as symbolized by a national response of the federal government that showed little leadership but introduced life-threatening disinformation into the handling of the U.S. COVID-19 epidemic. It became the responsibility of the states to individually and regrettably separately respond to a nation-wide epidemic.

The second aspect of our sense making effort that uses three complementary, but also different psychoanalytic theories has evolved across
time. We have learned that there is wisdom in using multiple theoretical perspectives to understand social, political, and organizational
dynamics.

Object relations theories offer many helpful ways to understand human
behavior individually, interpersonally, in groups, in organizations, and at
the level of societies.[1] We have also found Group Relations theorizing
offers complementary insights to better understand the role of unconscious
dynamics in groups.[2] Karen Horney's theorizing offers a third accessible and intuitive perspective that directs our attention of the unconscious
dynamics involved in moving against, toward, and away from others.[3] We
have learned that the three theories together offer different but compatible insights.[4,5] This once again speaks a learning curve on our part, and
we hope yours in terms of how these theories may be used to understand
the psychosocial nature of life in present day America.

Our sense making of the Age of Trump embraces the chaotic nature
of lived experience during the era by paying attention to unconscious
dynamics and by doing so it reveals dimensions of the Age of Trump
that other qualitative and quantitative methods do not. Psychoanalytic
theory provides a depth psychological understanding of individual and
group dynamics that other psychologically oriented and often socio-
logical perspectives lack. Much the same can be said of quantitative
methods.

Quantitative methods such as surveys and polling often suggest what
may be present in a group or society but often fall short of explaining *why*
it is there. What are the underlying group dynamics? These are left most
often to speculation. In contrast, the three psychoanalytically informed
perspectives used here offer depth psychological insights that substantially
differ from other methods. They reveal insights into human nature and
group dynamics that provide understanding and promote reflectivity, dis-
covery, and learning.

Our two learning curves conceptually combine in a double helix
much like DNA. Together they create something more than the sum
of their parts – a way of trying to understand and make sense of life,
and more specifically the complex tree-like branching resident in polit-
ical/social events in the second decade of the twenty-first century and
beyond. These complexities are embraced in our use of triangulations
for sense making that bring together the many diverse elements of the
Age of Trump that are usually considered separately and often as discrete phenomena. This complexity is then made sense of through insight
building that relies on the use of triangulated psychanalytically informed
perspectives.

In Conclusion

The abundance of books and essays that have already been written that attempt to "explain" Trump and his appeal, raise the question, what further insight could another book add? In this book, we uniquely address the dizzying complexity of this era. We bring to bear history, culture, economics, politics, organizational analysis, group process, and psychodynamics to attempt to "get our arms around" this complexity. That is why our metaphor of the planted field is apt and offers the reader an alternating closeness and distance that is needed to understand and explain the Age of Trump.

Our learning curve over the course of this book is far from complete – not only for us authors, but we hope, also for you, our readers. The Age of Trump and its meaning for American society will be unfinished work for many decades to come. We hope our efforts here have contributed in some measure to our shared learning curve.

Notes

1. Some of the books used to discuss object relations are:
   Grotstein, J. (1985). *Splitting and projective identification.* Northvale, NJ: Jason Aronson.
   Greenberg J. & Mitchell, S. (1983). *Object relations in psychoanalytic theory.* Cambridge, MA: Harvard University Press.
   Scharff, J. (1992). *Projective and introjective identification and the use of the therapist's self.* Northvale, NJ: Jason Aronson.
   Tansey, M. & Burke, W. (1989). *Understanding countertransference.* Hillsdale, NJ: The Analytic Press.
2. Bion, W. (1961). *Experience in groups.* London: Tavistock.
3. Horney, K. (1950). *Neurosis and human growth.* New York, NY: Norton.
4. Allcorn, S. & Stein, H. (2015). *The dysfunctional workplace: Theory, stories, and practice.* Columbia, MO: University of Missouri Press.
5. Stein, H. & Allcorn, S. (2020). *The psychodynamics of toxic organizations: Applied poems, stories, and analysis.* New York, NY: Routledge.

Acknowledgments

In a book, *acknowledgments* mean that we did not do it all ourselves – and that we openly recognize our indebtedness and our gratitude.

We wish to acknowledge with gratitude the many decades of our friendship and fruitful collaboration with Dr. Michael Diamond, a leader in the field of applying psychoanalytic perspectives to workplace organizational identity and change, and its dynamics in the larger psycho-political domain.

Our many years of association with members of the International Society for the Psychoanalytic Study of Organizations has made many contributions to our research and writing. This community of shared interest has been invaluable. We also wish to acknowledge Dr. Carrie Duncan's contributions to our mutually coauthored papers as well as her leadership in developing the Center for Psychosocial Organization Studies.

We both wish to thank Dr. David Lotto, psychoanalyst, and Editor of *The Journal of Psychohistory*. Dr. Lotto has championed our work and published many of our papers in his journal. He also offered meticulous editorial suggestions for our papers and for our book-length-manuscript which Routledge published in 2020: *The Psychodynamics of Toxic Organizations: Poetry, Stories, and Analysis*. We also want to acknowledge the fine editing and support of Susan Hein at the journal. Together David and Susan have inspired our writing by providing a creative space for us to imagine.

Howard wishes to acknowledge with gratitude his long membership and participation in conferences/retreats of the High Plains Society for Applied Anthropology, and The International Psychohistorical Association. Both organizations have provided opportunities for him to make presentations on topics Seth and Howard published in previous papers, and now in this book.

Research and writing are ultimately a solitary endeavor that, in our cases, has been grounded by the presence and comfort of two *cats*, now deceased, but inseparable from the creation of this book and many others. Far from being "pets," they were feline persons, almost always with us, whether we were sitting at our computers at a desk or in a chair with pen and pad of paper in hand. Lt. Savik and Luke remain with us, even as we keenly feel their absence. They were a true blessing.

We also wish to thank the team at Routledge for their capable work in bringing this book to final publication. Thanks.

Seth Allcorn and Howard Stein
December 2020

Permissions

The *Journal of Psychohistory* has generously provided permission to use in full or in part content from the following published articles.

Stein, H. & Allcorn, S. (2010). The Unreality of American Deregulation. *The Journal of Psychohistory* 38(1): 27–48.

Stein, H. & Allcorn, S. (2015). To Look or Not to Look: The Backward Engineering of Atrocity. *The Journal of Psychohistory* 43(2): 78–88.

Allcorn, S. & Stein, H. (2017a). The Post-Factual World of the 2016 American Presidential Election: The Good, the Bad, and the Deplorable. *The Journal of Psychohistory* 44(4): 310–318.

Allcorn, S. & Stein, H. (2017b). The Politics of Shame. *The Journal of Psychohistory* 45(2): 78–93.

Stein, H. & Allcorn, S. (2018). A Fateful Convergence: Animosity toward Obamacare, Hatred of Obama, the Rise of Donald Trump, and Overt Racism in America. *The Journal of Psychohistory* 45(4): 234–242.

Allcorn, S. & Stein, H. (2018). Donald Trump: Empty Vessel and Sum of All Projections. *The Journal of Psychohistory* 44(1): 3–16.

Allcorn, S. & Stein, H. (2019). Ideology, Bureaucracy, Hierarchy, and Human Nature in Psychohistory. *The Journal of Psychohistory* 47(3): 168–187.

Allcorn, S. (2020a). Sentience in Contemporary Conservative American Politics. *The Journal of Psychohistory* 47(4): 275–292.

Allcorn, S. (2020b). Cultures of Grievance: Creating Polarization from Chosen Traumas. *The Journal of Psychohistory* 48(1): 23–40.

Allcorn, S. (2021). White Supremacy and the Pursuit of Power. *The Journal of Psychohistory* 48 (4): 279–89.

1 Introduction

This is a book about recent times (2015–2020). To begin we must acknowledge that there are countless explanations and theories that attempt to account for Trump, his followers, his relationship with them, and his self-labeled Age of Trump. Given this rich buffet of often competing attempts to explain all this, our approach, which uses a triangulation-within-triangulation approach (Figure 1.1), requires a systemic examination of the relatedness of the many political and psychosocial elements of this period. This in-depth perspective offers the possibility of making sense of the many relationships within the complex milieu of the Age of Trump.

This book is about the triangulation of Trump, his narcissism, and his autocratic behavior relative to a second set of triangulated elements: his followers, his loyal sycophantic enablers, and his adherence to far-right ideological perspectives. We find that Trump is a narcissist[1] and an autocrat – a would-be dictator like those he admires around the world.[2,3] This tendency to be an autocrat and authoritarian follows from his experience as a developer who is in absolute control of his privately owned company and brand along with the banks and private investors that finance his projects. He can do what he wants, when he wants, how he wants, and with whom he desires including throwing anyone he chooses under the metaphoric bus – "You're fired." It is also the case that Trump is supported by loyal followers who are not offended by the idea of him shooting someone on a street in downtown New York City or for that matter separating infants and children from their mothers and parents and placing them in cages. These actions are intended to "signal" you are not welcome here. Trump's actions are enabled by those who work directly and indirectly for him (submit to his authority) who formulate means and methods to implement his decisions which are informed by far-right ideologies and the desire to bond with special interest groups.

Our contribution to making sense of all of this, the triangulation, has as its central focus the political context in which the elements of the triangles arise. We first provide an overview of this context before briefly exploring

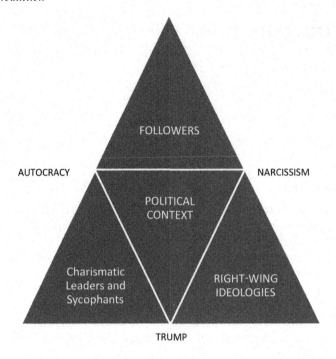

Figure 1.1 Triangulation of the Age of Trump

the six elements of the triangulation discussed throughout this book and provide a chapter-by-chapter overview of the book.

The Political Context

Anyone trying to provide a comprehensive overview of the social and political events during the last half of the second decade of the twenty-first century is on a fool's errand in that the sheer volume of lies, chaos, dysfunction, and toxicity will no doubt keep historians occupied for decades to come. To be expected will be the emergence of a fact-based narrative that is rejected by the right which will generate its own counter-narrative to justify its ideology and actions in defense of Trump. This inevitability underscores the political and social polarization present today.[4] We here humbly touch upon only some of the contextual elements to ground our use of the triangulation approach to sensemaking.

Ideological Rigidity

The Republican brand, the Grand Old Party (GOP), has been subjected to what some term a hostile takeover becoming what is now sometimes referred to as the Party of Trump (POT). Some conservative thought leaders of the past have dropped their membership in the GOP (registering as independents), and while remaining conservatives, they are now sometimes referred to as Never-Trumpers and perhaps participate in the anti-Trump Lincoln Project or similar groups that opposed Trump's reelection.

The groundwork for this outcome was laid in the reaction on the right to Barak Obama's election as president. This led to an immediate meeting by the GOP leaders to limit and undermine President Obama (Hell No!) hopefully reducing him to a one-term presidency as Mitch McConnell declared.

One major outcome of the response to Obama's election was the rise of the Tea Party, the emergence of Libertarianism, and the eventual creation of the Freedom Caucus. The Tea Party members advocate for a rigid adherence to political ideology on the right emphasizing libertarian principles such as minimal government intervention into the functioning of society and the lives of citizens. Illustrative of this is a 2010 Rand Paul interview with Rachel Maddow where he said he would have tried to change Title II of the Civil Rights Act that legally prohibits private businesses from racial discrimination, for example restaurants, because it violates the first amendment although he himself would not recommend discrimination. Ronald Reagan's go-to sound bite was that the government is not the solution; it is the problem that was operationalized as deregulation that helped to create the need for a massive savings and loan bailout under Reagan and an even more massive financial system bailout under the Bush/Cheney administration.[5]

The rigid and preferably unquestioned adherence to an ideology streamlines thinking providing a basis for mottos and sound bites and seduces adherents into believing it is the answer to all problems such as tax cuts as a universal cure-all. Ideologies are sometimes said to be a solution in search of a problem. They are at the minimum a method of unifying believers (brand identification) to pursue a cause which at an extreme can create social and political polarization and chaos. "We are right. You are wrong."

Brand Loyalty

Red state versus blue state, left versus right, urban versus rural, black versus white, old versus young, religious and less so, and special interest wedge issues that split the electorate such as pro-life versus pro-choice are examples where these social and political divisions create the basis for a concept like brand loyalty. These are some of the more notable realities of the contemporary political context.

Ideological purity is in some sense the brand of the Freedom Caucus and the Tea Party that was at one time referred to as neo-confederate having arisen in the southern states. Today the Republican Party is composed of the right and far-right libertarians and Trump loyalists. They have led the effort to move what is sometimes referred to as the former Republican Party further and further to the right while rejecting some former ideological boilerplate such as free trade. Politicians who would normally be considered mainstream conservatives (speakers of the house John Boehner and Paul Ryan and House Majority Leader Eric Cantor) as well as many conservative thought leaders such as George Will, Bill Kristol, Joe Scarborough, and Max Boot moved aside, opted out of the party, or were defeated in primaries.[6] The Tea Party, Trump, and the far-right, consistent with conservative ideology and values, strive to limit the size of the federal government, reduce regulation, cut government spending, and lower the national debt while opposing tax increases, excluding immigrants, and opposing abortion and gay marriage. Social programs and safety nets remain under attack as do foreign entanglements and participation in the United Nations and World Health Organization (WHO). To be noted these directions of movement are currently being pursued more energetically. However, also to be noted, many of the actions of the "right" today do not necessarily fit with what was formally thought of as traditional conservative values such as the use of tariffs versus free trade.

In sum the remarkably high approval ratings Trump has among those who identify as Republicans and with him is noteworthy in terms of the Trump brand appeal for this segment of voters. This branding and self-promotion are pursued by putting his name on everything from buildings, airplanes, products, and books to letters announcing government payouts to people during the pandemic recession.

Mobilized and Organized Special Interest Groups

The emergence of special interest groups left and right is an important feature in American politics (see www.hud.gov for a list of special interest groups). Groups like the Sierra Club and the National Rifle Association are prominent examples and at a more fundamental level so are what might be thought of as on the right movements opposed to: abortion (Americans United for Life, National Right to Life Committee); anti-LGBTQ (American Family Association, Liberty Counsel); and immigration framed as pro-white nationalism (Center for Immigration Studies, Federation for American Immigration Reform). These groups appear to be mobilized around fears of losing guns, degradation of marriage between a man and a woman, and being displaced by black and brown races which was a theme of the torchlight parade in Charlottesville 2017 that included neo-Nazis and opposition to Jews.

Fear is an organizing principle for these groups with the fearful and dependent seeking leaders to save them by delivering them security and safety and protecting their ideologies, values, and systems of belief.

A second organizer that these groups often share among their members and among similar groups is a sense of grievance that they are dismissed, looked down on, and considered to be uneducated and uninformed by "liberals," a word hurled as an insult. These grievances and the accompanying anger, discussed in Chapter 13, have been held for decades. They have been mobilized by Trump who promises to and often does pursue their interests in return for their loyalty to him.

Fear, anger, and grievance, it may be appreciated, form part of the foundation of the social and political polarization so visible today as the United States moves into the third decade of the twenty-first century. Polarization is our fourth and last foundational perspective for describing the political context in Figure 1.1.

Polarization in the United States

Steven Levitsky and Daniel Ziblatt in their book *How Democracies Die*[4] suggest democracies that die do so quietly. They slowly almost out of awareness decline. They also point out that this vulnerability is being exploited today by would-be autocrats who understand democracy can be used against itself.[7] They do not have to dislodge, defeat, or revolt against democracy; all they need to do is slowly co-opt it by compromising the information available to voters (propaganda), limiting those who can vote, removing or limiting rivals by any means available, manipulating the media and voting to get representatives that support them elected, and packing the judicial system with their appointees creating a loss of accountability.

These dynamics in the United States are fueled by fissures in our society, and anger and fear toward anyone who is not like "us" or does not agree with "us." These fissures promote intolerance and hostility about many aspects of American society and governance at the national, state, and local levels.[8] These fissures are not new. They have, however, been exploited to political advantage by Trump where his followers (voters) are highly motivated to protect, to the exclusion of other points of view, their interests, and often single-issue interests.

Alienation plays an important role in creating polarization. Alienation speaks to feeling cut off from oneself, others, organizations, communities, and even one's countries ("take my country back" is a common phrase). These feelings of being isolated and alone are especially profound when they pertain to what one holds as cherished values and beliefs. Many people especially in rural areas feel as though they are strangers in their own land.[9] They feel marginalized and that their views about abortion, gay marriage, race, and guns are ridiculed by the national media.

This is made even more possible by corporate-controlled news and social networking media that is being exploited to create polarization for profit.[10] Hate, anger, and fear are being mobilized on the right (to a lesser extent on the left) in the service of furthering the embrace of an ideology and an autocratic leader who said, "Only I can save you."

There has developed a breakdown of mutual toleration where respect for the political legitimacy of the opposition has been lost. The opposing side, progressives, and liberals are the enemy to be guarded against and preferably vanquished. There exists concern now (Fall 2020) that the results of a "fair" election will not perhaps be possible and the results not honored. This is underscored by a 2014 Pew Research study (pewresearch.org). The study found that the distrust that the Republicans and Democrats in Congress hold for each other is a mirror of our society. Liberals and conservatives live near their fellow partisans with whom they agree, and they are unhappy if their children marry someone with a different political viewpoint. This has the outcome of creating a divided society where liberals and conservatives prefer to live apart. Those with the strongest opinions are also the most motivated to vote in primaries and general elections furthering the politics of polarization.[11]

These elements of the current political context create an important framing for this book. We regret having to limit the scope of our analysis but clearly this is necessary given the vastness of the chaos, dysfunction, and toxicity that is "our" collective reality not to mention the 2020 pandemic and the demonstrations protesting racist policing and systemic and institutionalized racism.

The Six Elements

Figure 1.1 sets forth an analytical framework that captures the systemic complexity resident in understanding the social and political context of the Age of Trump in depth. The inner triangle helps to frame our understanding of Donald Trump as a person with a history, his narcissistic personal attributes, and his propensity to identify with strong and powerful autocratic leadership that may eventually compromise democracy in the United States. Part I discusses each of these three points in separate chapters that illuminate the psychosocial dynamics of the complexity by using the three psychodynamically informed perspectives (Chapter 2).

The larger triangle suggests Trump, as a person and narcissistically inclined charismatic autocratic leader who seduces followers to follow him or bends people to his will to fulfill right-wing ideologies, can only be understood by exploring these complex interrelationships. Parts II, III, and IV are devoted to an in-depth exploration of the complex relationships between leaders, followers, and ideologies using the three psychodynamically informed perspectives.

The Psychodynamic Perspectives

Our focus is to not only capture the content of the context but also analyze and interpret it using three psychoanalytic theories (also a triangulation) to explore the undiscussable, out of awareness, and unconscious creation of and polarized "us versus them" political and social context. These social and political as well as ideological dynamics can be studied from any number of perspectives. The contribution made in this book is to explore how psychological defenses such as denial, splitting, and projection; Group Relations perspectives; and Karen Horney's directions of movement contribute to understanding the polarization and the divergent realities that now exist.[12] Where did this context and conflict of realities come from? How is it so readily maintained? Where is it headed?

We now turn to describing how this book is organized providing a sense of direction that is in large part a product of our learning curve where we have over a number of years written papers exploring various aspects of the current political and social context. Not only were we working through the complex elements of our current political and social context, but we were also experiencing a learning curve in terms of locating psychoanalytic theory that was helpful to our gaining greater insights and learning to apply it in practice.

Book Organization

Chapter 1: Introduction

The introduction to this book in this chapter highlights the use of our approach of triangulating Trump, his narcissism, and his autocratic behavior relative to a second set of triangulated elements: his followers, his loyal sycophants, and his advocacy for far-right ideological perspectives. This approach we hope offers readers new conceptual dots to connect yielding new insights and respect for the complexity involved in understanding governments and their leaders who may pursue a vision that benefits everyone or a vision that divides the citizens against each other yielding the current state of polarization in the United States.

Chapter 2: Introduction to Psychoanalytic Theory in Making Sense of the Age of Trump

Psychoanalytic theory has a lot to contribute toward understanding human behavior and the behavior of individuals who hold positions of immense power and control including the role of the president of the United States. Our introduction to the three psychoanalytically informed perspectives that we use – Object Relations, Group Relations, and Karen Horney's tripartite theory – makes accessible what can become abstract discussions of theory somewhat detached from how it may be applied in practice. We provide concrete examples of how the use of the three perspectives can be operationalized both in organizations and at the level of national government and leadership.

Part I: Trump the Man, the President

Chapter 3: Overview of Trump's Business and Political History

This chapter provides historical perspective on Trump himself and connects the dots, so to speak, between many strands of the organizational, cultural, political, and historical story that explain Trump's successes, failures and bankruptcies, and the relentless effort by Republicans and the right to repeal the Affordable Care Act (ACA). We link this persistent battle to the widespread hatred of President Obama, the Republican Party's determination to obstruct Obama's legislative initiatives, the rise of Donald Trump, the emergence of open racism (birtherism), and the successful effort to further split the country creating social and political polarization.

Chapter 4: Narcissism

Trump's narcissism mirrors the narcissistic injuries and grievances of his followers. He, like them, is aggrieved and enraged about it as illustrated by his constant disregard for public civility (termed derogatorily as political correctness), denigration of liberal elites, and criticism of himself as "fake news" and fake science. News that does not match his narrative of grievance must be neutralized.

Trump identifies with and exploits the dark, raw emotions of a large group of Americans who feel their values and desires are disregarded by the political establishment and often looked down on by political elites – liberals. This has surfaced and authorized a very real sense of narcissistic rage, hatred, envy, and fear of a disappearing white middle and underclass who have lost the promise of a brighter future for themselves. These dynamics are accompanied by the shameless pursuit of and use of power not only by Trump but also Republican politicians. Shame also is an aspect of far-right economically oriented strivings that require reducing government involvement in commerce and daily life (safety nets) including deregulation of banks and the environment. These dynamics can be better understood by using the three triangulated psychodynamically informed perspectives.

Chapter 5: Autocracy

Autocracy as a word encompasses those who use threatening and bullying tactics as well as lawbreaking to govern. Authoritarians and authoritarianism are closely allied with autocracy and are often used to describe Trump and the right and far right including in other countries, such as Russia, China, Brazil, Poland, and Hungary. Autocrats who eliminate all opposition can be said to "live by the sword" and rightly fear dying by the sword. This fear on the part of a leader who sees in others his or her own autocratic and authoritarian tendencies leads to the necessity of creating a loyal, admiring, and preferably unquestioning cadre of followers and sycophants. This dynamic is enabled by propaganda that promotes fear and dependence on this leader as a savior and most recently the creation of two realities driven by a post-factual world of for-profit media.

Part II: Charismatic Leaders and Their Sycophants

Chapter 6: Charismatic Leaders

The charismatic leader offers followers an individual who is bigger than life thereby becoming a target for idealizing splitting and projection that magnifies the leader while diminishing followers. This magnified individual thus becomes seductive. These leaders often rely on a pattern of motivation based on fear. They continually locate evil others such as terrorists and immigrants, liberals, competitors and threats to stockholder value, international aggressors, and legal threats aimed at, for example, limiting the number and types of guns that may be owned. The promotion of fear by identifying many threats and enemies is discussed from the perspective of paranoia and more specifically paranoid charismatic leadership.

Chapter 7: Sycophants and Their Charismatic Leader

Most attempts to understand and explain Donald Trump have focused on his personal characteristics and traits. The crucial role of Trump's followers in the creation and sustaining of Donald Trump are often overlooked. The mirroring process between Trump as leader and his loyal followers can be better understood from the role projective and introjective identification play in this dynamic. The critical role of Fox News in intensifying this mirroring and group polarization must also be appreciated. The dynamics of the triangulation of Trump, Fox News, and Trump's followers are critical to understanding 2015–2020.

Chapter 8: The Reality of Chaotic Leadership

Trump as a paranoid charismatic and autocratic leader sees enemies, resistance, and disloyalty everywhere (the "deep state" for example). There is a real sense of paranoia that many people, organizations, and forces are out to get him which resonates with his voter base that feels much the same. They are all victims and aggrieved. Trump has proven willing, especially since his failed impeachment, to fire, force out, and otherwise replace anyone who is not loyal to him more so than to the constitution or country. Everyone in the executive branch of the U.S. government is at risk. To be appreciated is that the more anxious he becomes when confronted with accurate reality testing that does not support his expansive sense of self, the more mobilized he becomes in terms to vanquishing all offenders by any means available without regard to creating collateral damage to democratic governing institutions.

Part III: The Power of Ideologies

Chapter 9: Introduction to Ideology

Ideology, bureaucracy, hierarchy, and human nature are often discussed as individual, bounded concepts from an academic perspective. Human nature is influenced by ideology and in turn influences ideology. Human nature and ideology are determining factors in the creation and operation of bureaucracies and the hierarchies they are composed of. When it comes to human nature also to be considered is the dark side of human nature and how it introduces repetitions of destructive societal events (genocide is an example), where learning from errors and mistakes is largely absent. This appreciation is especially relevant when it comes to paranoid charismatic leaders who continually create havoc throughout history. Human nature and unconscious psychological defensiveness aimed at reducing anxiety combines with ideology, bureaucracy, and hierarchy to create dysfunctional historical repetitions.

Chapter 10: Contemporary Right-Wing Ideology and Its Relationship to Shame

The psychodynamics underlying contemporary American politics that culminated in the election of Donald Trump to the U.S. Presidency can be explored from several perspectives. Pursuing one's self-interest and a political ideology of limited government and social support systems suggest that some shame must arise relative to this "me first" approach to life. The feelings of shame are distressing and must be denied as existing, split off, and projected toward others and institutions to maintain self-comforting thoughts and self-images. Right-wing ideologies often seem to lack compassion toward others which is underscored by George W. Bush's effort to rebrand conservatism as "compassionate conservatism." The hard edge to conservatism, where economics is emphasized over social well-being, suggests that feelings of shame are resident in conservatism and the beliefs in the accompanying ideologies.

There are also linkages between authoritarianism, unbridled self-interest, a pervasive attitude of me-first/us-first, our sharing of a national culture of historical shame (slavery, the ethnic cleansing, and genocide of American Indians), and a lack of compassion toward others (not us). These social and psychological dynamics must be acknowledged or else they will likely remain a constant presence creating social and political polarization.

Chapter 11: Deregulation as a Right-Wing Ideology

This chapter explores the group psychodynamics of coping with anxiety that induces psychological regression and losses of accurate reality testing that form the foundation for the American ideology of deregulation. Deregulation has dominated the American economic and political landscape since the early 1980's. The theoretical perspective, of "unreality," is explored to better understand the psychodynamics underlying the emotional lure of deregulation despite its many failures.

Part IV: The Followers of Trump

Chapter 12: The Sentience of Followership

Conservatism according to conservatives often embraces inconsistent and conflicting ideological perspectives. The foundations of conservatism are based on shared feelings and sentiments that vary over time and help to account for the changing and conflicting basis of conservative thought. One way to explore these sentiments is to rely on Wilfred Bion's concept of sentience-based basic assumption groups – fight or flight, dependency, and pairing. These groups and their underlying theoretical foundations contribute to understanding not only conservative ideologies but also liberals' systems of beliefs. An appreciation of the role of sentiments and sentience in politics and ideologies is essential for understanding the past, present, and future of the United States.

Chapter 13: A Culture of Grievance: Creating Polarization from Chosen Traumas

Understanding the consistently high approval rating for President Trump among his followers is the subject of much speculation. This challenge to understanding can be in part met by reviewing the work of two authors (Thomas Frank[13] and Arlie Hochschild[9]) who explore the nature of the red state cultures of grievance that has been so successfully exploited by Trump. Trump speaks for them and in doing so exploits their sense of being an aggrieved group that has suffered at the hands of a liberal elite. The voice this gives is documented by these authors of books on Kansas and Louisiana. The sense of grievance is then further explored from the perspective of revisionist historical social traumas being resurfaced, recast, and used to mobilize the Republican voter base.

Chapter 14: White Supremacy and the Pursuit of Power

Understanding the importance and depth of Trump's and the far-right's embrace of white supremacy and structural and systemic racism is a critically important subject for American society as well as in many countries around the globe. The use of the terms "white supremacy" and "white nationalism" must be explored to appreciate the siren call of white supremacy and nationalism in the service of maintaining white privilege and domination of society, economics, and government. White supremacy is grounded in the ethnic cleansing of American Indians and slavery. Despite the freeing of the slaves by President Lincoln, Jim Crow laws and segregation were not seriously challenged until 100 years later by the Civil and Voter Rights legislation of the mid 1960's. In response white supremacy evolved to embrace housing red lines to keep the suburbs white limiting wealth accumulation, racist dog whistles, voter suppression including efforts to compromise the 2020 census, and many forms of systemic and structural racism. These psychosocial dynamics can be better understood using the three psychodynamically informed perspectives.

Chapter 15: The Learning Curve

This book represents a learning curve regarding understanding U.S. politics for the period 2015–2020 as they unfolded. The learning curve applies equally well to learning how to use the three psychanalytically informed perspectives to interpret these events. The theories used are among some of the most accepted in terms of understanding group dynamics, leader and follower relations, and individual psychodynamics. Looking back over the book's chapters suggests that critical thinking has been encouraged by the triangulation informed by psychodynamically informed analyses; sense making to better understand the Age of Trump and this period of American history and politics.

Conclusion

This book is a complex undertaking in terms of trying to make sense of the political and social culture of the United States 2015–2020. The use of the triangulation methodology (Figure 1.1) merged with the use of three complimentary psychodynamically informed perspectives we hope will promote reflectivity and critical thinking. Making sense of the Age of Trump by using this approach casts light onto what may be considered one of the darker periods in American history.

Notes

1. Lee, B. (2017). *The dangerous case of Donald Trump: 27 psychiatrists and mental health experts assess a president.* New York, NY: Thomas Dunne Books.

2. Freedland, J. (2018). This mafia style of government makes Trump a role model for all autocrats. *The Guardian.* https://www.theguardian.com/commentisfree/2018/aug/18/mafia-style-government-trump-role-autocrats.
3. Sit, R. (2018). Trump meets every criteria for an authoritarian leader, Harvard political scientists warn. *Newsweek.* https://www.newsweek.com/harvard-political-science-professor-donald-trump-authoritarian-how-democracy-778425.
4. Levitsky, S. & Ziblatt, D. (2018). *How democracies die.* New York, NY: Broadway Books.
5. Stein, H. & Allcorn, S. 2010. The unreality of American deregulation. *The Journal of Psychohistory,* 38(1), 27–48.
6. Chinoy, S. (2019). What happened to America's political center of gravity? *The New York Times.* https://www.nytimes.com/interactive/2019/06/26/opinion/sunday/republican-platform-far-right.html.
7. Applebaum, A. (2020). *Twilight of democracy: The seductive lure of authoritarianism.* New York, NY: Doubleday.
8. Klein, E. (2018). How democracies die, explained: The problems in American democracy run far deeper than Trump. *Vox.com.* https://www.vox.com/policy-and-politics/2018/2/2/16929764/how-democracies-die-trump-book-levitsky-ziblatt.
9. Hochschild, A. (2018). *Strangers in their own land: Anger and mourning on the American right* [Kindle Edition]. New York, NY: The New Press.
10. Allcorn, S. & Stein, H. (2017). The post-factual world of the 2016 American Presidential election: The good, the bad, and the deplorable. *The Journal of Psychohistory,* 44(4), 310–318.
11. Cohn, N. (2014). Polarization is dividing American society, not just politics. *The New York Times.* https://www.nytimes.com/2014/06/12/upshot/polarization-is-dividing-american-society-not-just-politics.html?_r=0.
12. Hetherington, M. & Weiler, J. (2009). *Authoritarianism & polarization in American politics.* New York, NY: Cambridge University Press.
13. Frank. T. (2005). *What's the matter with Kansas? How conservatives won the heart of America.* New York, NY: Picador.

2 Introduction to Psychoanalytic Theory in Making Sense of the Age of Trump

This chapter begins our project for making sense of what it is like to live during the Age of Trump by addressing the central question of our book: How can a psychodynamic perspective help us to understand and explain an entire socio-political cultural and historical era? In the past, we have used three psychodynamic perspectives to discuss individual, interpersonal, group, and organizational dynamics. These perspectives also provide insights into local, regional, and national groups of many kinds including social identity groups and political parties in the Age of Trump. Psychoanalytic theories contribute to understanding human behavior and the behavior of individuals who hold positions of immense power, including the role of the president of the United States.

Three psychoanalytically informed perspectives – Object Relations, Group Relations, and Karen Horney's tripartite theory – when applied in practice, make accessible the many present-day individual, group, and political dynamics. These three perspectives, supplemented by others, analyze, and interpret the toxic nature of Trump, his supporters including GOP politicians and the ever-present high approval ratings of his followers. We explain the three theoretical perspectives in this chapter and make them accessible by providing concrete examples that operationalize them both in terms of understanding organizations and dynamics at the level of national government and leadership.

Understanding Psychoanalytic Theory

We use various schools of psychoanalytic theory to understand leaders, organization members, and organizational dysfunctions at the individual, group, and organizational level. There is a growing literature on the three perspectives used here. We provide references for each at the beginning of their respective sections and accessible definitions and descriptions of the theories. We also note that we are not psychoanalyzing Trump but rather relying on the theory to better understand the individual and group psychodynamics of the Age of Trump as a psychosocial phenomenon.

We now explain the three theoretical perspectives with attention given to linking them to understanding the Age of Trump.

Object Relations Theory

Leadership and followership have been discussed from many perspectives. Object relations theory can be used to examine the workplace and leadership. It also contributes to understanding the current U.S. political context. In our discussion, we use the work of a few of the more established authors.[1]

We begin by introducing the concepts of denial, splitting, projection, projective identification, and transference. Concrete examples are provided to ground them in lived experience at work.

Denial

Denial is a common psychological defense mechanism that disposes of distressing experience relative to oneself or one's group by suppressing awareness. Awareness, however, is not entirely banished by denial, and the individual must invest some conscious effort in maintaining the denial, especially when the "facts" become progressively harder to ignore. Denial is often spotted by others and perhaps pointed out to the person in denial, which can become problematic in that it may promote more defensiveness in turn reinforcing the denial.

Denial is a common psychological defense. We may observe denial in others and groups where everyone acts as though a distressing situation is not happening or a problem does not exist. This is illustrated by not wearing masks, not practicing social distancing, and reopening the economy too early to prevent the spread of the COVID-19 virus in 2020. Denial is an integral part of splitting and projection.

Splitting

Splitting is an unconscious psychological defense. It divides oneself or a representation of another individual or group formulated in one's mind into all good and all bad. This usually results in feeling good about yourself and "knowing" the representation of the other, based on the evacuated bad part of yourself, as bad. Splitting starts with denial of the distressing experience that is to be split off from the self. We may, for example, deny we are feeling concerned or threatened by what is going on. At the same time, in our minds, we may locate these same thoughts and feelings in another person or group who is then thought to feel threatened and anxious. We feel calmer because our anxiety is now suppressed from awareness. An individual may appear anxious but deny it. Another individual may be thought of as anxious but not appear to be anxious.

The sequence is that first the distressing self-experience is denied, and then it is split off, which creates the possibility of locating (projecting) the experience onto someone else or another group (them) in one's mind. I am not angry; you are. Splitting creates the basis for projection and projective identification, to be discussed. Theoretically, it is important to consider splitting and projection as occurring together as in this discussion.

Splitting is complex enough to merit more discussion. Splitting is an unconscious mental process that can be shared with others, given that there is a shared distressing experience – a historical grievance or immigrant invasion. I or we are good and being attacked by a bad other person or group. This process is so common and natural that we do not pay much attention to these dynamics in our lives. We simply feel we are being attacked or victimized by another individual or group. The world becomes divided into a black and white landscape often with little to no middle ground. The world becomes filled with evil empires, axes of evil, and polarization. Within organizations, for instance, the finance department and its mission to manage costs can create an oppressive experience for other departments that need resources to do their work. In a nation such as the United States, the "good" white Christian Europeans are threatened by non-white others who, it is believed, will replace "us" and soil "our" white ethnicity with foreign blood.

Splitting may also happen in the reverse. For example, we might see ourselves as weak and ineffective and therefore unworthy. We may also see someone else or a group as better and acting effectively. The other person or group is then worthy of admiration and respect and we or I are not. For example, when we are in the presence of a powerful leader, we might feel anxious, diminished by comparison, and vulnerable. The leader is in our minds bigger than life, and we are small and weak. Only the leader might be able to save us, as Trump said. We have split off and projected our own self-efficacy onto the leader.

Splitting combined with projection occurs frequently enough that they affect how we experience ourselves and others. The splits are durable in part because they are out-of-awareness psychological defenses. As a result, they are not particularly open to self-inspection unless something happens that challenges these defensive patterns, such as accurate reality testing. In these cases, it may be the case that the splits are defended and evidence to the contrary ignored.

In sum, splitting is common and degrades accurate reality testing. We create in our minds a context that is not accurate, but it is comforting. The split context in our minds helps us to cope with distressing anxiety in the moment. It is also important to appreciate that splitting promotes thinking and feeling that can lead to actions that are destructive of other individuals or groups. "Others" may become despicable or a threat, e.g., Trump's rapists, murderers, and terrorists, who should be defended against or destroyed. Splitting is the basis for interpersonal dominance and submission, and for cultural dislocations such as genocide, ethnic cleansing, and family separations.

An Example

Throughout this chapter, we will be using a fictional company executive "Christine" and her employees to illustrate how psychodynamic defenses manifest themselves in organizations. We encourage readers to imagine how these also play out in your organizations and life experience, and in the recent political dynamics of the United States relative to Trump and his many types of followers and collaborators.

In this example the focus is on splitting. However, as noted it cannot be entirely understood without also considering *projection* (discussed next).

Christine owns a food service company with nearly 30 employees. She is admired and respected by everyone. She founded the company with the vision of serving a niche market for Spanish cuisine. As a result, her company occupies a safe market niche with no other major competitors. Her employees feel secure. They enjoy their work, feel appreciated, and are fairly compensated.

Her staff feels she is a good leader. She feels good about her employee approval. James, a new employee is not too eager to join in this shared admiration. He needs to see that the admiration is merited. He feels he is not willing to deny and split off his experience of himself as competent or deny and split off aspects of Christine that do not support idealizing her. Some of his colleagues are aware of his unwillingness to join with them in idealizing her. He is also aware of their pressure to validate their psychodynamics.

This context contains collusion and coercion. Christine acts in ways to draw positive projections. In striving for perfection, she splits off those aspects of herself that are less than admirable and competent and projects them onto her staff, leaving her feeling capable and perhaps at times arrogantly so. James' sense of these dynamics is that Christine encourages (pulling projections) but also merits some positive and idealizing projection onto her. This is how they like to see her. She is also omnipresent because she closely monitors the quality of the work and service. She is clearly the "decider." Her bigger than life presence and her attention to quality encourages idealizing her.

In sum, employees, whether Christine's or Trump's, are encouraged to split off and project some of their own competencies onto their mental representation of their leader. Christine, being aware of this at least to some extent, encourages them to do so. This dynamic makes her feel better about herself by receiving the idealizing projections, but she also splits off and projects awareness of her more marginal competencies onto her employees. In the case of Trump, others are only there to serve his needs for admiration and submission, as illustrated by Trump referring to Attorney General Jeff Sessions as Mr. Magoo (a hapless cartoon character) when he failed to "measure up" to Trump's expectations. For example, everyone must be loyal, submit, and follow his dictates. Everyone needs to be closely overseen, which for Trump and others means guarding against the "deep state" (federal bureaucracy) and disloyalty.

Projection

Projection arises when denial and splitting are present. Projection *disposes* of denied and split off distressing self-experience by creating a representation in one's mind of the other individual(s) or group and locating the denied experience in this representation. The representation is then available to be manipulated at will in one's mind. We often "know" others and groups in this way. This is natural and happens out of awareness. Denial, splitting, and projection, as psychological defenses, are not particularly open to reflection but can be acknowledged if pointed out to the individual, perhaps in therapy or by trusted friends. These mental representations are unique to each person, yielding different views of one individual (or group) who may be "known" by others in many different ways – some good and some bad. Groups can also share this dynamic and collectively create a shared, largely mental, image of a threatening group such as immigrant terrorists, rapists, and drug smugglers pouring across our borders.

Projection concurrently alters not only one's sense of self but also one's sense of another individual or group. Projection occurs when a hard-to-resolve internal conflict arises between our good and bad qualities or self-experience and, in turn, we wish to be rid of usually the bad qualities or experience. A leader who claims to be strong and powerful and omniscient (the smartest guy in the room) has split off and projected weakness, lack of control, and ignorance onto others (followers). This may also occur, as mentioned, relative to our good qualities and experience being projected, creating our idealized charismatic leader.

In sum, denial, splitting, and projection occur relative to others *as mental representations*. We might also be initially aware of another person or group having both good and bad qualities. However, we have a bias or preference for knowing the individual or group in a particular way. To achieve this, we split off the undesirable qualities. For example, denying the good parts of the other allows us to feel good about ourselves (as conservatives) by comparison. Most often splitting and projection involve experiencing oneself as good or as an aggrieved victim, and the other person (as liberals) as bad or the victimizer. This outcome leads to an unconscious commitment to maintaining polarizing splits and projections. Information that does not support this dynamic may not be attended to (selective attention and recall) or denied, bending reality to one's own psychologically defensive needs. The result is hard, impermeable, and defended boundaries.

It is also important to appreciate that splitting and projection that take place in one's mind leak out into the interpersonal world, leading to our actions in ways relative to the other person consistent with our splitting and projection. This person (or group) who is the focus of the projections may sense that he or she is thought to be a certain way (as bad or a victimizer) that may not be consistent with his or her own self-conception. This is common in interpersonal and intergroup relations. And, since it occurs at the margins of awareness, it is rarely open to discussion. Challenging this dynamic by the individual or group that is being targeted may paradoxically validate the inner experience that the person or group is bad, reinforcing the splits and projections.

An Example

Continuing with the previous example, organization members sometimes feel inferior to Christine. They tend to assume roles of dependency on her, and she does not discourage this. Christine is also influenced by a constant press of leaked idealization projections from her employees. Others often wait for her to make decisions. Their waiting encourages her to make them. This is a subtle process that, while observable, is usually unacknowledged. To the extent that she fulfills their expectations, she completes what amounts to interpersonal contracting and collusion. On those occasions when James has called this into question, others defend their conception of Christine, seeing James as bad for raising questions. Trump similarly seeks to dominate others who must support him in his many lies and distortions, leading to losses of personal integrity on their part. For example, no one may question the size of his crowds.

Projective Identification

Projective identification takes splitting and projection to a new level: that of trying to control the other person by getting him or her or the group to become like (accept, take in or introject) the projections. The subject is actively encouraged to feel, think, and act in accordance with the projections. The outcome is that the other individual or group may act out the projections, confirming their accuracy. People in the Black Lives Matter movement, by protesting peacefully, invite being labeled by those on the right as rioters who must be vigorously policed, thereby provoking resistance to the police and validating the projections.

For the recipient of the projective identification, the pressure to become like the projected content is subtle but also distressing. Others make clear the individual or group is not meeting their expectations. This sense of pressure is diminished by embracing the projections. This relieves the anxiety associated with the resistance to the projections. Of course, if the projections are positive the person or group may welcome and embrace them.

It is important to emphasize that all of this is natural and that these dynamics are going on all the time. Think for a moment of a father and daughter. The father, in his mind, wants to see his daughter as the perfect little girl. He acts as though she is and actively encourages her to feel this way. She is also punished when she fails to fulfill his mental representation of her. With time and persistence, she or the other person or group often becomes as desired. All is well as the gradual reshaping of the other fulfills and confirms our projections, creating a false sense of self on their part. To be noted, the opposite of an idealizing dynamic may occur where projective identification creates a bad "other" person or group that is continually coached (baited) into acting in bad ways consistent with projections such as being accused of or actually victimizing others.

An Example

Continuing with the example, Christine is idealized by her employees. Why not? She created the company. This idealization is in part based on projective identification. Christine often acts, thinks, and feels like her employees imagine her to be. This reduces her anxiety about not meeting their expectations. It also reduces their anxiety by providing them with some sense of control over her. They know what to expect from her and she from them.

The employees may do more than merely wait for Christine to make decisions. They encourage her to feel that she is the only person who can make them. Politically the equivalent is that only Trump can save us. She is complimented and coached into becoming the leader who they desire. She preferably makes all the major decisions and shelters everyone from distressing operating problems by assuming responsibility. She relieves her employees of personal responsibility for solving problems on their part. This constant press of projections, when accepted, encourages Christine to experience herself not only as an outstanding manager and leader but also as the only person who can make the important decisions.

It must also be appreciated that for Christine to believe that she can and must make most of the decisions, she must eliminate self-experience that is not consistent with being able to do so. Her imperfections and limitations may be split off and projected onto her marginally capable employees. By her dominating decision making, they feel less than capable. As a result, they must be managed and even micro-managed. This outcome fulfills the unconscious contract and collusion implicit in projective identification. Dynamics like this appear to be omnipresent at Trump rallies, where adoring fans applaud their charismatic leader who will lead them to safety and make America great again.

However, James and those around Trump need to be careful. They might evoke anxiety in followers by questioning these dynamics by pointing out imperfections and unresolved operating problems. Her employees and Trump's followers may easily feel threatened by anyone who does not support their splitting and projection. Denial and overlooking of Christine's or Trump's imperfections maintains the idealization. If something goes wrong, it is most likely her employees who will think they are at fault, fearing the possibility that one of them will be scapegoated and thrown under the metaphoric bus, as is often the case for many in Trump's orbit.

Transference

Interpersonal and intergroup dynamics are filled with many thoughts and feelings. Some of these are not related to the present moment. Transference involves the unconscious transfer of past experience and the accompanying feelings onto the present. This often energetic transfer creates confusing distortions for others. A leader, who resembles a past abusive, manipulative, or emotionally unavailable parent or past authority figure may readily surface unconscious feelings that are consistent with this past experience. The leader and his or her behavior evoke transference. This response is learned by trial and error by the child or adult to cope with abusive and un-nurturing parental figures or a leader. This often-stable defensive pattern "normalizes" what is a powerful and unconscious coping response to manage anxiety in interpersonal relationships, groups, organizations, and even in nations.

Splitting and projection contribute to this dynamic. The leader is experienced as *familiar* having been created in one's mind. The mental representation evokes overly strong thoughts and feelings, even though they are not entirely consistent with the leader's self or actions. The response to this "bad" representation is disproportionate. There may be an overly fearful, submissive, enraged, or withdrawn reaction. The leader and others may wonder, "What just happened?" Also, to be considered are "good" representations where the transference includes idealization and adoring and loving feelings. The leader may, in this case, also be left to wondering what just happened.

An Example

Christine is a much-admired founder of her company. She is idealized by her employees often in ways that are not always consistent with accurate reality testing. Further, she has likely selectively accepted positive employee projections and tries to "measure up." This collusive process includes Christine encouraging or pulling positive employee projections and transference associated with their experience and feelings for past authority figures who provided good enough nurturing and caretaking. This allows most employees to feel good about Christine and themselves and each other. Christine's transference may resemble that of a parent who provides caretaking for her employees.

In sum, within this psychodynamic context there may be good self and other feelings – sometimes described as a happy family. The employees feel safe since they are joined with Christine who is the wise and caretaking parental figure. We once again point out that this same dynamic can also create a "bad" leader where the employees are "good." For example, if Christine fails to fulfill employee expectations, the idealizing projections and positive transference may begin to collapse, evoking disillusionment and anger and the possibility of destructive organizational dynamics.

We now turn our attention to the two remaining helpful theoretical perspectives. Each makes a unique contribution to understanding group, organizational, and national dynamics.

Group Relations Theory and Wilfred Bion

Organizations including political and identity groups (religious, ethnic, national) are composed of individuals who live and work in one or more groups.[2] These groups may be working on tasks or have their work diverted to meet the defensive needs of their members. Wilfred Bion developed in the 1940s concepts that provide insight into what groups are doing or not doing and how to understand these group dynamics.[3] He suggests that there are three defensively oriented "basic assumption groups" and a fourth group, the work group that is intentional and reality-based. His focus on group dynamics contributed to the development of the Group Relations movement and, in the United States, the development of the A.K. Rice Institute. The Institute sponsors Group Relations conferences that provide experiential learning opportunities for understanding unconscious group dynamics.

Basic Assumption Groups

Bion described three group dynamics that arise in response to psychological regression where anxiety increases relative to perceived threats and other stressors. Group members, who share the regression and seek a defensive response (which characterizes a basic assumption group) compromise work on the group's task(s). A feature of this group dynamic is that group members have particular defensive tendencies or "valences" to retreat to one of the three basic assumption groups to relieve group anxieties. Margaret Rioch writes, "In his [Bion's] concept of valency he is saying that everyone has the tendency to enter into group life, in particular into the irrational and unconscious aspects of group life, and that people vary in the amount of tendency they have in this direction."[4] The entire group may not join in the regression and join in a basic assumption group. These individuals and perhaps the leader may also resist the retreat to a defensive basic assumption group.

We now describe the three types of basic assumption groups: fight/flight, dependency, and pairing. These basic assumption groups provide a conceptual framework that contributes to understanding group dynamics, whether the group is small, large, or a national group that contains tens of millions of individual members such as in a political party, a religion, or social movement.

Fight/Flight

Fight/flight is a familiar response to distressing anxiety associated with perceived threat. It can lead to intense responses such as attacking the source of the threat or turning away in flight. When fight or flight groups arise, thinking and reflectivity are often lost. This group seeks out a leader who shows hate or fear toward the "enemy," one that may be seen to be within the group or organization or outside the group where fight and flight are prominent in international relations. The leader and group members are also willing to accept member casualties. Some members may be viewed as part of the problem and may be singled out for discipline or possibly termination. They may also be left behind as the group moves on, as might occur during an organizational restructuring. This basic assumption group is not particularly reflective, preferring to focus on *acting against* the threat or *moving away* from it (see Karen Horney below).

Fight and flight are common individual and group dynamics that, if they are to be avoided, must first be acknowledged by the leader and group in order to redirect this basic assumption group back to working on its task. In the United States, the pressing need to locate a fight/flight leader was fulfilled by Trump, who as a paranoid charismatic leader, located enemies and threats everywhere. In national and global affairs, the fight/flight group dynamic is common where groups and nations wage war, conduct ethnic cleansing, and engage in genocide.

Dependency

The dependency group's dynamic is one of meeting to attain security by being protected by someone, usually a leader. Group members act as though they are less than competent and unable to manage operating problems that have been encountered. When an individual is identified to lead the group out of harm's way, he or she may be readily followed and idealized. Everyone waits expectantly to receive direction from their leader. Splitting and projection of personal competencies onto the leader, and the leader's identification with these projections, contributes to idealization and dependency as in the example of Christine in the previous section.

If a leader is neither identified by the group nor self-identifies (steps forward), the group waits for the leader to emerge. The waiting may create enough anxiety in the group from not dealing with the threatening problems, that eventually a member decides to try to lead to relieve his or her own anxiety about waiting. However, the new leader is faced with the probability that this dependent group cannot have its dependency needs fully met. This may be more likely if the waiting has allowed the problems faced to reach hard to respond to proportions. Failures to meet the group's dependency needs lead to disappointments and to hostility toward the leader. This may result in a fight or flight response and the termination of the leader in the hope a new and better leader will be found.

Also, to be noted is that collusive dynamics may arise in hierarchical organizations when dependency basic assumption groups create the basis for a culture of autocratic command and control, enabled by subordinates who seek submissive security. These dynamics lead to creating autocracies that are reinforced by the leader who promotes fear and anxiety and psychological regression to dependency. These dynamics are especially prominent in the Republican Party and the Age of Trump – the belief that only Trump can save them.

Pairing

This group hopes a leader, new idea, or new strategy will save the group from perceived threats. This group's members are attentive to each other. The focus is on the *hope* that the future will be better. However, group members are unwilling to invest much effort or take risks to deal with the threats themselves. Paradoxically the rise of a leader who expects the group members to act is also threatening, in that by providing the directions, the leader is experienced as coercive. Resistance to receiving direction and acting becomes the basis for maintaining the status quo. Problems and threats are merely accepted. Little to no action is taken to deal with the threats. This outcome is a common feature of all forms of government, including many organizations and countries. The resistance to change has been flagged by Trump as the "deep state."

Psychodynamically it is important that the leader, the better idea, or new strategy remain unborn and unthought. The hope is that change which deals with the anxiety arising from the threats will magically occur. Everyone seems to be waiting for something good to happen. Hope is abundant and does not include having to think and act to deal with the threats in order to reduce the anxiety that promotes regression to this regressive group defense in the first place.

Within the political area, the constant turnover of leaders creates a context where there is no clear sustainable direction. This leaves citizens and organization members hoping times will get better. During the Age of Trump, many people expect America will almost magically be made great again. However, if the problems and threats posed by Trump eventually become intolerable, a change is needed, as evidenced by the election of November 2020. A fight/flight basic assumption group occurred to resist a charismatic authoritarian leader who led American conservatives, for example, to fend off protesters, imagined terrorists, and masses of supposedly criminal immigrants from impoverished countries.

The Work Group

Rioch asserts the work group, is "very rare and perhaps even non-existent in pure culture."[5] This group possesses maturity and can engage in reflection and work on clearly defined tasks. Rioch also notes, "Each member of the group belongs to it because it is his will and his choice to see that the purpose of the group is fulfilled. He is therefore at one with the task of the group and his own interest is identified with its interest."[5] The group tests its assumptions, acquires the data and knowledge it needs, and continually questions its methods how to better achieve work on its tasks. In sum, it learns from experience.

These group dynamics lead to avoiding group regression to basic assumptions. A work group is, however, not necessarily free of stress and anxiety. The group has a leader and members who resist individual and group regression. The work group may be observed to be in operation in organizations, nations, and globally when accurate assessments of operating problems, threats, and opportunities occur. Action plans are collaboratively developed and implemented, and they are monitored for the satisfactoriness of their outcomes.

Discussion of Basic Assumption Groups

Bion's basic assumption groups increase our awareness of irrational and unconscious group dynamics that compromise working on the group's official mission and tasks. Basic assumption groups such as dependency and pairing are especially likely to arise during stressful times when leaders are looked to for providing clear and reassuring direction to deal with threats.

Equally important, however, is the frequent presence of fight and flight group dynamics. Fighting back against intrusions on one's turf (such as border crossings) is a common response for nations and organizations. If the incursions are perceived as or said to be dangerous by an elected leader, flight into fantasy, intellectualization, denial, and rationalization and action based on them may develop. These individual, group, and national dynamics then promote greater dependency on a fight/flight leader who is willing to try to save the organization or nation from perceived threats.

We now turn to discuss the third theoretical perspective provided by Karen Horney.

The Tripartite Theory of Karen Horney

Understanding human behavior in nations and large or even small organizations can be challenging without a conceptual road map to understand what one observes.[6] Karen Horney offers us a thoughtful framework for understanding behavior in small and large groups that can mobilize millions of members such as a political party. The underlying psychodynamics of these groups have their origins in inadequate parental nurturing and toxic adult experiences.[7] Instances where there are serious and persistent caretaking failures in infancy, childhood, at work, and living life in one's country, yield well-organized and durable individual and group defensive reactions (strategies) that introduce dysfunctions.

Childhood and Personal Development

These psychodynamics and their accompanying individual and group dysfunctions arise from insufficiently caretaking that creates anxious attachment to parents or to one's job that, in turn, lead to finding ways to cope
with these threats and anxieties. Karen Horney speaks to problematic,
anxious, and painful attachments by offering three psychologically defensive solutions to the anxieties.[7] The child might respond by not giving up
on seeking secure attachment by becoming more submissive and changing
one's self in the service of seeking attachment, including to a group, leader,
or larger cause. This is a *movement toward* others and is also described as
is the appeal to love and the self-effacing solution to anxiety. In an adult
life, these dynamics lead to the pursuit of attachment to an organization,
community, ethnic or religious group, or to a particular social identity.
The "drive" to belong and be accepted is strong.

A second possibility in the interpersonal world is to fight back and resist
unacceptable caretaking by others. Horney describes this as *moving against*
others – the appeal to mastery and the expansive solution to anxiety. This
response represents an abandonment at least in part of the hope of being
securely attached. If there is little hope, the child or adult has little to
lose if others are alienated. This creates a self-fulfilling outcome of not
being nurtured and loved, and perhaps failing that, at least feared. Moving
against other groups of all kinds (not us) can include other nations, races,
and the global community. This is a reoccurring theme in the United
States, most often attributed to right-wing politicians and parties underscored by Trump's motto "America First."

A third possible direction of movement is *movement away* – the appeal to
freedom and the resigned solution to anxiety – from others when the child
(and adult) abandons the hope of being loved and receiving adequate caretaking. In this case, achieving meaningful attachment is too difficult and
painful to try by moving toward or against others, the appeals to either love
or mastery. These directions of movement are opposites, and the individual, group, or nation cannot resolve the conflict of choosing a direction or,
having tried both unsuccessfully, give up. In sum, when an individual (or
group) accepts that he or she is not worthy of being loved (moving toward
others), and that fighting back against others (moving against others) is too
stressful and futile, the choice of moving away from others (withdrawal)
is a viable option. The expression – "taking your ball and going home" –
speaks to this directional movement. The feeling of wishing to be left
alone to not have to deal with the interpersonal world is a common experience. On a larger scale, movement away also happens in large national
groups, sometimes referred to as isolationist politics and protectionism.

In sum, these three directions of movement are psychologically defensive responses to stressful interpersonal and group relationships. They are
coping responses that can threaten attachment to others as well as to one's

self-integrity. They can become steadfastly and compulsively pursued to allay anxiety. We now discuss these three directions of movement in more detail. To be noted these discussions are framed as individual directional movements, but they also apply to groups of all sizes, including political parties and nations.

Movement Toward

Movement toward others is the opposite of moving against others. This individual or group that moves toward others avoids feelings of being superior to others and has no wish to dominate and control others.[7] Feelings of inferiority are present, and self-contempt may be experienced (unworthiness) including some sense of self-hate. Feelings of self-pride and superiority are shunned, replaced by a willingness to subordinate oneself to others as well as being submissive in order to make oneself lovable, worthy, and loyal to secure attachment. This individual or group has an idealized self-image that consists of lovable qualities such as goodness, generosity, humility, and sacrifice. In groups, these pursuits may focus on others who possess power and authority and who are feared and admired much like parental figures.

Denial, splitting, projection, and transference contribute to this outcome. Submission may be relied on to gain attachment to powerful others. Splitting off and projection of self-efficacy reinforces the dominance and control that can be imposed by the desired object of attachment. Every effort may be made to sustain this solution to anxiety, including avoiding thoughts and feelings that the powerful other is dominating, abusing, and degrading. Ultimately, maintaining a balance between depleting one's inner self and losing personal integrity created by submission, is a challenge.

Observers might see an individual (or group) who is willing to do whatever it takes to acquire and maintain attachment. Personal sacrifices that are embedded in this interpersonal "contract" abound. Common expressions for this dynamic are, "sucking up," sycophancy and a perverse sense of loyalty, idealization of the leader and unquestioning submission to a charismatic organizational or political leader who may suggest that only he or she can save us, as Trump said.

Immigration to the United States is an example of moving toward. Immigrants make many sacrifices especially at the border with Mexico to be accepted into the United States. Immigrants are willing to suffer many indignities such as family separations and confinement in private prisons in the hope of having their exceptional vulnerability transformed into a welcoming embrace.

Movement Against

Movement against others is a defensive response that often includes aggressively manipulating others in the pursuit of narcissistic supplies.

It also has interpersonally aggressive and destructive elements that arise when an expansive sense of pride is harmed (narcissistic injury). This individual's idealized self is felt to be able to accomplish just about anything and to solve any problem – Trump is "the smartest person in the room." This inflated sense of self-importance and arrogance often seems to be the right person to be in control to take care of anxious and regressed, dependent group members. However, the arrogant pride is easily injured (thin-skinned), and this can lead to interpersonal aggression, where anything may be risked to achieve vindicative triumph. There is often present an enemies list where payback is always "on the table." Groups or nations may also have an expansive sense of "exceptionalism" that, if reality tested, is easily threated, requiring countermeasures.

For many people, organizational positions and political offices that receive a lot of attention, and possess status, authority, and power resident in the position, are especially desirable to have. These positions fulfill the narcissist's desire to appear charismatic, and in Trump's words "strong and powerful" and, therefore, worthy of fear and admiration. These positions provide the means to vindicate and repair injured narcissism and expansive pride. Empathy, interpersonal authenticity, and the ability to connect with others are often lacking or absent. The Age of Trump illustrates this. These individuals in role as charismatic narcissistic leaders are affectively disconnected from others although they pay a lot of attention to their loyal followers who are sought after for narcissistic supplies.

In practice, these individuals often manipulate and dominate others, creating admiration and dependency and the hope of being taken care of by the leader. This dynamic is nurtured along by the leader who spots many threats and enemies. However, as noted, arrogant-vindictive responses that focus on using the power that resides in a hierarchical position to get even or gain control will often alienate others. Vindictive uses of power "cuts both ways."

This leader often appears to be self-righteous and tends to attract adoring, self-effacing followers (movement toward) who are willing to submit to the leader to achieve secure attachment. These followers become enabling sycophants and "cult members." For this leader, others become objects to be used.[8,9] Employees within the organization may describe this leader's behavior as bullying, threatening, and intimidating – descriptions often used to describe the Trump Administration. However, if positive attachments are not particularly sought after, being feared is a viable option. Getting even with offending others becomes a priority that is pursued with enough energy to become self-destructive at times. These dynamics may also create excessive fear and anxiety on the part of others, where avoiding offending the leader becomes a top priority – bearing bad news and speaking truth to power must be avoided. Movement against others, we suggest, offers a lot of explanatory power in terms of understanding some of the more common and prominent workplace and current U.S. political scene dysfunctions.

The zero-tolerance policy for immigration that has led to sending a message to immigrants you are not welcome here is one of the high visibility Age of Trump benchmarks of aggressively moving against others described as rapists and murders and a few good people. The lack of compassion shown immigrants from around the world and especially at the border with Mexico is exceptionally attention-getting. Trump also moves against anyone or any organization that threatens his preferred self-narrative with accurate reality testing. The counter-attacks against the "fake news" and the organizations that generate it that includes exceptionally disparaging language is noteworthy.

Movement Away

Movement away from others is a response to the stresses of the interpersonal world by dropping out.[7] This person gives up trying to cope with others and prefers a solitary life. This response is chosen when moving toward and against others has not resulted in better attachment, or because the person is conflicted about these two directions of movement. Perhaps this person fears rejection from moving toward and is fearful of what might happen from moving against others. Movement away may include reducing striving to achieve, and they embrace philosophies that renounce non-essentials. As a result, life becomes streamlined and less complex. There is often a lack of self-confidence that reinforces avoiding striving to succeed in one's life. Being alone and being left alone are comforting when compared with the potential of interpersonal conflicts. America First and other "go it alone" strategies such as withdrawing from the Iran nuclear agreement or challenging China without engaging other nations and allies in the cause, are consistent with this direction of movement.

This defensive positioning in the interpersonal world avoids attempts at influence, pressure, coercion, and change. In a workplace filled with these eventualities, others understand that this individual prefers to be left alone to do his or her work. Supervisors may be confronted with sensitivity to and resentment of efforts to impose due dates and performance expectations (accountability). Routine work and work not subject to change are preferred. At the national level, these dynamics are reflected in avoiding foreign entanglements, including treaties and coalitions like NATO or the UN, and foreign wars which is a libertarian cause.

In sum, movement away from others toward personal or national freedom is encountered in the workplace and political arena where advocacy for unencumbered personal autonomy (not wearing protective masks during pandemics) is regarded as a national right not to be compromised by government mandates. Movement away may also apply to some leaders who find their responsibilities stressful and may appeal to freedom.

They may have the responsibility but avoid assuming the responsibility that comes with it. They may depend on others to make tough decisions and deal with messy tough problems embroiled in interpersonal conflict. They are strong on delegation, making clear that they just want to be left alone perhaps to focus on financial analyses or political ideology (a policy wonk) in splendid isolation. This direction of movement, it may be appreciated, may be expressed in many ways.

This direction of movement is illustrated by the many people fired often by tweets or who have voluntarily left the Trump administration and government service. Leaving an organization that is toxic is often a good choice in terms of maintaining self-integrity and self-esteem. Fighting back (moving against) and submission in dependency (moving toward) are not good options for those who are not receptive to unethical and immoral decisions and actions and being bullied, threatened, and intimidated. There is often a very real sense of relief from the freedom of "getting out."

Mixed Models of Movement

It is problematic to speak of pure types in a typology. People and groups and the context create complexity, to which are added systems of psychological defenses that compromise logic or rationality. While some defensiveness is to be expected, when it becomes rigidly adhered to, it may create a dysfunctional group, organizational or national culture. And given the complexity of human nature, more than one of the defensive responses may be relied on. A typical mixed model we have found in the workplace is vacillation between moving against and toward others.

For example, a leader may prefer to move against others by seeking domination and control within the workplace or within a political party. Anyone who gets out of line may be disciplined or discharged, which is made more likely based on how easy it is to offend this leader. This leader, when confronted with a major operating problem, resistance to his or her direction, or messy inter-group conflict, may suddenly seek reassurance, nurturing, admiration, and even love from others – the movement toward others as illustrated by Trump rallies. An inner circle of enablers and sycophants may also shore up this fragile sense of self in the moment in order to permit the leader to feel self-assured, admired, and back in control, which in turn restores the leader to an idealized but also dominating and potentially abusive state.

Movement against others may also be paired with movement away during stressful periods. The leader lashes out at others but then takes a business trip or goes golfing, as Trump did after losing the election. This absence creates soothing downtime away from the stress associated with attacking others. Leaders who most often move toward others may, rather than move against others, move away, withdrawing into an office with the door closed and stop responding to emails and phone calls – essentially becoming unavailable for leadership.

In sum, Karen Horney's three directions of movement – toward, against, and away – offer an intuitive framework that helps to account for many psychodynamic aspects of interpersonal, group, organizational, and national life. These three defensive directions of movement provide a basis for understanding the dynamics of the Age of Trump that are the subject of this book.

In Conclusion

We conclude our discussion of the three psychodynamically informed perspectives with a strong dose of humility. Trying to understand the immense complexity resident in human nature, groups, politics, and social dynamics will come up short. The three theoretical approaches used in this book do not represent all possible approaches that might be used. In fact, we do use other theoretical perspectives to further illuminate our discussions. If anything can be said about using psychoanalytic theory to understand the Age of Trump, it is that the theory provides vitally important ways to organize and interpret the data that one finds when observing human behavior that includes the darker side of human nature.

We now turn to Part 1 and its exploration of the *inner triangle* within Figure 1.1 – Trump, Narcissism, and Autocracy – using these three psychodynamic perspectives to try to make sense of and better understand the Age of Trump.

Notes

1. Some of the books used to discuss object relations are:
   Grotstein, J. (1985). *Splitting and projective identification*. Northvale, NJ: Jason Aronson.
   Kohut, H. (1984). *How does analysis cure?* A. Goldberg (Ed.). Chicago, IL: University of Chicago.
   Segal, H. (1973). *Introduction to the work of Melanie Klein*. London: Karnac.
   Greenberg J. & Mitchell, S. (1983). *Object relations in psychoanalytic theory*. Cambridge, MA: Harvard University Press.
   Scharff, J. (1992). *Projective and introjective identification and the use of the therapist's self*. Northvale, NJ: Jason Aronson.
   Tansey, M. & Burke, W. (1989). *Understanding countertransference*. Hillsdale, NJ: The Analytic Press.

2. Some of the books used to discuss Group Relations are:
   Allcorn, S. & Diamond, M. (1997). *Managing people during stressful times: The psychologically defensive workplace*. Westport, CT: Quorum Books.
   Colman, A. & Bexton, H. (1975). (Eds.). *Group relations reader*. Sausalito, CA: Grex.
   Colman, A. & Geller, M. (1985). (Eds.). *Group relations reader 2*. Washington, DC: A.K. Rice Institute.
   Czander, W. (1993). *The psychodynamics of work and organizations*. New York, NY: Guilford.
   Diamond, M. & Allcorn, S. (1990). The Freudian factor. *Personnel Journal*, 69(3), 52–65.

3. Bion, W. (1961). *Experience in groups*. London: Tavistock.
4. Rioch, M. (1975). Group Relations: Rationale and Technique in Colman, A. and Bexton, W. (Eds.) *Group relations reader*. Washington, DC: A.K. Rice Institute Series, pp. 11–33, 29.
5. Rioch, M. (1975). Group Relations: Rationale and Technique in Colman, A. and Bexton, W. (Eds.) *Group relations reader*. Washington, DC: A.K. Rice Institute Series, pp. 11–33, 23.
6. Some of the books and articles used to discuss Karen Horney are:
   Diamond, M. & Allcorn, S. (1984). Psychological barriers to personal responsibility. *Organizational Dynamics*, 12(4), 66–77.
   Diamond, M. & Allcorn, S. (1985). Psychological dimensions of role use in bureaucratic organizations. *Organizational Dynamics*, 14(1), 35–59.
   Diamond, M. & Allcorn S. (1985). Psychological responses to stress in complex organizations. *Administration& Society*, 17(2), 217–239.
   Diamond, M. & Allcorn S. (1986). Role formation as defensive activity in bureaucratic organization. *Political Psychology*, 7(4), 709–731.
   Kets de Vries, M. (2006). *The Leader on the couch: A clinical approach to changing people and organizations*. San Francisco, CA: Jossey-Bass.

7. Horney, K. (1950). *Neurosis and human growth*. New York, NY: Norton.
8. Babiak, P. & Hare, R. (2006). *Snakes in suits: When psychopaths go to work*. New York, NY: Harper.
9. Schouten, R. & Silver, J. (2012). *Almost a psychopath*. Boston, MA: Harvard University.

Part I

Trump the Man, the President

Our approach of triangulating the many possible elements of recent national and political events offers a way to make sense of the period 2015–2020. The inner triangle (**Figure 1.1**) is the subject of Part I. We set for ourselves the task of examining Trump as a businessman and executive, his self-evident excessive narcissism, and his equally observable autocratic and authoritarian tendencies. This is not to say other obvious elements do not merit consideration, for instance, his lack of morality, questionable ethics, lack of a clear overarching set of ideological principles (other than himself), racism, xenophobia, homophobia, and aggression toward women as possible and important topics.

The buffet of possibilities overflows the serving table. We focus here on Trump, narcissism, and his autocratic leadership style primarily because, from our perspective of a history of writing about dysfunctional and toxic organizations, we believe these are among the core elements to be considered.[1,2]

We will explore this from a psychodynamically informed perspective that allows us to inspect in depth what may be readily observed. This work involves adapting and applying psychoanalytic theory to understand organizational, social, and political dynamics to make sense of events, but also what everyone is processing as self-experience evoked by these recent events. We hope how we organize our context and then explore it contributes to sensing making on everyone's part.

Notes

1. Allcorn, S. and Stein, H. (2015). *The dysfunctional workplace: Theory, stories, and practice*. Columbia, MO: University of Missouri Press.
2. Stein, S. and Allcorn, S. (2020). *The psychodynamics of toxic organizations: Applied poems, stories and analysis*. New York, NY: Routledge.

3 Overview of Trump's Business and Political History

Historical perspectives contribute much to understanding the past, present, and future. This is especially important when considering the Age of Trump. The magnitude of the political and social dislocation and polarization suggests that the next decade will be challenging if not tumultuous. The likely lingering effects of SARS-CoV-2 will be arrayed with a lingering major recession and the now overt white supremacy/white nationalism of the right. These eventualities raise for post-Trumpist conservative thought leaders the problem of "where to from here."

The sweeping nature of the pandemic of bad news defies any effort to encapsulate and fully understand it at the present. In this chapter, we provide limited and selective historical perspectives of Trump himself, the Age of Trump, and the transformed political and social context of the United States as we begin the third decade of the twenty-first century. We begin by "connecting the dots" of Trump as a businessman and real estate entrepreneur and more recently as a politician in this chapter.

Any overview of Trump's business history is a complex project and here we wish to only briefly highlight this history preferring to focus on his political history. These parallel histories are, however, intertwined in that his loyal voters see him as a successful business executive who owns his own companies.

A Brief Business History

Our effort here does not include how his wealthy developer father set him up in business although Trump's fabrications and distortions of this are noteworthy. The brief overview that follows highlights his business failures and bankruptcies to illustrate that many of the Trump-branded projects and products that are invariably financed by third parties are often losers. He also earns income from licensing his name as a brand that is now tarnished by his politics and being removed from buildings.

Michael Cohen's testimony before Congress also highlighted what are possibly illegal actions on Trump's part such as inflating his net worth to borrow millions of dollars, deflating his net worth to avoid taxes and successfully, and consistently shifting losses from his losing enterprises to his investors.[1] Currently, New York's attorney general is pursuing possible Trump corruption across a broad front.

Fawaz and Stuart summarize Trump's business failures and bankruptcies by fact-checking Trump's expansive sense of himself as an outstanding businessman.[2,3] We briefly highlight these.

Trump's Less than Successful Businesses

Trump Airlines

In 1988, Trump took out a $245 million loan to purchase the planes and routes of Eastern Air Shuttle. Trump ultimately defaulted, surrendering ownership of the airline to his creditors.

Trump Travel Site – GoTrump.com

Launched in 2006 as what some considered to be a vanity site with low money-making expectations, it folded in 2007.

Trump Vodka

The trademark was abandoned in 2008, and the liquor was out of circulation by 2011.

Trump Mortgage

This company was shuttered in September 2007. According to the *Washington Post*, the company never paid a $298,274 judgment it owed a former employee.

Trump Magazine

Trump launched his magazine in late 2007 to capitalize on the booming advertising market for high-end commodities. It did not survive the great recession closing by 2009.

Trump University

Trump University (2005–2010) was a series of wealth-building seminars considered to be a sham. Trump settled the lawsuit for $25 million in 2016 after he was elected.

Several other business efforts are occasionally mentioned as examples of failures.

Trump Network

Trumpnet started in 1990 never got off the ground; the trademark was abandoned in 1992.

Trump Steaks

This 2007 enterprise marketed through the Sharper Image lasted about three months before folding. *Gourmet Magazine* described the steaks as mediocre.

Trump: The Game

Originally released in 1989 it was at best a modest success and was discontinued. It was released a second time in 2004 in conjunction with Trump's *The Apprentice* TV program. Sales were once again marginal. The game is now considered to be a collector's item.

Trump Ice Natural Spring Water

Trump Ice (1995–2010) was originally available on Trump properties and eventually was distributed more broadly. It is still thought to be available exclusively on Trump properties and Trump famously had some Trump Ice delivered to rival Marco Rubio in 2015 when he said Rubio sweated too much.

Also, to be noted, a few Trump companies sought bankruptcy protection:

> Trump has filed for bankruptcy a total of 6 times with the following three being prominent. Trump Taj Mahal filed in 1991 and was $3 billion in debt after just one year in operation. In 2004 filings occurred for Trump Marina and Trump Plaza casinos as well as a riverboat casino in Indiana that together had a debt burden of $1.8 billion. These were part of a reorganization into Trump Entertainment Resorts that four years later missed an interest payment on a million bond and declared bankruptcy.

These bankruptcies and reorganizations, Buettner and Bagli noted, led to business partners having to write off billions of dollars of losses while Trump avoided personal bankruptcy and in fact often profited from these bankruptcies by taking upwards to $82 million in compensation.[4]

In the interest of being "fair and balanced" Tom Worstall, reporting for *Forbes*, notes that while two-thirds of Trump's approximately 60 business endeavors failed or at best partially succeeded with many burdened by lawsuits, government investigations, conflicts with partners, and market downturns, still one-third of his enterprises met or exceeded expectations including his successful reality TV program *The Apprentice*.[5]

The personal ability to continually strive for success when faced with frequent failures may be fueled by "productive" narcissism. Looking good and being admired even in failure is important in terms of maintaining an expansive sense of self.[6] As is evident with Trump, the stable genius and the smartest guy in the room, the ability to think of himself in these terms with few pangs of conscience is remarkable. This ability is associated with entrepreneurs and marketeers who sell the "sizzle" with self-assurance bonding others to the individual and to related endeavors or products. In plainer English, they will say and do just about anything to close the sale without feelings of conscience including selling products, financial schemes, and business opportunities that do not exist, cannot be delivered, or are known to be likely failures preferably leaving everyone else holding the losses as is the case with bankruptcies.

When narcissism is combined with arrogance and vindictiveness anyone standing in the way must be defeated and any injuries to expansive narcissistic pride must be vindicated sometimes for Trump ten times over. The pursuit of vindication may know few limits as can also be observed when Trump pursues anyone in the government, judicial system, or military to damage their careers or have them fired. These dynamics promote fear throughout the government, the GOP as a political party, and among foreign leaders, business partners, friends, colleagues, and even extended family members.

These psychodynamic considerations lead to considering the imagery of his mob boss-like (autocratic, authoritarian) behavior occasionally mentioned as part of the sea of media coverage he receives.

Trump as Mob Boss

Some journalists have concluded that Trump, in addition to supporting a plutocracy, functions like a mob boss where he takes out opponents and expects others to figuratively kiss his ring (sycophants) to obtain favors, stand in the brilliant light of his radiance, and at the minimum keep their jobs. Their approval and admiration of him counterbalance negative "fake news" coverage that he often complains about including saying he does not receive the credit he deserves. There are also elements of a kleptocracy where everyone around Trump stands to benefit financially sometimes at the expense of the country such as huge government contracts being given to small companies as a political favor. Images from movies such as *The Godfather* movie series capture the mob boss where crossing this boss can most definitely lead to termination (You're fired.).[7] And to be noted is that rule by an insular mob or tribe that pushes the limits of being unlawful sabotages legitimate government and public confidence in government and its institutions such as Congress which is held in low regard.[8]

We now turn to the question of what exactly Trumpism is since it is frequently mentioned in discussions of the Age of Trump, Trump's brand,

and his loyal followers who, in part, are loyal out of fear (conservative politicians fear his base).

The Four Characteristics of Trumpism

David Edward Tabachnick provides a succinct overview of what Trumpism constitutes.[9] Trumpism has its roots in a uniquely American intertwining of contemporary and traditional political trends that is distinct from the European Fascism of the last century.

Celebrity

Celebrity is a factor in two ways. First, Trump's televised persona (brand) as a CEO and tough decision-maker (You're fired.) was extended to his desired political image. This self-branding has proven to be exceptionally durable despite unrelenting evidence to the contrary (discounted as fake news). Second, this celebrity branding has appealed to a large "audience" and Twitter following composed of disaffected people and social groupings where he has succeeded in expanding his brand to embrace their unsatisfied wants and dreams thereby creating a motivated voter base.

Nativism

Trumpism includes nativism which has its roots in the mid-nineteenth century Know-Nothing agitation that combined anti-immigrant sentiment with conspiracy theories about foreigners. Trumpism has some of its origins in birtherism and Trump's 2011 demand for Obama to release his full birth certificate, which endeared him to his base voters. This conspiratorial fear of foreigners has been extended to "build the wall" and deportation of all illegal immigrants and restrictions on legal immigration. And to be noted the harsh treatment of families including children has been intended to send a message that immigrants are not welcome (Jeff Session's speech Scottsdale, AZ May 7, 2018).

The Outsider

Trump as a brand is anti-establishment and takes up positions opposed to the entrenched power structure and the imagined conspiratorial "deep state" that must be destroyed. Paradoxically he is often opposed to his own administration – his appointees and their positions. He, in a sense, has mastered the political expression of "talking out both sides of his mouth at the same time." This is one of the sources of the sense of chaos that grips the government and country where today's direction may be reversed tomorrow and initiatives are often mandated but without any planning or preparation, which has stranded passengers in airports and overwhelmed immigration systems and confinement. To this may be added the appearance of not being dependent on big-money donors like the Koch Brothers and lobbyists while simultaneously serving their interests – clean coal that does not exist being an example.

Trump also consistently attacks the mainstream media, his political opponents, and disloyal conservatives. This consolidates his narrative that he is a threat to the established power structure and a savior of the disenfranchised.

Populism

Trumpism may be conceptualized as rhetorical resentment based on a long list of grievances and as a mash-up of patriotism (wrapped in the flag), economic nationalism (America First) combined with aggressive foreign policies that include compromising international organizations such as the United Nations, NATO and the World Health Organization. Trumpism also includes commitments to the *white* middle class such as returning manufacturing to the United States and keeping it here to create jobs. This last point is underscored by his responses to race and police brutality and the chant "Black Lives Matter" by saying "All Lives Matter" and labeling protests as riots and protestors as terrorists that require brutal suppression by law enforcement (Chapter 14).

"Is Trump a populist" is a question asked and answered by Paul Krugman, the economist who points out that Trump's economic policies are the opposite of populist.[10] He has continually supported plutocrats by ramming through big tax cuts for corporations and the rich that create massive public debt. At the same time, he is trying to repeal Obamacare which takes away health insurance from poor and working-class families during a pandemic. Also, contrary to a populist position, he has pursued deregulating protections for the environment, food chain, animals, and consumer rights and safety. He has also opened federal lands for exploitation.

In sum, these four characteristics of Trumpism make it a unique political phenomenon that has broad appeal across the political spectrum that extends beyond Trump himself. Much to the consternation of Republican elites, it also stands well outside of accepted conservative political ideology.

We now turn to a more in-depth examination of our primary focus, Trump's political contribution to history and the United States.

Trump's Political History

Trump, in his pursuit of narcissistic supplies and enablement of his autocratic – sometimes described as "mob boss" – governing style, has gradually forced people out of the government and appointed positions and fired those occupying temporary appointments, replacing them with loyalists.

These actions have gradually allowed him to carve out a cadre of loyal enabling sycophants who carry out his orders and ideas and decisions.

Trump has steadily bonded special interest groups with their respective ideologies to him. To list a few: NRA and gun enthusiasts, white supremacists/Neo-Nazis, various leaders of western religious sects, the Right to Life special interests as well as anti-LGBTQ who are opposed to same-sex marriage, adoption, service in the military, and of course bathroom privileges.

Many aspects of this bonding are supported by changing government rules and regulations (family separations at the border) or not complying with them or possibly breaking the law (pardons promised). In many of these instances, the changes are being successfully challenged in court. Much of this activity is screened out of the press and public awareness by the continuous creation of distracting chaos. Many times, Trump will speak to, for example, appropriate rules of conduct during the pandemic followed by urging people to violate those rules. Personal attacks on public figures and businesses, democrats, former presidents and government officials, and sports figures who protest are combined with endless propagation of insults hurled at anyone who crosses him including families of fallen soldiers, international allies and historical enemies, and impromptu reallocations of troops in foreign lands are examples. The chaos creates "red meat for the right" that the left disapproves of. This disapproval reinforces the world view on the right that Trump is doing their work and that everything said is "fake news" and evil.

What is written about Trump and contemporary events fills many books about democracy and authoritarianism (Chapter 5) and an unlimited amount of media coverage. This is underscored by the appreciation that some of what Trump and his allies (Shawn Hannity and Tucker Carlson of Fox News are examples) have to say is often intended to key off (bait) a reaction on the left. Much of this in-depth reporting and analysis is riveting to read. However, it creates little change beyond bearing witness and forming a repository for future historians to research.

Weiner offers several insights regarding Trump surrounding himself with sycophants (Chapter 7).[11] Trump speaks of his aides as flatters who seldom if ever just say "no" to him which is thought to serve him poorly. This suggests Trump lacks the self-confidence to deal with others who challenge him. As reported in Weiner's article is that General John Kelly, the former White House chief of staff, warned Trump not to hire sycophants who are not willing to speak truth to power. When it comes to media coverage Trump is invested in getting Fox News personalities to submit to him and follow the narrative he sets for them.

Once again to be noted is that Trump's overdetermined self-centered narcissism is the underlying psychodynamic that is juxtaposed to followers seeking out a powerful and authoritative leader from a role of dependency. They move toward him in the hope he will save them from the many threats that he identifies as existing (Chapter 6). When viewed from a Group Relations perspective this leader becomes a fight or flight leader who is essential when fear is used as a group and social motivator.

This brief orientation to Trump as a political leader leads to examining Trump's racist birtherism and unrelenting attacks on Obama, his accomplishments, and his allies.[12] To be explored here are the connections between the many attempts to repeal and comprise the Affordable Care Act (ACA, Obamacare); the long felt often race-based animosity for President Barack Obama held by many on the right, the political ascent of Donald Trump, and last the upsurge of white male supremacy, white nationalism and open racism in the United States.

The Long Congressional Struggle to Repeal the Affordable Care Act

The many-year-long effort to repeal/replace Obamacare ultimately defeated by John McCain's theatrical thumbs down, while ostensibly about health care access, costs, inclusion, freedom of choice to purchase health insurance or not and not pay a penalty for not purchasing coverage, is at a deeper societal level, about something disturbing. While healthcare is the focus of the argument, *Obamacare as a brand* is also a highly charged symbol of a black man's influence on American politics and culture.

Obamacare as a target for unbridled opposition on the right extends beyond rational discussion and political compromise (the despised C word)[13] Vindictive language was and is used to describe its many failures and the President who led the creation of the despicable legislation that violates many rigidly held conservative and libertarian principles.[13,14] Starting January 19, 2011 there were dozens of votes to repeal and replace Obamacare and becoming a rallying cry for the 2016 election cycle. The crusade to eradicate Obamacare has been relentless. There is now a major 2020 case pending before the Supreme Court brought by 20 Republican-led states that Trump supports. The case asserts that the ACA is illegal because the individual tax penalty has been eliminated. Why so much vitriol?

The key to understanding why Obamacare is both so hated and beyond discussion is the effort on the part of many white Americans and white nationalists, both politicians and non-politicians, to rid the United States of President Barack Obama's legacy of legislation. Obamacare is one of the most visible symbols of Obama's presidency.[14,15] This intense long sustained effort to repeal Obamacare can be understood to contain unconscious and undiscussed in the public arena motivations that are an effort to eradicate the blackness of Obama as an African American President and remove his administration from the White House and from the government and relegate it to a forgotten distant past.[16,17]

Walsh writes that President Obama reflected in 2010, race was still a problem.[17] In May 2010 during a White House dinner he commented that race was an important element of the rising conservative opposition to his presidency as represented by the "Tea Party" movement surging across the country. This movement spoke to middle-class and working-class whites who felt aggrieved (Chapter 13) that the federal government was helping other groups, bankers, corporations, and minorities during the great recession, but was not helping them nearly enough.

Gandin similarly notes that Obama is the only American president who has faced an opposition convinced that he is not a legitimate president as underscored by "birtherism."[18] Gandin suggests this was racism that did not die with the end of slavery but rather is an extension of the pervasive presence of America's white supremacist roots and slave holding by the founders.[18]

That an African American could and did twice win the presidency of the United States can be viewed from the right as a shameful stain on the cherished image of America as a white nation.[16,18] Eliminating Obamacare and other policies associated with President Obama can then be understood to contain a symbolic cleansing of the stain, and a reversal of this shame back into pride in white America to "Make America Great Again" and to keep it that way by walling off any further immigrant stains on white society. Obamacare is thus about far more than healthcare.[19] It is in fact about a twisted kind of "social medicine," the aim of which is to cure America of blackness symbolized by Barack Obama's election and legacy.

Linking the Unlinked

The triangulation approach used in this book allows us to understand the relentless Republican Congressional effort to repeal Obamacare. Trump's hatred of President Obama, and the upsurge of racism against African Americans but also anyone of color including Muslims, are related if only based on what Trump tweets and says. The first element of this race-based triangle is: Shortly following the election of President Obama in 2008 there was a meeting of Republican Party leaders at which they vowed to oppose, block, and reject everything that President Obama did, which came to include repealing and replacing the Affordable Care Act of 2010.[20] The Republican Party single-mindedly rejected the entire Democratic platform. "Hell No!" as John Boehner said on the floor of the House. Hatred of Obamacare effectively became a target of displaced hatred and aggression toward President Obama.

The Republicans saw a path out of the political wilderness. By blocking Obama's policy initiatives, they could win the broader messaging war simply by remaining unified and fighting him on everything – the victory of "no."[20]

The second element of the triangle is: An explosion of unfettered racism. Almost concurrent with Obama's election the Tea Party movement arose which was overtly racist and was supported by the wealthy Koch Brothers.[21] A predominantly Southern-based grassroots movement was thus mobilized to complement the efforts of the Republican Party.[22,23] Many Tea Party members were ultimately elected to Congress, becoming the Freedom Caucus. During this same time there appeared posters in mass gatherings and cartoons of President Obama and Michelle Obama, and T-Shirts of President Obama as the children's book monkey character Curious George, that made them look like monkeys, clearly a racist depiction of blacks as lower-than-human.[24,25,26,27]

Discussing a study in *Race and Social Problems*, by Angie Maxwell and T. Wayne Parent,[28] Morgan Whitaker[29] writes that "Tea Party members are not necessarily more racist than typical white Americans, but the movement's supporters are more likely to be ...." Further, Tea Party members "were significantly more likely [than white non-members] to believe President Obama is a Muslim and to favor harsher immigration controls. Maxwell and Parent also found [Tea Party] members were more likely to agree that 'whiteness, the ability to speak English well, and native-born status' were especially important in 'what it means to be fully American.'" The "subterranean agenda" of Tea Party members was white supremacist at its core.

This is underscored by the Southern Poverty Law Center documenting a rapid expansion in the number of racist hate groups after Obama was elected.[30] In short, white racism was fanned and encouraged during the years leading up to Trump's ultimate mobilization of these racist social elements, by drawing upon historical white grievances and racial hatred. Donald Trump capitalized on this by courting the Tea Party and alternative right (alt-right), fanning the flames of racism, and by tacitly supporting racist, white supremacist, organizations – the KKK and Neo-Nazis. Trump's August 2017 comments referring to good people on both sides regarding the Charlottesville marching and violence are illustrative. By contrast, Obama was loath to "play the race card," preferring rather to self-edit and take the high road that his wife Michelle often refers to.[31,32]

The third element of the triangulation is Donald Trump's election to the U.S. presidency in November 2016. By 2011, Trump had become the most visible spokesperson for the birther movement which was understood to be an effort to delegitimize Obama as President. Trump and many others portrayed themselves as refusing to believe that Obama was born in the United States and was therefore not legally the President of the United States. They also insisted that Obama was not Christian.

Some think that the decisive moment Trump decided to run for the presidency was the annual Washington Post gala White House Correspondents' Dinner on April 30, 2011, in which President Obama "roasted" and publicly humiliated Trump, a reality TV celebrity, with his relentless humor.[33,34] Trump is easily offended (thinned skinned), although he thinks nothing of offending others. He has often sought revenge against Obama – ten-fold as Trump is heard to say at a public humiliation of a former Miss Universe, Jennifer Hawkins in 2011.[35]

In a sense, Trump's quest for the presidency was not so much about politics, but about getting even and destroying the man who publicly shamed him. His personal grudge and appeal to white supremacy groups ignited the historical grudge of many whites, especially in the South. President Trump predictably rejected the interpretation that his decision to run for president was triggered by Obama's roast and that his presidential ambitions began years earlier.[36] Still, Wang writes that "Video from the dinner would later show Trump seemingly frozen in the audience, lips pursed, staring straight ahead with his face set into something between a squint and a hard scowl."[36]

The triangulation completed at this point offers many insights. Trump's personal vendetta against Obama was enacted and operationalized by resurgent anti-black white supremacist groups and by the Republican Party, Tea Party, and Libertarians, all of whom, in turn, drew upon the deep well of racial hatred of African Americans and fear of foreign terrorists and rapists. Obamacare embodied and condensed the irrational animosity into a single easily identified symbol.

Vowing to destroy the Affordable Care Act, Trump wrapped his personal vendetta in the ideology of white supremacism. As Ta-Nehisi Coates writes:

> His political career began in advocacy of birtherism, that modern recasting of the old American precept that black people are not fit to be citizens of the country they built. But long before birtherism, Trump had made his worldview clear .... It is often said that Trump has no real ideology, which is not true – his ideology is white supremacy, in all its truculent and sanctimonious power. Trump inaugurated his campaign by casting himself as the defender of white maidenhood against Mexican 'rapists,' only to be later alleged by multiple accusers, and by his own proud words, to be a sexual violator himself. White supremacy has always had a sexual tint.[16]

For Trump psychological splitting and projection is commonplace. To be noted Democratic presidential candidate Hillary Clinton further inflamed this problem when she characterized Tea Party members and white supremacists as "deplorables," who embraced sexism, homophobia, xenophobia compounding their sense of shame and their vow to reverse it into shamelessness and pride and political mobilization.[37] Many Trump supporters in fact wear "deplorable" t-shirts with pride in addition to many other flags and symbols of the far-right.[38]

Simply put, the personal and cultural mobilized the political. The Tea Party, alternate right Republicans, and white supremacists have sought to undo and avenge the affront that President Obama was to their racial ideology of white supremacy. Destroying Obamacare was a readily available and highly visible target to destroy and declare victory for white nationalism.

The Psychodynamics of Polarization and Political and Social Destruction

Racism, white nationalism, and white supremacy are a dark undercurrent of much of the political rhetoric on the right, including long sustained efforts to eliminate the Affordable Care Act as Obama's signature legislation, but also everything associated with him. The conviction that he as black is bad or evil and they as white are good is a reality supported by denial, splitting, and projection. Obama as black is created in mind by individuals and large groups as representing all that white racists wish to disown in themselves – lazy, ignorant and stupid that are stereotypes cast at people of color historically and at the present but in a more coded (politically correct) way. The result is the creation of a simplified black and white world (conceptually and figuratively) that when combined with right-wing ideologies is reassuring to those who embrace the splitting and projection.

There is also the presence of a fight/flight leader who everyone depends on to save them from all these threats and evils. So long as their fears and anxieties can be manipulated, they will faithfully follow a leader who offers hope for deliverance from these threats. They move toward the leader from a position of deeply felt anxiety and dependency that only the leader can take care of them. They are willing to follow even an imperfect leader like Trump so long as some of the promised hope still seems attainable. This is also self-evident even when some followers admit their leader is morally and ethically deficient. Loyalty, however, is sustainable only so long as he pursues their interests such as Supreme Court and judiciary appoints believed to be favorable to their goals. The underlying psychologically and socially defensive dynamics are powerful and sustainable only when many threats are identified by a charismatic and paranoid leader who promotes fear and anxiety on the part of his followers and voters.

In Conclusion

This chapter has provided a historical perspective on Trump himself and connected the dots, so to speak, between many strands of the organizational, cultural, political, and historical story that explains the relentless effort by Republicans and the far right to repeal and destroy Obamacare and Obama's presidential legacy. The Republican Party's determination to obstruct Obama's legislative initiatives, the rise of Donald Trump, his experience of humiliation by President Obama, and the emergence of open racism are readily documented and will be the subject of much research and writing to come. Our triangulation approach relied on here represents one way to understand the emergence and consolidation of this movement and its relentless and irrational determination to rid the United States of Obamacare.

Chapter 4 turns our attention to a very often mentioned aspect of Trump's sense of self that contaminates his interpersonal world. Narcissism that is excessive and even malignant is often ascribed to him by psychologists, psychiatrists, and psychoanalysts. Narcissism appears to consume him and drive self-centric political thoughts that are on full view on Twitter.

Notes

1. Greenberg, J. (2019). The 6 essential cons that define Trump's success: A playbook of deceit starts with the "origin lie" that made him richer than he was. And it's still being written. *Washington Post.* https://www.washingtonpost.com/outlook/2019/02/22/essential-cons-that-define-trumps-success/.
2. Fawaz, S. (2016). Here are all of Trump's bankruptcies and failed businesses. *Labor 411.* http://labor411.org/411-blog/here-are-all-of-trump-s-bankruptcies-and-failed-businesses/.
3. Stuart, T. (2016). Donald Trump's 13 biggest business failures. *Rolling Stone.* https://www.rollingstone.com/politics/politics-news/donald-trumps-13-biggest-business-failures-59556/.
4. Buettner, R. & Bagli, C. (2016). How Donald Trump bankrupted his Atlantic City casinos, but still earned millions. *The New York Times.* https://www.nytimes.com/2016/06/12/nyregion/donald-trump-atlantic-city.html.
5. Worstall, T. (2016). Only one third of Trump's new businesses succeeded – that's actually a pretty good record. *Forbes.* https://www.forbes.com/sites/timworstall/2016/10/06/only-one-third-of-trumps-new-businesses-succeeded-thats-actually-a-pretty-good-record/#30c852c2486a.
6. Maccoby, M. (2003). *The productive narcissist: The promise and peril of visionary leadership.* New York, NY: Broadway Books.
7. Woodward, B. (2018). *Fear: Trump in the White House* (2nd ed.). New York, NY: Simon & Schuster.
8. Capehart, J. (2018). I used to be afraid to call Trump a mob boss. Not anymore. *Washington Post.* https://www.washingtonpost.com/blogs/post-partisan/wp/2018/08/24/i-used-to-be-afraid-to-call-trump-a-mob-boss-not-anymore/.
9. Tabachnick, D.E. (2016). The four characteristics of Trumpism. *The Hill.* https://thehill.com/blogs/congress-blog/presidential-campaign/264746-the-four-characteristics-of-trumpism.
10. Krugman, P. (2020). Trump takes us to the brink: Will weaponized racism destroy America? *The New York Times.* https://www.nytimes.com/2020/06/01/opinion/trump-george-floyd-police-brutality.html.
11. Weiner, G. (2019). Trump's sycophants are his worst enemies. *National Review.* https://www.nationalreview.com/2019/11/donald-trump-sycophants-endanger-his-presidency/.
12. Stein, H. & Allcorn, S. (2018). A fateful convergence: Animosity toward Obamacare, hatred of Obama, the rise of Donald Trump, and overt racism in America. *The Journal of Psychohistory* 45(4), 234–242.

13. Marcotte, A. (2015). The Obamacare fight has always been about race and gender anxiety. *TPM.* http://talkingpointsmemo.com/cafe/obamacare-fight-race-and-gender-anxiety-michael-carvin.

14. Daily Kos (2013). Calling the Affordable Care Act "Obamacare" Just Exacerbates Public Confusion, So Stop Doing It. *Daily Kos.* https://www.dailykos.com/stories/2013/9/19/1239651/-Calling-the-Affordable-Care-Act-Obamacare-Just-Exacerbates-Public-Confusion-So-Stop-Doing-It.

15. Taddonio, P. (2017). How "Obamacare" became a symbol of America's divide. *Frontline.* http://www.pbs.org/wgbh/frontline/article/watch-how-obamacare-became-a-symbol-of-americas-divide/.

16. Coates, T. (2017). The first white president: The foundation of Donald Trump's presidency is the negation of Barack Obama's legacy. *The Atlantic.* https://www.theatlantic.com/magazine/archive/2017/10/the-first-white-president-ta-nehisi-coates/537909/.

17. Walsh, K. (2011). Obama says race a key component in Tea Party protests. *USNews.* https://www.usnews.com/news/articles/2011/03/02/obama-says-race-a-key-component-in-tea-party-protests.

18. Grandin, G. (2014). Obama, Melville and the Tea Party. *The New York Times.* https://www.nytimes.com/2014/01/19/opinion/sunday/obama-melville-and-the-tea-party.html.

19. Stein, H.F. (2017). The Obamacare fight isn't about health. *Tulsa World.* http://www.tulsaworld.com/opinion/opinionfeatured/howard-f-stein-the-obamacare-fight-isn-t-about-health/article_e08199a1-05a3-5f29-8c4c-b6eb23caac2f.html.

20. Grunwald, M. (2016). The victory of no. *Politico.* http://www.politico.com/magazine/story/2016/12/republican-party-obstructionism-victory-trump-214498.

21. Rich, F. (2010). The billionaires bankrolling the Tea Party. *The New York Times.* http://www.nytimes.com/2010/08/29/opinion/29rich.html.

22. Lotto, D. (2016). The south has risen again: Thoughts on the Tea Party and the recent rise of right-wing racism. *Journal of Psychohistory* 43(3), 156–166.

23. Tea Party movement (2021, May 21). In *Wikipedia.* https://en.wikipedia.org/wiki/Tea_Party_movement.

24. Burkeman, O. (2009). New York Post in racism row over chimpanzee cartoon. *The Guardian.* https://www.theguardian.com/world/2009/feb/18/new-york-post-cartoon-race.

25. Chan, S. & Peters, J. (2009). Chimp-stimulus cartoon raises racism concerns. *The New York Times.* https://cityroom.blogs.nytimes.com/2009/02/18/chimp-stimulus-cartoon-raises-racism-concerns/?mcubz=.

26. Haines, E. (2008). Obama/Curious George T-shirt draws protests. *Washington Post.* http://www.washingtonpost.com/wp-dyn/content/article/2008/05/14/AR2008051403613.html.

27. Cheezburger. (2017). Barack Obama Totally Looks Like Curious George. *Cheezburger.* http://cheezburger.com/1522639104/barack-obama-looks-like-curious-george.

28. Maxwell, A. & Parent, W. (2013). A "subterranean agenda"? racial attitudes, presidential evaluations, and Tea Party membership. *Race and Social Problems,* 5(3), 226–237.

29. Whitaker, M. (2013). Study: Tea Party supporters more likely to exhibit racism. *MSNBC.* http://www.msnbc.com/politicsnation/study-tea-party-supporters-more-likely-ex.

30. Neo-Confederate. *Southern Poverty Law Center (SPLC).* https://www.splcenter.org/fighting-hate/extremist-files/ideology/neo-confederate.

31. Thrush, G. & Brown, C. (2013). Obama weighs in on race, reluctantly. *Politico*. http://www.politico.com/story/2013/07/obama-weighs-in-on-race-reluctantly-94495_Page2.html.

32. Henry, C., Allen, R., & Chrisman, R. (2011). Editors. *The Obama phenomenon: Toward a multiracial democracy*. Champaign, IL: University of Illinois Press.

33. Taddonio, P. (2016). Inside the night president Obama took on Donald Trump. *Frontline*. http://www.pbs.org/wgbh/frontline/article/watch-inside-the-night-president-obama-took-on-donald-trump/.

34. Gajanan, M. (2017) A history of President Trump being trolled at the White House Correspondents' Dinner. *Time*. http://time.com/4756751/donald-trump-white-house-correspondents-dinner/.

35. Grim, R. (2016). Video shows Donald Trump sexually humiliating woman before large audience. *Huffington Post*. http://www.huffingtonpost.com/entry/donald-trump-jennifer-hawkins-video_us_58137b85e4b0390e69cfbbba.

36. Wang, A. (2017). Trump denies 2011 White House correspondents' dinner spurred presidential bid. *Washington Post*. https://www.washingtonpost.com/news/arts-and-entertainment/wp/2017/02/26/did-the-2011-white-house-correspondents-dinner-spur-trump-to-run-for-president/?utm_term=.61d-8205b39ed.

37. Allcorn, S. & Stein, H. (2017). The politics of shame. *The Journal of Psychohistory* 45(2), 78–93.

38. Hatewatch Staff (2017). Flags and other symbols used by far-right groups in Charlottesville. *Southern Law and Poverty Center*. https://www.splcenter.org/hatewatch/2017/08/12/flags-and-other-symbols-used-far-right-groups-charlottesville.-

4   Narcissism

In this chapter, we consider Trump's narcissism, his vulnerability to narcissistic injuries, and his vindictive responses. Trump attracts a lot of attention to himself, very often dominating the 24-hour news cycle. He wants to be the center of attention regardless of whether it is good attention or bad – all publicity sometimes is considered to be good publicity. He has a long history of continually promoting himself by putting his name on buildings, products, and services. He also professionally manipulates the media into covering his every thought, feeling, and action including his tens of millions of Twitter followers. And to be noted, he received exceptional free coverage during his campaign against Hillary Clinton, so much so that it was a factor in his election.

Narcissism has a vast literature, indicating it is a common personality and character disorder. We begin our inquiry by providing an overview of some of this literature, followed by an exploration of how narcissism informs understanding Donald Trump. We conclude by using the three psychodynamically informed perspectives (Chapter 2) to further understand the role narcissism plays in the Age of Trump, and within business organizations in general, since Trump is foremost a businessman.

Clinical Theory and Perspectives on Narcissism

Clinically narcissistic personalities are described with a fairly common consistency. James Masterson writes:

> The main clinical characteristics of the narcissistic personality disorder are grandiosity, extreme self-involvement, and lack of interest in and empathy for others, in spite of the pursuit of others to obtain admiration and approval. The patient manifesting a narcissistic personality disorder seems to be endlessly motivated to seek perfection in all he or she does, to pursue wealth, power and beauty and to find others who will mirror and admire his/her grandiosity. Underneath this defensive façade is a feeling state of emptiness and rage with a predominance of intense envy.[1]

This clinical picture is a good explanation for what may be observed relative to Donald Trump. Keywords that are noteworthy are: grandiosity, the pursuit of admiration, power, and beauty, accompanied by rage that Trump acts on by "getting even many times over" when narcissistic injuries occur. His pursuit of offenders is relentless. One last keyword is envy, which seems to be especially apparent regarding Barack Obama who, for example, received the Nobel Peace Prize while Trump continues to strive to receive it.

Andrew Morrison in his edited book *Essential Papers on Narcissism* highlights some of the complexity of this personality disorder.[2] Early development may include narcissistic injuries (the withholding of approval and love by parental figures). In response, there may develop an expansive sense of self, bolstered by seeking approval and love in response to hard to control feelings of helplessness, vulnerability, anxiety, and rage.[2] The child and adult may be said to be compensating for a narcissistic deficit and is always seeking from others admiration and love to compensate.

The narcissist may therefore oscillate between feelings of grandiosity and worthlessness and dejection. In this regard, these shifts in self-regard and self-esteem suggest that vulnerability may well be the key underlying deficit, and that grandiosity may be thought of as a compensatory defense mechanism. There may also exist an oscillation between a healthy sense of narcissism necessary for effective functioning, and excessive or pathological narcissism that introduces confusion and toxicity into relationships.

Morrison highlights some of what may be observed in narcissists. There is a high degree of self-reference and self-promotion paradoxically paired with the pursuit of approval, loyalty, and admiration. Emotional life is often shallow, and concern for others is lacking. Narcissists may idealize people from whom they expect to receive approval and admiration (narcissistic supplies) and conversely punish and exclude (fire) those who do not provide these critically important supplies. This underscores that narcissists, being self-centered, exploit those around them, including being observed to develop a parasitic relationship with those closest to them.[2]

Masterson and Morrison offer similar insights that reinforce the clinical understanding of narcissism. Elsa Ronningstam in her book *Identifying and Understand the Narcissistic Personality* extends these insights into the workplace, whether it is a business or the White House.[3] She notes: "Vocational activities and professional careers are usually associated with healthy narcissistic investment. For most people, the capacity to work – that is, to create, produce, collaborate, accomplish, achieve, and succeed – is a source of personal pride and satisfaction."[3] Healthy narcissism and adequate self-esteem are important contributors to having a vision and sufficient self-confidence to pursue it with suitable levels of assertiveness, where becoming overly aggressive is usually counterproductive. Being able to tolerate the many stresses associated with leading change particularly in organizations and politics, without becoming overly anxious and psychologically regressed that, in turn, surfaces less healthy narcissistic traits, is an essential element for successful leaders.

Michael Maccoby in his book *The Productive Narcissist* explores narcissism from the perspective of whether the narcissist is productive or not.[4] He notes several traits successful narcissists have. Maccoby also makes a point of saying that narcissists who are not productive are often removed from organizations – you're fired. The exceptions to being removed are CEOs who own their own company (Trump) or dominate their corporation (Dennis Kozlowski, Tyco). Productive narcissists have traits that may be summarized as:

- Passionate vision and independent thinking
- Willing risk-taking
- Motivated to create change and able to tolerate related stress
- A focus on achieving results, winning, and the doable
- Willing to use all available resources including people to achieve success
- Alert to threats especially from others who are not supportive
- Charming and manipulative

We see in this perspective narcissism is not "all bad." We often see major innovators who, while being exceptionally self-absorbed and self-promoting, are seemingly able to tolerate the stress of meeting exceptional challenges to succeed, that many others would eventually give up on. However, the challenges may also evoke anxiety and psychological regression toward less desirable narcissistic traits, thereby introducing interpersonal and organizational dysfunctions.[5] Donald Trump's performance as a businessman resembles this as discussed in Chapter 3. So might the careers of Steve Jobs and Elon Musk. To be noted outcomes like Enron are also possible where the "smartest guys in the room" were uninhibited in their pursuit of fame and profit, but ultimately proved not to be all that smart. We now take a moment to explore narcissism in the workplace as a way of better understanding Trump.

Narcissism and Organizational Life

Narcissism is a common presence in our daily lives at work. Our organizations are economically based, and we like to think that the people who work in them, are rational, realistic, objective, and make decisions based on productivity, profitability, and efficiency. Yet a lot of things that happen at work defy reason. Often "ego" rather than economics prevails. An example is a manager orienting new employees who says that employees are expected to work hard, underscored by also saying that every employee is expendable – with many people waiting to take the job. This is not a welcoming speech. It is a threat to the new employees who have not even started to work. This manager is making clear that he or she is strong and powerful (a common Trump phrase), and you are not. This explicit threat can be understood to be made for the sake of feeling powerful and in control, which is grounded in a narcissistically oriented need for self-importance.

This is not to say that all organizational leaders and managers are like this, but rather to point out that management by bullying, threatening, intimidation, and irrational decision-making, are more common than we would like to acknowledge. Anyone with work experience likely knows, based on first-hand experience, the effects of self-important narcissists hungry for admiration, power, and control.

This overview, while providing many cogent points about narcissism, is necessarily incomplete and has not delved into the many different depth psychological perspectives that endeavor to "unpack" narcissism for clinical treatment. Even so, the discussion has highlighted many of the traits of narcissists that can be experienced, observed, and felt in terms of their effects on others. We now turn to how this literature can be applied in practice to understand Donald Trump and the Age of Trump.

Narcissism in the Age of Trump

Trump's narcissistic qualities are often mentioned in the media and by academics. Dr. Bandy Lee's, book *The Dangerous Case of Donald Trump*[6] and Dan McAdams' article *The Mind of Donald Trump*[7] offer two complementary ways of understanding Donald Trump and how we got to where we are in 2020. They provide in-depth understanding of the relationship between excessive narcissism, clinical narcissism, and pathological narcissism.

The Dangerous Case of Donald Trump

Dr. Bandy Lee, a forensic psychiatrist, edited *The Dangerous Case of Donald Trump*.[6] The book includes many thoughtful analyses by professionals who research, write about, and treat people who suffer from narcissism that disturbs interpersonal, family, group, organizational dynamics, and beyond. Provided here are two illuminating discussions in a condensed form.

Thomas Singer, M.D.

Dr. Singer is a psychiatrist and psychoanalyst who examines contemporary political and social movements from a psychodynamic perspective. His contribution to Lee's book focuses on the relationship between Trump's narcissism and his loyal followers who identify in him the promise that their narcissistic injuries will be healed and their needs for appreciation and recognition fulfilled (Chapter 13). Trump's narcissism amounts to a compensatory mirror for their narcissistic injuries and needs as he articulates his own. He and his followers are aggrieved and enraged about it. His constant disregard for public civility (termed derogatorily as political correctness), liberal elites, and criticism labeled as *fake* news, including science and any other information that does not match his narrative of grievance, mirrors his followers' sense of neglect and injury.

Trump exploits the dark, raw emotions of these Americans who feel their values and desires have been disregarded by the political establishment and that they are often looked down on by political elites – liberals. This exploitation has surfaced a very real sense of rage, hatred, envy, and fear within the despairing white middle class who feel they are losing the promise of a brighter future for themselves.

Psychodynamically, there exists a process of identification with this image of an all-knowing and powerful leader who allows his followers to imagine themselves as powerful as well. Identification with Trump helps them to heal their narcissistic wounds. At the same time, this powerful unconscious process that involves splitting, projection, and identification with the projections of self-efficacy deposited in their leader in their minds tends to compromise their knowing, reasoning, and conscience (empathy). This, in turn, can lead to shameful, immoral, and criminal actions on his and their parts with a sense of impunity. For instance, they feel entitled as well as authorized by Trump to punish and throw out demonstrators at rallies. The lack of personal and group accountability, which is evident in 2020, is in part the result of the predictably failed impeachment. This dynamic has created ever greater norm violations, criminality, and authoritarianism, supported by Attorney General William Barr. However, at the same time, a leader who relies on promoting fear, lies continually, and betrays in many ways the public trust, becomes progressively more isolated from the public and accurate reality testing, requiring ever greater loyalty from supporters to stave off paranoid and persecutory anxiety.

In sum, Trump symbolizes for his followers the embodiment of a negative world view of America and of their needs to be made great again along with America. For his followers, Trump's continuous self-promotion of himself as a brand and his readily discerned arrogant self-pride that is easily injured (thin-skinned) that leads to vindictive bullying of anyone who crosses him, is part of this process. His insensitivity to others' feelings and needs and his insulting everyone and anything, highlights his needy toxicity while echoing this follower's thoughts and hurt feelings that require vindication. Trump, by putting himself and America first in international relations, has turned many Americans against the historical and symbolic meaning of America as welcoming immigrants and supporting the world community. Trump's followers believe that it is time for them and Trump to receive their rewards for their hard work and perseverance.

Harper West, Licensed Psychotherapist

West offers insight into Trump's narcissism by exploring the notion of Other-blamers who suffer from low self-worth and poor shame toler-ance. Poor shame tolerance West associates with vindictive anger, poor self-reflectivity, a lack of being held accountable, in addition to attributes, such as lying and dishonesty, reckless impulsivity, entitlement that comes with great wealth and power, and low empathy. These enable Trump's ruthless punishment of others combined with continuous self and brand promotion, often dissociated from the reality of past performance.

Trump as an Other-blamer is focused on seeking out others who are willing to be controlled, manipulated, or intimidated, aided by his con-stantly firing people until the "right" person is found. Michael Cohen, during his testimony before Congress, referred to Trump as eating your soul one bite at a time. This dynamic of turning over people until submis-sive people are found gradually assures him that fewer and fewer people will "speak truth to power" and challenge or correct him. They also, at the same time, become targets for blaming as the need arises (thrown under the bus). Here again, the lack of a sense of wrongdoing and self/ other awareness leads to low accountability for himself and his followers, who as a result are more willing to act out their fear and rage. This opens up the possibility of a cycle of ever-increasing destructiveness where the opposition is depersonalized and dehumanized, allowing for their unmer-ciful punishment and even elimination – firing or more recently interna-tionally, poisoned, shot or murdered, and dismembered (Jamal Khashoggi, the murdered Washington Post journalist).

In sum, there is then to be appreciated a largely unconscious resonance between Trump and his followers (identification) grounded in a mutually shared sense of grievance (Chapter 13) of being discounted and looked down on by a liberal elite and a political system that overlooks their needs to have their own values and ideals recognized and enacted into laws (abortion is an example). Dan McAdams further explores these dynamics that have at their core overdetermined narcissism and narcissistic injuries that demand vindictive triumph over others who harm this fragile expan-sive sense of self.

The Mind of Donald Trump

Dan McAdams who is a professor of psychology at Northwestern University, offers many insights into Trump in his *Atlantic* article, "The Mind of Donald Trump."[7] McAdams explores Trump's narcissism, disa-greeableness, and grandiosity.

Trump, McAdams observes, is callous, rude, arrogant, and lacking in empathy. He has, for example, at rallies and elsewhere encouraged his followers to attack protesters, which they have done. Trump appears to be motivated by anger, and he speaks angrily, fueling malice toward others. Because he lacks a moral compass and is not thought to be very ideological, he has no problem waffling between conservative and liberal positions. This frees him up to seize upon positions to dominate the news cycle not infrequently in the moment without consulting with those affected by his pronouncements. His pragmatism in pursuing his self-interests and his willingness to continue to switch positions often allow him to achieve his goals. He may speak for and against the same position on the same day or week depending on the moment and his audience.

McAdams points out that Trump's disagreeableness seems to be motivated by anger, making him at times a ruthless and aggressive decision-maker who wants to succeed at all costs. He ignores how damaging his behavior is to others and other organizations, governmental entities, foreign nations, and international agreements. Winning at any cost is the goal. This intense pursuit of success may be thought of as not only self-consuming and self-centered but also as diminishing other aspects of himself, such as his empathy and a willingness to voluntarily coordinate with others. Business and social dominance is his strategy.

Narcissism is also self-evident in his highly accomplished pursuits of drawing attention to himself – best, the greatest, strong, and powerful are words he often speaks of relative to himself. He desires to be loved and admired or, failing that, feared – the Mob Boss. Striving to be seen by others as brilliant and powerful promotes a sense in others who feel they are vulnerable a willingness to accept being manipulated by this self-important narcissist. They feel they are in the presence of greatness. As a leader who is charismatic and paranoid, Trump spots threats and enemies everywhere, and by doing so he continually promotes fear on the part of his followers increasing their dependency on him. Perhaps it is indeed the case that only he can save them.

In sum, Trump's disagreeableness combined with a willingness to violate social and historical norms and values leads to considering a concept such as authoritarian personality (Chapter 5). This pattern involves embracing self-defined social norms and values consistent with held ideologies. This dynamic, combined with the submission of followers to an authority figure, reinforces these ideologies, systems of belief, norms, and values. Everyone is onboard. The result is that historical social norms are displaced, extinguished, and preferably forgotten. The new status quo must then be protected at all costs. This leads to greater dependence on a strong and powerful leader who will dominate events, thereby securing the sacredness of the ideology and the new social norms and values. This pattern is consistent with conservative values that oppose progressive change such as embracing immigrants, Muslims, and the LGBTQ community.

Narcissism and Its Relationship to Shame

Lee's and McAdam's insights lead to the conclusion that a narcissist who sees the world as dangerous must defend against and dominate enemies. Compassion and shame are largely absent and perhaps even counterproductive to dominating others. This closely resembles Trump's but also the GOP's behavior in the Age of Trump. In Trump's case, everyone around him and all his past, present, and likely future business partners are subjected to the same behaviors where dominance and submission are at play. Winning at almost any cost and punishing anyone that crosses him are the norm. And to be noted, this norm is also consistent with Karen Horney's formulation of the expansive solution to anxiety which includes perfection, narcissism, and vindictive triumph over those who harm his arrogant pride.

Shame is an important perspective for understanding the worldview, philosophy, and political ideology of the political right that underpins Donald Trump. Chapter 10 is devoted to more fully exploring the relationship between right-wing political ideologies and the lack of a sense of compassion and shame that seem to be implicit in embracing a world view of individualism free of masks and personal responsibility. This is especially relevant in a society that has historically created inhibitors and discrimination that forestalls, for example, and people of color from pursuing a fulfilling life (Chapter 14). Further, shame and the denial of shame help to explain the tenacity with which the right embraces its ideological understanding and interpretation of the world. Consistent with this point of view we note that much of what the right does politically may be viewed to be unethical (promoting conspiracy theories is an example) and not consistent with generally accepted human values. Healthcare is, for example, considered by many on the right to be a privilege and not a right. Positions like this taken by the right must therefore be concealed or spun to sound less anti-social, uncaring, and undesirable to others while staying consistent with their political beliefs.

Our contribution to this understanding is to explore these many psychosocial dynamics from the perspective of a compromised ability among many conservatives to feel empathy and shame where shameless behavior on Trump's part is striking. All too often there appears to be no sense of wrong-doing, conscience, or regret when positions are taken that harm others (imprisoning immigrant children) or limit or eliminate social programs such as Obamacare, food stamps, food for children, and extended unemployment benefits. Ideology and party come first.

The toxic fusion of narcissism with shamelessness pervades the Age of Trump and Trump's life itself. A recent illustration of Trump's all-consuming narcissism and lack of sense of shame is his response to his own diagnosis of COVID-19 in early October 2020. He insists on not wearing a protective mask at White House meetings and gatherings (e.g., the September 26th Rose Garden event in which he introduced his nominee for the U.S. Supreme Court), and at his political rallies, including early in October, when medical staff in the White House already knew he had tested positive for COVID-19. His disregard for others' health, life, and potential death, as Dr. Fauci noted, makes him a potential "super-spreader." He is contemptuous of any of his associates who wear a mask and regards it as a sign of weakness. Narcissism could hardly have more dangerous consequences.

In sum, a willingness to risk the lives and health of those around him to fulfill his self-image of being powerful, strong, and manly is pursued without, it appears, a sense of shame, compassion, or empathy regarding his actions that potentially can bring harm to others. All these psychosocial dynamics are better understood by using the three psychoanalytic informed theories in Chapter 2.

Applying Psychodynamically Informed Theory to Psychosocial Polarization

Narcissism and the Age of Trump invite inspection from the three theoretical perspectives presented in Chapter 2. *Object relations* perspectives suggest that unconscious processes and defenses create a black and white world with self-created-and-perpetuated evil others (birtherism, for example, that speaks to fear of the alien other). Consider the phrase, "Take my country back," as has been used by the left and the right. This speaks to the polarization of a deeply split-apart society, holding worldviews amplified by television's quasi-news/propaganda that is now heavily relied on for knowing about and understanding the world around us.

Within this context, the opposing side of the polarization is constantly held up for contempt and condemnation and as a threat to one's very existence. Evil others lurk everywhere, including in the immigrant communities that we, until recently, welcomed into our midst. Fear is continually activated by using black and white imagery that promotes splitting and projection and transference of past traumas and anxieties onto the present context, as portrayed on TV and other news media, including internet platforms such as Facebook and Twitter.

It is also the case that splitting and projection have driven much of our national history, as discussed earlier. Fundamental splits in our society such as black versus white, north versus south, rural versus urban, old versus young, poor versus rich, and middle class versus the poor and the rich all have their origins "in mind" where the "other" is held in contempt and fear. Hence law and order are needed. These splits have been exploited by politicians and political parties since the founding of the country, when well over half of the founders owned slaves, and some were farmers from rural areas (Washington and Jefferson). Politicians invariably and shamelessly tell supporters what they want to hear. These splits are there.

They feel "natural." They are filled with unconscious dynamics that promote, maintain, and further them.

The populist ethnocentrism and economic national-centrism that have arisen not only in the United States but also around the world are exploited by political leaders who induce fear, which in turn encourages psychological regression and the use of psychological defenses such and splitting and projection. It is a world of us versus them and good versus bad. Splitting and the accompanying transference of emotions help to explain authoritarianism on the right, that is one side of the current political and social polarization. The "me first" worldview and white supremacy implicitly contain shame that must be coped with via denial and compensation in the form of grandiosity and an expansive pride system. Hillary Clinton's "deplorables" on T-shirts at Trump rallies highlight how Trump's supporters embrace this pejorative label with pride. Distressing self and group experience may also be split off and projected onto people branded as worthless, incompetent, and who should feel ashamed for calling us "deplorable." This is "as if" to say: They deserve what they get from Trump.

In sum, object relations theory contributes to creating and maintaining the polarization described by Hetherington and Weiler, and the undoing of shame in our cultural history.[8] The us versus them and the good versus bad dichotomies can be better understood by using object relations theory. It is essential to appreciate the conscious and unconscious psychodynamics that make those on the right feel set upon, rejected, and considered to be as holding unacceptable values, that are anti-social in nature – as is manifested by the me-first selfishness promoted by the right are important to appreciate.

Group Relations perspectives also contribute insights into the fight or flight basic assumption group that requires a strong and powerful leader to lead it to win out. This group benefits from a narcissistic charismatic leader who locates threats everywhere (paranoia) that require action. Those who form this group accept authoritarianism willingly if not preferably.[9] Having found their leader, his group becomes dependent, and it is willing to accept casualties among its members either harmed by the opposing force (beaten and shot) or not infrequently by the leader for not being loyal.

In sum, individual and group regression to this basic assumption group stifles critical thinking and adherence to customary social value systems thereby freeing the leader and group members to act aggressively toward the identified enemy (liberals, protestors, or immigrants). There may also be a sense of flight from the threat that may, for example, require walling off and out the threatening group, or throwing offenders back over the wall. The creation of alternate facts (Fox News) forms the basis of confirmation bias that serves to make the embrace of an ideology consistent with this basic assumption group reassuring.

Karen Horney's movements against (expansive solution to anxiety) and movements toward (self-effacing solution to anxiety) also contribute insights. Similar to the fight or flight leader, a leader like Trump must possess an expansive sense of self that knows few limits in terms of what might be considered and acted upon. He, the stable genius, knows more than experienced state department officials and senior military officers. For him, having no limits is important. This bigger-than-life individual easily attracts the attention of those who project their self-efficacy onto him, and therefore feeling less capable of dealing with problems and threats. These followers can become dependent, seeking their "just" rewards for their hard work and perseverance (Chapter 13), and possibly becoming submissive and little more than sycophants discussed in Chapter 7.

In sum, it is common for individual and group regression toward these directions of movement to occur when major threats are perceived to exist. When the threats are magnified by a powerful leader thought to be strong, these regressed dynamics further empower the leader. The result may be dependent and even submissive followers who further expand the already narcissistic expansive sense of self the leader already possesses. At this point, the leader is authorized to do whatever is necessary to save everyone from the threats (the chosen one), and most often they will unquestioningly follow – the "lock her up" and "build the wall chant."

In Conclusion

In this chapter, we have explored some of the psychodynamics of narcissism underlying contemporary American politics and the Age of Trump. The worldview of pursing one's self-interest under the banner of a political ideology can become itself a societal problem. The omnipresence of continuous lying, distorting, and misleading voters about the outcomes – for example, of repealing and replacing the health care system (no Republican plan has ever been put forward) may well disenfranchise many millions of citizens from receiving healthcare – is a product of pathological narcissism where anything goes that serves the narcissist's self-interest. One wonders how these actions can be denied or rationalized.[10]

We have explored linkages between unbridled self-interest, a pervasive attitude of me-first/us-first, and a lack of compassion toward people that contribute insight into the denial and rationalization. We conclude this chapter by noting that unless these social and psychological dynamics are acknowledged and held up for inspection, reflection, and discussion, they will likely remain a constant toxic presence, creating social and political polarization.

Chapter 5 continues this journey into creating psychodynamically informed insights by examining autocracy and authoritarianism and what is a clear emergence of these dynamics in 2020 following the failed impeachment of President Trump. The failure encouraged a no limits world view by Trump accentuated by the right's growing sense of anxiety and desperation during 2020 regarding being reelected.

Notes

1. Masterson, J. (1981). *The narcissistic and borderline disorders: An integrated developmental approach.* New York, NY: Brunner/Mazel, 7.
2. Morrison, A. Ed. (1986). *Essential papers on narcissism.* New York, NY: New York University Press.
3. Ronningstam, E. (2005). *Identify and understand the narcissistic personality.* New York, NY: Oxford University Press, 135.
4. Maccoby, M. (2003). *The productive narcissist: The promise and peril of visionary leadership.* New York, NY: Broadway Books.
5. Allcorn, S. and Stein, H. (2017). *The dysfunctional workplace: Theory, stories, and practice.* Columbia, MO: University of Missouri Press.
6. Lee, B. (2017). *The dangerous case of Donald Trump.* New York, NY: Thomas Dunne.
7. McAdams, D. (2016). The mind of Donald Trump. *The Atlantic.* https://www.theatlantic.com/magazine/archive/2016/06/the-mind-of-donald-trump/480771/.
8. Hetherington, M. & Weiler, J. (2009). *Authoritarianism & polarization in American politics.* New York, NY: Cambridge University Press.
9. McWilliams, M, (2020). Trump is an authoritarian. So are millions of Americans. *Politico.* https://www.politico.com/news/magazine/2020/09/23/trump-america-authoritarianism-420681.
10. Morrison, A. (1970). *The culture of shame.* Northvale, NJ: Jason Aronson.

5   Autocracy

This chapter's title is Autocracy, which encompasses the autocrats who create autocracies and the means and methods they employ to do so that are described as fascist and authoritarian.[1,2] The means and methods in the United States include the creation of a post-factual world explored in this chapter. Authoritarian leadership and its outcome authoritarianism are closely allied with autocracy and autocrat. These are words often used to describe Trump and the right/far-right. There is implicit in the use of these means and methods the presence of paranoia in that those who "live by the sword" also fear dying from the sword, perhaps left swinging by their feet from a bridge (Mussolini), suicide and burned (Hitler), or arrested and tried like Chile's dictator Pinochet or Sudan's Omar Hassan al-Bashir. This fear, where the leader sees in others his or her own autocratic and authoritarian tendencies (driven by splitting and projection and an alternate media reality), leads to the necessity of creating a loyal, admiring, and preferably unquestioning cadre of followers (sycophants) discussed in Chapter 7.

Our discussion here of the autocratic outcomes of these means and methods will of necessity be abbreviated given their hundreds of years and worldwide presence. The mention of the loyal followers and the autocrats who carefully groom their followers illustrates that ultimately all the topics in this book are interrelated and reinforcing from a systemic point of view. This chapter contributes insight and sensemaking for understanding autocrats and authoritarian regimes around the world (Brazil, Hungary, Egypt, China, Russia are examples) as well as examples from world history (Germany and Italy, fascism) and the enabling provided by propaganda and the right-wing media.

We begin this process of "peeling the onion" by briefly defining autocracy and authoritarianism, which are similar and found together but are not the same things.

Linguistic Distinctions

Linguistically autocracy is a noun; a form of government in which unlimited power is held by a single individual. Autocrat is an adjective (autocratic is a noun) that relates to a leadership style and structure in which governmental power is held absolutely and may be used arbitrarily by an autocrat. Authoritarian when used as an adjective relates to a way of achieving obedience to the authority of an authoritarian (noun). Authoritarianism is a noun that describes a leadership style and structure on which absolute authority (power and control) is achieved through tyrannical means in the service of submitting others to the authority (obedience).

At the risk of oversimplifying these fine-tuned differences, the similarities are striking in their overlapping meaning in terms of how they are played out in societies around the world. The meaning of these words as forms of governance is important to understand.

Autocracy Defined

A review of definitions and discussions to be found on the internet leads to the following definition including approaches to achieving it. Autocracy is generally regarded as a system of governance in which a single person (autocrat) or a party dominated by a single person who, in either case, possesses supreme and absolute power. What the autocrat does is not limited by external legal restraints or forms of popular control with the exceptions of revolutions and insurrections. Absolute monarchies (such as Saudi Arabia, Qatar, and Vatican City) and dictatorships (formally Iraq and currently Egypt and North Korea) are contemporary examples. Totalitarian and military dictatorships that try to control all aspects of civil life may have an absolute leader but may also take the form of single-party rule bound by ideology.

Modern autocrats often use democracy against itself by achieving gradual but near-absolute control over political parties, legislatures, elections, the military, police, and the judicial system to lessen their risk of being overthrown or held accountable.[3] How this is accomplished varies considerably. There are similarities but also differences depending on history and culture, but they ultimately share in the approaches and methods used to strive for this level of near-absolute control of all the levers of government and society. Successful cooption of democracy and democratic elements often assures long-term success masquerading as democratically elected leaders (Putin is an example) as compared with autocrats who have seized power and who have not gained this level of legitimacy and control.

Authoritarianism Defined

Authoritarianism as a form of government is characterized by centralized power often in the form of a single-party or military rule and limited political freedoms. Authoritarian rule may be either autocratic or oligarchic in nature. Control is often maintained by fraudulent and non-competitive elections, appeals to emotion that encourage identifying the leader or party as glorious and caretaking or, at least, protecting civilians from some form of harm or threat from a feared other.[4] Opposition groups that may include forms of religion and special interests are usually suppressed and those leading them are eliminated. The exercise of the centralized power varies based on the circumstances at hand (opportunism), indicating that the governing principle is to maintain power and not rigid adherence to an ideology or set of overarching norms and values. This dynamic closely resemble Trump's form of rule over his political party, his gradually taking over control of the government, and his polarization of American society. These considerations lead to exploring autocracy and authoritarianism as it applies to the Age of Trump.

Autocracy: The Essence of Autocratic Rule

Burn in her paper *The Perils of Trump's Autocratic Leadership Style* offers insights that are informative.[5] She considers Donald Trump to have the characteristics of an autocratic (authoritarian) leader who uses and abuses the extensive and coercive powers of the presidency. He seems entitled to demand respect and submission as compared with earning it. He is clearly willing, because he is the smartest person in the room, to make flash decisions with little or no consultation, often surprising those around him including the traditional allies of America around the world.

His leadership style is one of demanding compliance or failing that doling out punishment, threats, and firing resistors. Observed by many is the fact that using threats and intimidation (the sword) to obtain loyalty can result in a superficial sense of loyalty and respect, but only so long as he possesses unilateral power of coercion. Even then subordinates will often speak their minds "behind his back" or openly testify before Congress at their own risk of being taken out later. A partial list of fired or resigned under pressure is: Rex Tillerson, Jeff Sessions, James Comey, H.R. McMaster, John Bolton, Sally Yates, Reince Priebus, Sean Spicer, and five inspectors general.[6] Bob Woodward in his book titled *Fear: Trump in the White House* underscores well-documented uses of what amounts to tyrannical power.[7] Another outcome of an autocratic approach is voluntary subordinate turnover because they do not like the intimidation or agree with Trump. Turnover like this gradually creates a homogeneous group of loyal supporters as vacated positions are filled.

Also, to be noted in U.S. politics is that coercive leadership strategies often fail when the opposition (Democrats) also has power. Continued efforts at coercive pursuit of win–lose strategies creates resentment and lose–lose outcomes, sacrificing long-term relationships based on cooperation (win–win).

Yet another problem is that autocratic leaders tend to make unilateral decisions and change direction without sufficient or many times no consultation with experts. This unilateral and not infrequent arbitrary use of power tends to alienate those responsible for carrying out the orders, which leads to the above firings (they did not do it right) or voluntary departures (they do not agree with the decision). Problems such as these are responded to by ever greater insistence on unquestioning loyalty on the part of those around Trump, where sometimes these individuals seem to be "yes men" and "nodding heads." The expression "going along to get along" applies in these instances where going along also insures employment and the protection and support of the autocratic leader. A notion such as groupthink also contributes to understanding faulty decision making and implementation, where the leader is described as surrounded by yes-men and -women who embrace the same or similar ideologies. These individuals and groups often overestimate their abilities, knowledge, and power and reject information to the contrary. This is supported by creating "alternate facts" and by news media that are aligned ideologically (Fox News, Breitbart News).

Burn concludes that Trump's role as the CEO of his own company allowed for an authoritarian style and intuitive decision-making.[5] He is in complete control and master of his universe. Trump's role as president, however, does not provide him absolute power as evidenced by the impeachment, successful lawsuits against his policies, and the house in the hands of the opposition. This underscores that the division of powers approach to governance can function to prevent a complete takeover of the country by an autocratic president with an authoritarian leadership style.

Authoritarian Leadership

Ryan Sit summarizes Trump's authoritarianism building upon the work of Professors Steven Levitsky and Daniel Ziblatt who authored *How Democracies Die*.[3,8] Sit notes that no U.S. politician other than Trump has conducted himself in a way consistent with the four markers of an authoritarian leader.

- Rejecting or compromising democratic rules.
- Denying the legitimacy of political opponents.
- Encouraging violence against opponents and resistors.
- Stifling civil liberties of opponents, including the media (fake news).

These tendencies were in clear view during the campaign but nonetheless, voters on the right voted for Trump. Once elected Trump wielded the power of the presidency to operationalize the four markers. This ongoing reticence to disavow Trump that is associated with fear of him precludes overcoming the intense political and social polarization that has split the country, creating fertile ground for an authoritarian to play off one side against the other to achieve and maintain power.

Freedland and others often refer to Trump as a gangster using mafia-style approaches to gain and defend political territory (taking no prisoners).[9] Trump is familiar with gangsterism, having worked as a developer in New York City and New Jersey (casinos). And to be noted, consistent with protection rackets, the protector first instills terror, then offers protection from it. This is a prominent feature of a paranoid charismatic leader (Chapter 6) who sees threats everywhere, such as "Radical Muslims," immigrants, labeling those protesting dysfunctional policing of citizens of color as terrorists, and often trafficking in threatening conspiracy theories (QAnon). These dynamics are enhanced by splitting and projection when one's own corrupt, immoral, and unethical motives are projected onto others who are then thought to be threatening.

Autocratic authoritarian leaders are highly dependent on having a loyal, obedient followership – people who are willing to take a bullet for their leader, such as Michael Cohen, Trump's fixer, said he would. The presence of a cadre of sycophants contributes to understanding these leaders.

Sycophants

Some mention here of sycophants is important although Chapter 7 deals with this topic more completely. Autocrats and authoritarians need loyal, unquestioning followers who admire the rich, famous, and powerful and enjoy the thrill of affiliation but also hope of gaining advantage for themselves by relying on the leader as an imperfect instrument to fulfill their goals. Examples are Steve Bannon, Stephen Miller, and the Religious Right who see Trump as "the chosen one." Sycophants often achieve a special status relative to the leader by invariably agreeing with the leader and not offering opinions or information inconsistent with what is thought the leader wants to hear. They must also be certain to not step into the spotlight, casting "shade" on Trump who is the star of his own production (The Apprentice, The Presidency). These individuals are many times thought of as shameless self-promoters and in coarser language "suck ups" and "ass kissers." Personal loyalty to Trump rather than to the country or constitution has become a prerequisite for seeking and keeping one's job.

The loyal followers who by their loyalty and admiration protect the leader's expansive and fragile expansive sense of self (thin-skinned) are essential. These leaders can dish it out, but they can't take it. And, as will be discussed, denial, splitting, and projection play an important role in terms of followers feeling dependent on the leader to direct and protect them. Trump asserts, "Only I can save you." Those around the leader enable, protect (willing to take a bullet for him), and carry out wishes, orders and commands with panache, which currently translates into "in your face" statements to rile up left-wing politicians and the media. This appreciation revisits the points made in Chapter 4 on narcissism.

We now turn to exploring the post-factual world that has arisen that serves to enable Trump as an autocrat. One of the key elements in terms of autocrats rising to power is neutralizing civil unrest in the population and further bonding loyal followers to the autocrat's agenda. Here we examine the foundational nature of creating a viable alternate reality for followers to believe (propaganda) in preferably unquestioningly. In the United States, this has been referred to by Kelly Conway, Counselor to the President, as "alternate facts." This reference has been discussed as a "post-factual world" where everyone is entitled to their own facts to support their point of view and discount all those that do not (fake news).

Creating a Post-factual World in Support of Autocracy

The emergence of a post-factual world in the United States (2015–2020) is something that for many critical observers is something you could not make up. Who could have imagined? The polls all favored presidential candidate Hillary Clinton who, it seems, won every battle and lost the war.

There are many complexities that can be explored about contemporary political events now and in the future. Two realities will likely emerge, one on the left and one on the right. This eventuality of multiple realities raises for consideration, where can one go to obtain objective news? We have arrived at the point that everyone used to have their own *opinion*, but everyone was not entitled to their own *facts*. Now the two realities have their own facts, supported by a burgeoning for-profit industry of social media to support vastly different "facts" and opinions. There is, from the perspective of psychoanalytic object relations theory, dual-polarized good and bad realities and arousal of fight or flight dynamics and movement against others. Trump's followers are dependent on an autocratic, paranoid, charismatic leader who promotes fear and anxiety, bonding those who feel this way to him – he will save them. The C-word has been banished. Comprise has not often been possible. There is only the "Hell No" of Obama's presidency and ideological purists within the Freedom Caucus. It has become "my way or the highway." America First in international affairs and allies second.

The world and the United States have arrived at a dysfunctional dark period where the threat of many things – pandemics, terrorists, Sharia law, global warming (or not), loss of jobs to lower-cost labor markets across international boundaries, danger in the streets, and the smoking Twin Towers that are burned into our collective consciousness to name but a few. These many threats have created fear and a corresponding willingness in 2020 to accept a police state-like government that invades the streets of large cities, and our privacy, and has made a "strong and powerful" autocrat a reality or – once again, maybe not, depending on who you talk to.

Psychodynamically informed perspectives make an important contribution toward understanding the polarization and the divergent realties that exist.[10] Where did this context and conflict of realities come from? How is it so readily maintained? Where is it headed?

Invention of Facts

What happened? This is the question. Anyone endeavoring to offer his or her best efforts to answer the question is confronted with a chaos of conflicting information and perspectives and a vast constellation of ever-changing data points that may or may not be true or accurate. After all, in the twenty-first century, as already mentioned, everyone is entitled to not only their own opinions but also their own facts. Assertions, myths, and conspiracy theories often blur into facts. "Spin" is reality. Orwellian Newspeak and the Unreality Principle (believing a lie to demonstrate loyalty) are being realized. The triad of regression, magical thinking, and omnipotence of thought has prevailed on the right contaminating everything around it.

For example, Ingraham reviews three studies focused on the conservative media's role in fostering confusion about the seriousness of the coronavirus.[11] The findings reveal a media ecosystem that amplifies misinformation, entertains conspiracy theories, and discourages audiences from taking concrete steps to protect themselves and others. The virus as Trump states will go away (eventually), and from this perspective, we are all dead in the long run anyway. Personal freedom (libertarianism) to not wear a mask "trumps" social responsibility.

Anyone trying to make sense of our new universe of alternate facts must preferably embrace humility in that what may be said to be known or factual, may from an alternate reality, be said to be untrue. This points to an underlying appreciation that the different realities the members of the two American political parties live in more closely resemble a duality than a shared culture.

The sensemaking we endeavor here begins with the deepest appreciation that we now live in a post-factual world – a world in which spin becomes fact.[12,13,14] If we accept this as one possible reality, we are left to wonder what sense can we make of anything, ever. This being the case the non-rational and irrational that compromise accurate reality testing must be explored. The tools relied on here for sensemaking are based on psychoanalytic theory and object relations theorizing in particular. Object relations theory is a way of thinking about intra-subjective and inter-subjective experiences of self and others, including groups and large organizations and even nations. We thus begin our sensemaking project of *nonsense* with the deepest appreciation of the hard-to-know and understand aspects of human nature.[15] Object relations theory can help us to make sense of nonsense.

Object Relations and the Projective Construction of Reality

Object relations theory provides a context for understanding that others as well as groups exist as objects or presences in one's mind. We make them up to fit our unique needs in the moment (reality is ours to create) based on our biased and incomplete awareness of others, including our, at times, distorted and often fragmented sense of ourselves. We are free to manipulate these" others" in mind as much as we like. We add to this that over time these manipulations leak out into the inter-subjective interpersonal world. When we have created an object in mind, and we prefer that the external object be much the same as what we imagine, and we act accordingly. The other person comes to have a sense of this and that how he or she is being treated does not necessarily match how they know themselves to be (in their own mind). What a quandary, and one that psychotherapists encounter daily.

There is one more consideration. The person who has created the other(s) in mind and has this content leak out may with more unconscious intent seek to affect external relationships via projective identification. It may be important that the other person become like the mindful image. This dynamic (projective identification) is a coercive, forceful effort to take over the other person or group.[16] The external object, the other, is continually treated as though he or she is the internal object. Compliance is rewarded. Deviations from the plot are not acceptable and may be punished. The other must be hammered into the shape of the internal object. Projective "Reality" is created and enforced, which helps us to understand how such extreme polarization has arisen in the United States. We now turn to psychodynamic sense-making of a nonsensical world of national chaos and good versus bad polarization.

Applying Object Relations to the Post-factual World

The post-factual world offers unlimited opportunities to fuel polarization based on creating a good and even victimized self and a bad and evil other and victimizer. These dynamics also introduce consideration of fight or flight groups and movements against and toward leaders and others who see the world and each other very differently. We highlight this by offering the following partial list of prominent splits in our collective consciousness.

- Us (white America) versus them (alien non-white others)
- Fear (Trump) versus Hope (Obama)
- Strong (Trump) versus Weak, the apology tour (Obama, H. Clinton)
- Tough talk, military action, and drone assassinations versus diplomacy
- Not PC (politically correct) and white male supremacy versus PC
- Wire Bear versus Cloth Bear – conservationism (immigrant children in cages) versus liberalism (welcoming immigrants)

- A tall great beautiful wall at the border with Mexico versus the Statue of Liberty
- Entrenched conservative ideology versus progressive change

Splits like these and many others have made peaceful family and social group gatherings problematic. The clash of post-factual divergent realities supported by splitting and projection and energized by transference has created hard to manage conflict. The post-factual world that lies before us now as an intense and confusing national split has created a pain-filled dysfunctional fragmentation that in some ways revisits the Civil War era.

Descent into Chaos: Applying Object Relations to the Age of Trump

This fragmented world is one of chaos. The chaos we are experiencing within and without is essential to understanding Trump's behavior and his interaction with his followers. The chaos is not a coincidental byproduct of his campaigning and leadership style. His language stokes the fires of bitter hatred and divisiveness where divide and conquer seem to be the overarching strategy. He inflames his base of largely white followers to revisit their grievances and the accompanying anger and rage (transference) in the service of seeking revenge against others (the left, minorities, immigrants). They are bad and we are good. These others must be voted out, rounded up, locked up, disposed of, and expelled beyond a wall – real or metaphoric. They are never to return in fact or in mind. For some if not many the white race is saved from "bad blood." There is not much in life that is emotionally more primitive than this disturbing experience of recent events. Denial, splitting, and projection fuel these group and national dynamics.

Amidst the flames and billowing smoke of recent protests, Donald Trump offers himself as their only savior (the chosen one) who can "Make America Great Again." He offers himself as the solution to the chaos he has generated. In psychodynamic language, Trump induces a trance of regression and deep dependency on him on the part of his followers who are strongly encouraged to idealize him. He then promises to be the redemptive parent-god to rescue and redeem them. In him they are born again, not as vulnerable, hapless, looked-down-upon-by-elites working-class victims, but as having a future where they and he will triumph as avenging victors. They will get their white identity, jobs, and country back. He offers them a mirror transference in which they see themselves anew as renewed. They bask in the bright, shining radiance of his greatness – his greatness, not theirs. He is, in a sense, a modern shaman who understands their suffering and knows the secrets of their hearts but also exploits them for his self-aggrandizement.

As a nation, we have come to experience a shared cultural split into opposing "camps." When this occurs in workplace and social and political groups the two opposing groups may wonder why they are divided and have "bad" feelings toward each other. They may enter a reflective period where they come to understand there are few good reasons for the split and realize that they are playing out the divisions inside their own minds that have been allowed free reign to create a threatening and evil other. They are acting upon the other-in-them that has been created by splitting and projection, sometimes enabled by projective hooks offered by others to draw the projections. When both sides of the split are engaged in splitting and projection, there arises a vicious downward and self-fulfilling spiral made all the more worse by the opposing groups incorporating the projections (projective identification), thereby acting out the worst fears of the opposing group. Add to this the transference of strong emotions drawn from past similar experiences and you have a perfect storm that tosses all boats around.

On a vaster social and political stage there exists a psychological "contract" between Trump and his followers who "find themselves" in him. Also, to be considered is that the chaos he sows (creating distractions) offers him relief and a degree of resolution-through-externalization of chaotic parts of himself. Both he and they need and complete each other – a form of interpersonal and social contracting. Within this circularity is personal validation for all that, once achieved, must be protected at all cost, including accurate reality testing. Trump's followers' cult-like idealization of and devotion to him requires of them that they experience the regression, chaos, despair, and feelings of dependency that he induces. Fear is made real by factory closings with jobs shipped overseas, feelings of being disposed of and left behind by the elite others, and the now pervasive threat of the out of control spread of a highly infectious virus and its social and economic consequences. Trump's followers also experience ethnic existential fear that leads to white nationalism or more darkly white male supremacy.

In sum, there is embedded within this polarized reality the post-factual nature of this reality. It is true? Must change be feared (for conservatives) or embraced (by liberals)? We are once again humbled by the multiplicity of realities supported by their own facts and the likely inability to locate a mutual or negotiated reality. The loss of social cohesion yields not only paranoia fueled by an autocratic charismatic leader who promotes splitting but it also yields a continuous cycle of *fight and flight* and strong *movements against* others and *vindication of past wrongs*. Is there any hope that fear can be overcome?

In Conclusion: Imagining the Future

What can then be made of a society that is polarized good versus bad that enables an autocratic leader? We conclude with a perspective that seems to be one possible scenario of reality. We have it entered a period of *polarization for profit*. Our news media is largely dominated by major for-profit corporations selling advertisements with news that is exciting and engages their viewers and readers. The better the story the more income per advertising minute is earned. If it bleeds it leads is a mainstay of journalism. Bad news sells. It sells even better if everything becomes magnified to the point of social toxicity, amplified by governmental dysfunction. And to be noted we continually reelect the people who create the dysfunction which is a sign of the much deeper split in our nation's collective sense of a shared culture.

There is then, in this appreciation, a self-sealing feedback loop (an echo chamber) that has become self-sustaining enabling an autocratic leader. Must we join the unquestioning passengers in the car on their trip to Abilene that no one agreed to?[17] Have we not as a nation arrived "here" without knowing how we got here?

Is polarized fragmentation all there is for the future? Any healing that can take place must confront the endless pursuit of political power at any cost aimed at imposing one's worldview and ideology upon the country using hand-crafted facts. How might this "confrontation" be accomplished? Humility is a starting place that puts omnipotence of thought in perspective. The confrontation begins with the self: a vigilant refusal to be drawn in. It takes place one minute at a time, by allowing the pseudo-facts to flow by, as if one is standing in a swift river of fiction. To stand and not drown in this onslaught of pseudo-facts is no small thing. Failure is not a good option.

Chapter 6 further explores this subject matter by providing a more in-depth discussion of the role paranoid charismatic leaders play in creating group and national toxic leader and follower dynamics. Making sense of this leader may be the ultimate challenge.

Notes

1. Applebaum, A. (2020). *Twilight of democracy: The seductive lure of authoritarianism.* New York, NY: Doubleday.
2. Stevens, S. (2020). *It was all a lie: How the Republican Party became Donald Trump.* New York, NY: Knopf.
3. Levitsky, S. & Ziblatt, D. (2018). *How democracies die.* New York, NY: Broadway Books.
4. Gerson, S. (2020). *How fascism works: The politics of us and them.* New York, NY: Random House.
5. Burn, S. (2019). The perils of Trump's autocratic leadership style. *Psychology Today.* https://www.psychologytoday.com/us/blog/presence-mind/201901/the-perils-trump-s-autocratic-leadership-style.
6. Cohen. R. (2019). All the president's shrinking sycophants: In Trump's White House, staffers have lost all sense of dignity. *New York Daily News.* https://www.nydailynews.com/opinion/ny-oped-all-the-presidents-shrinking-syco-phants-20190618-nx44xj4egvcrjhuuc2e5h6xkiy-story.html

7. Woodward, B. (2018). *Fear: Trump in the White House* (2nd ed.). New York, NY: Simon & Schuster.
8. Sit, R. (2018). Trump meets every criteria for an authoritarian leader. *Newsweek.* https://www.newsweek.com/harvard-political-science-professor-donald-trump-authoritarian-how-democracy-778425.
9. Freedland, J. (2018). This mafia style of government makes Trump a role model for all autocrats. *The Guardian.* https://www.theguardian.com/commentisfree/2018/aug/18/mafia-style-g.
10. Hetherington, M. & Weiler, J. (2009). *Authoritarianism & polarization in American politics.* New York, NY: Cambridge University Press.
11. Ingraham, C. (2020). New research explores how conservative media misinformation may have intensified the severity of the pandemic. *Washington Post.* https://www.washingtonpost.com/business/2020/06/25/fox-news-hannity-coronavirus-misinformation/.
12. Applebaum, A. (2016). Fact-checking in a "post-fact world." *Washington Post.* //www.washingtonpost.com/opinions/fact-checking-in-a-post-fact-world/2016/05/19/d37434e2-1d0f-11e6-8c7b-6931e66333e7_story.html.
13. Davies, W. (2016). The age of post-truth politics. *The New York Times.* http://www.nytimes.com/2016/08/24/opinion/campaign-stops/the-age-of-post-truth-politics.html?_r=0.
14. Gold, H. (2015). Fact-checking the candidates in a "post-fact" world. *Politico.* http://www.politico.com/blogs/on-media/2015/12/fact-checking-the-candidates-in-a-post-fact-world-216790.
15. Greenberg, J. & Mitchell, S. (1983). *Object relations in psychoanalytic theory.* Cambridge, MA: Harvard University Press.
16. Grotstein, J. (1993). *Splitting and projective identification.* North Vale, NJ: Jason Aronson.
17. Harvey, J. (1988). *The Abilene paradox.* San Francisco, CA: Jossey-Bass.

Part II

Charismatic Leaders and Their Sycophants

The relationship between leaders who are autocratic and authoritarian and people who are attracted to them and willing to personally benefit from their relationship, as well as to submit to the leader, creates a familiar, somewhat understandable but also toxic and dysfunctional dynamic, both in a national sense and also within public and private organizations. Powerful and controlling leaders who can be demanding and threatening very often possess charisma and a larger-than-life presence. This presence that is frequently accompanied by interpersonal and organizational dynamics that contain for the leader a sense of paranoia of being fired, overthrown (or assassinated), as well as being actively and passively resisted. This paranoid edge leads to careful recruitment of others to serve the leader who are expected to be obedient if not enthusiastic administrators of the leader's will. Going overboard in carrying out a directive of the leader is often welcomed. This leader would rather reign in a bulldog as compared with constantly having to push, prod, and threaten others less inclined to be aggressive. Problems created by over zealousness are usually overlooked or minimally addressed such as asking the person to "dial it down a bit."

The chapters in this section first explore the paranoia and charisma of Trump and his autocratic and authoritarian approach to leading. This is followed by an examination of the nature of sycophancy as is evident in those surrounding Trump and this type of leader. These individuals are often responsible for translating big attention getting ideas into plans that can be implemented, such as building a wall, locking up immigrant children, as well as zealously promoting freedom of religion, limiting abortions, and suppressing LGBTQ rights.

We conclude by exploring the nature of the chaos that Trump and these types of leaders create. The creation of chaos, that is a distraction, is enabled by their authoritarianism and a loyal unquestioning cadre of sycophants who offer little balancing resistance to sudden changes in direction. For Trump ill-considered changes in internal and international policy are magnified by a universe of confusing, contradictory, and chaotic tweets that lack a sense of self-regulation and fore thought.

6 Charismatic Leaders

It is impossible to comprehend Donald Trump, the national large group dynamics that made his presidency possible and the consolidation of his power without recognizing the central role of charisma in the evolution of his role as a leader. Charisma is not so much a property of a leader, but rather it exists in the in-between co-creational space of leader and the follower dynamics. Successful organizational and political leaders often attract a lot of attention to themselves. Everyone may notice when they enter a room. Their reputation and their accompanying mythology precede them. For many, awareness of these leaders is not created based on the first-hand experience of the leader but rather by mentally constructing the leader out of a biased information selection process where myth, opinions and concrete evidence are sifted to create in one's mind the preferred leader. This "sifting" process amounts to selective attention and confirmation bias. At the same time, the leader may intentionally pull follower projections encouraging, voters, and subordinates to magnify his or her presence and greatness.

Close observation of attention-getting leaders often reveals a preoccupation with self-presentation including the length and color of ties or scarfs, the design and fit of clothing, and what is said and how and when it is said, including the staging and props such as background flags and troops. The particular type of leader explored here – is a charismatic leader who motivates others by promoting fear. This leader's paranoia locates threatening others and events that must be defended against and preferably defeated or expelled "go home to your country of origin."

Charismatic Leaders as a Type of Leader

The charismatic leader offers followers an individual who is bigger than life, which is seductive for those who seek a strong and powerful leader to protect them from the many threats the leader identifies and magnifies. This seduction combines with a pattern of motivation based on fear, that relies on continually locating evil others such as terrorists and dangerous immigrants, competitors and threats to stockholder value, international aggressors, and legal threats aimed, for example, at limiting the number and types of guns that may be purchased and owned. This promotion of fear and identification of many threats and enemies are the basis of the paranoid charismatic leadership style. The location of one or many threats combines with the charismatic leader's ability to motivate others and groups to follow him or her into the breach to fend off the threat(s). Mob leaders, as portrayed by Hollywood, provide a reasonable facsimile, where everyone is encouraged to feel strongly and irrationally about the threat or offending other(s) and the necessity to protect their turf. Extrajudicial lynching and killing of people of color by white mobs is a historical example, but also an inner presence where a noose is not merely a piece of rope.

Better understanding this leadership style that Trump exhibits requires exploring charismatic leadership fused with paranoid leadership and their relationship to the current state of affairs in the United States. The left and liberals are held up as despicable and a threat to "traditional" society and conservative ideologies and values. These social and political dynamics must be eliminated as a threat by any means available, such as voter suppression and gerrymandering.

What Is the Charismatic Leadership Style?

There are different ways of defining, describing, and operationalizing charismatic leadership conceptually and in practice. What follows is an overview constructed with a deep appreciation that many authors and researchers have written about charismatic leaders.[1,2]

Max Weber, a German sociologist, and philosopher of the early twentieth century described charismatic authority that derived from a larger than life leader whose authority is different from legal authority and traditional authority. This leader possesses a personality that sets the person apart from most others who are willing to endow this individual with exceptional abilities and a willingness to submit to the leader's direction and dominance over them. These leaders are charming, persuasive, and skilled communicators who access the deeper emotional lives of followers by their passion and ability to arouse emotions. They can "read the room." They usually possess strong convictions and an unwavering commitment to fulfilling their compelling vision.

They are sometimes referred to as transformational leaders who put forward an inspiring vision. The leader's successes and ability to pass off failures inspires the idealization, loyalty, and obedience of followers. The leader's authority depends on the perceived subjective legitimacy of this individual's personal authority which may also be in part grounded in rational-legal authority arising from hierarchical bureaucratic positions (scalar authority) and traditional authority arising from social customs that are generally followed, such as authority invested in a religious leader or elder. While these authorities may exist and be relied upon based on the context, the charismatic aspect predominates.

In this regard charismatic authority, while grounded in character traits of the charismatic leader, depends on the intersubjective and unconscious relationship between the leader and his or her trusting followers and less on rational appeals and logical calls to action. The charismatic leader *inspires* followers to perform in contrast to autocratic leaders who rely on legal/rational and traditional/coercive authority to *demand and enforce* performance. However, as noted charismatic leaders may resort to autocratic methods when inspiration is not achieving the desired results. It is common to find instances where, if charisma does not obtain results, there is a resort to an autocratic leadership style to force submission and change – militarized police state tactics. In the near-term the results of the charismatic and autocratic leadership styles may be similar. In the long term, they generate different group, organizational and national cultures each with its unique societal and political dysfunctions and toxicities.

Charismatic and autocratic leadership styles often create a lot of intensity that may eventually lead to burnout both for the leader and followers. The leader may become burdened with ever more dependent followers who hold unrealistic fantasies for what the leader can accomplish (movement toward). These expectations can become demanding and an exhausting experience for the leader, who will never possess enough power and control to allay all follower fears and anxieties (the proverbial feet of clay). This dynamic may encourage the leader to delegate to expendable others difficult and problematic decision making that threatens to alienate followers or create enemies. They can be scapegoated and thrown under the bus (fired). Similarly, the leader may avoid making decisions where there is a clear risk of a wrong outcome that might compromise the idealization of this omnipotent (genius) leader by followers, for example, responding to a pandemic is risky. This burdened and at times anxious leader may occasionally be observed to be stressed out, suffering and angry. When this occurs the response on the part of followers motivated by fear of the anger may well be loving and caretaking support as well as defending the leader at any cost to self or group. Devoted followers will voluntarily fall on their metaphoric sword sacrificing themselves by taking a bullet for their reader. Conversely, follower may become disillusioned and have less faith in the omnipotence of the leader. They may be alienated by the leader's angry, vindictive, threatening, and punishing responses toward them relative to unresolved problems, when invariably the leader believes the problems are the fault of incompetent and inferior followers. These dynamics are accentuated by beliefs that there is a conspiracy against the leader. Loyal followers may feel victimized and aggrieved not only by the leader and not infrequently by his or her most loyal followers, but also by threatening others (victimizers) that the leader has identified.

These leaders, supported by unquestioning, loyal followers, can become personally disorganized in that they feel they are all powerful and controlling and that the normal rules of civility, fair play, and following the laws of the land are optional. Many of Trump's actions indicate that he does not think the Constitution and laws apply to him or minimally so. He is enabled by loyal appointees and sycophants eager to please him. Followers who are carefully selected for their loyalty may also not feel obliged to, like their leader, follow the laws and historical customs and conventions.

In politics, charismatic rule is often found in authoritarian states, autocracies, dictatorships, and theocracies. Maintaining their larger than life charismatic presence and authority is often enabled by the creation of a personality cult with their name and image everywhere. State-controlled news media obligingly support the cultish rule, with Iran and North Korea being examples.

The experience of a charismatic leader in the moment for followers is that, while listening to their leader's pronouncements, they feel attached to the leader and convinced by the leader's stated directions and methods. Possibly later for some, after the leader departs, there may arise, upon discussion and reflection, an awareness of what was said, that while inspiring, lacked relevance and sufficient substance and direction to permit acting. In a sense, it was a "con job" which is something that is descriptive of Trump's self-representation and how his businesses are operated. Narcissistic charismatic leaders may ultimately be implicitly only interested in themselves and their careers, creating wealth and being elected or reelected. This consideration revisits Chapter 4, where narcissism is discussed.

In sum, the seduction of these leaders is based on their manifestation of considerable self-importance and grandiosity (bigger than life) which is irresistible to followers who move toward the leader, wishing to be saved and led. It is also the case that when the leader dies naturally or otherwise or leaves office, and a new charismatic leader does not appear, the "regime" is likely to fall unless it has become routinized in the form of ideology and bureaucracy and is sustainable by bureaucratic "power" or traditional authority.

Charismatic Leaders and Group, Organizational and National Psychosocial Dynamics

Groups, organizations, and countries often seek out an omnipotent and powerful charismatic leader who will save fearful and anxious members and citizens, and restore national pride, making the country great again by controlling most aspects of adverse experience including repairing historical harm and healing grievances. The leader is expected to provide clear and inspirational direction that will defend against threat, dominate others, and undo historical traumas. The leader rewards loyal followers while punishing those who defy or challenge the leader's direction and control. Any resistance on the part of followers must be vanquished. Within this context problems that evoke anxiety are interpreted by followers as the leader not having enough power and control. Group members become unquestioningly supportive of their leader (loyal and submissive) in the belief (hope) by doing so they are helping the leader to achieve enough power and control to fulfill their expectations even if laws and norms are violated.

Ultimately, aggression from followers or a superior to whom the charismatic leader reports may lead to the symbolic murder of the leader should the leader fail to meet follower or the superior's performance expectations. In the case of a CEO, this is the governing board and indirectly the stockholders, and for politicians the voters (constituents). When this happens, another charismatic leader may be sought or perhaps, if the group learns from experience, a more participative and inclusive leader who engages and empowers followers to achieve in their own right may be located.[3,4]

Discussed below is the psychological tendency to project one's good self-aspects such as personal integrity and efficacy onto this bigger than life leader who then identifies with the idealized projections. This becomes a self-fulfilling prophecy when followers find they need the leader to direct and save them, and the leader experiences an inflated and expansive sense of self that arises from idealization that is accompanied by power and control arising from the submission of followers. Citizens, group, and organization members having located and "created in mind" this charismatic leader, feel less responsible for themselves, each other, the group, the organization, and the country. The phrase, "basking in the warm glow created by their leader" applies.

Paranoia and the Charismatic Leader

Paranoia is a sense or thought process linked to feelings of fear and anxiety. Anxiety is a form of a bodily signal (signal anxiety) of a fear orientation that is magnified to the extent that delusional qualities are present. Threats may be perceived to exist that are associated with a belief that there is a conspiracy against the leader by distrusted and disloyal others (the deep state). Random events and actions of others may become invested with fears of imagined and even fantastic intentions of others who threaten to harm the leader. And to be noted, this in-the-mind dynamic (paranoid ideation and cognition) may also be "hard won" in that the social context may reasonably contain threats worthy of concern that promote anxiety that reinforces the sense of paranoia. Paranoia, it should be noted from a clinical perspective, is associated with depression, social anxiety, feelings of powerlessness, and victimization, as well as acting out in the form of persecution of others (getting even) and litigiousness that uses the legal system to attack others (law suits) who are perceived to be a threat. These dynamics are also often linked to excessive narcissism and self-entitlement, where narcissistic injury inflicted by others intentionally or not, and resistance from others to being obedient and submissive, become an ever-present personalized threat. The result is that the self is never to be blamed for problems and failures – others are invariably held to be responsible and scapegoated and thrown under the bus. Mistakes are never made and apologizing for harm to others is not necessary and may be interpreted as weakness that may provoke personal attacks.

Object relations perspectives contribute insight into these psychological dynamics within the paranoid leader.

A Note on the Paranoid–Schizoid Position

In object relations theory, the paranoid–schizoid position (a concept of Melanie Klein) is a state of mind of children during the first six months to one year of life. Object relations points out that for the infant there exists an interpersonal world of part objects and no awareness of an independent other as a "person" or even a sense of self. Instead there is a blooming buzzing confusion of experience. This developmental phase remains present throughout life and can be reactivated at any time relative to stress and anxiety-induced psychological regression. The paranoid–schizoid position is a more primitive position than its successor, the depressive positions where whole object relations arise relative to the experience of an independent autonomous other. Omnipotent control of the other in mind is lost. It is normal to move back and forth between the two positions depending in large part on the amount of perceived stress (threat), anxiety, and psychological regression.

Schizoid refers to the defense mechanism of splitting (the separation of the good object from the bad object). Paranoid anxiety and the fear of an invasive malevolence can be understood in terms of anxiety about imminent annihilation. Splitting is useful because it protects the good from being destroyed by the bad. In the depressive position that follows the ability arises to integrate good and bad relative to a "whole" other. The loss of the mindful idealized good object is mourned, and the child or adult must cope with the world and others as possessing both good and bad features, including this appreciation applies to the self.

These intrapsychic processes involve projection in addition to splitting good from bad. While it is more common to retain the good and split off and project the bad onto (in mind) or into others (projective identification), the reverse may also be true. Projection of the good becomes the basis for idealization of the other and the charismatic leader, which may be especially relevant when one assumes a role of dependency. Soldiers in battle must make a "leap of faith" in terms of trusting that their leaders will not unnecessarily place them in harm's way. Effective military generals are often idealized (Eisenhower, Patton, Schwarzkopf). In contrast, the projection of badness onto or into the object is the basis of racism, stereotypes of dangerous immigrants, homophobia (LGBTQ), and the irrational hatred of another group, creating a pure form of "not us" (liberals, conservatives, Northerners, Southerners).

The depressive position compared to splitting schizoid defenses represents the loss of omnipotent control of the object in mind. It allows for experiencing others as subjects and autonomous and that the good and bad split can be seen as different aspects of the same object.[5,6] The world of whole object relations requires movement toward mutual respect and acceptance, tolerance of ambiguity (a world that is not black and white), and efforts at interpersonal and group coordination, including the necessity to compromise on fulfilling one's desires and wishes that avoid fight and flight interpersonal and group dynamics.

There is one additional perspective to be borrowed from Group Relations theorizing that also contributes insight into leaders who see threats everywhere and that promote fear and anxiety in followers, thereby creating the basis for strong motivations to fight back against or flee from threats.

The Paranoia of Fight or Flight Leaders

Fight and flight are responses to threats that are invested with usually strong emotions such as fear, panic, anger, and rage.[7] Wilford Bion formulated the concept of three basic assumptions groups and the fight/flight group is one of these groups.[8] The other two are the *pairing group* that hopes two members will pair and provide direction and the *dependency group* that has the goal of being taken care of by someone. A fourth ideal group is the *task group* that is more self-aware and intentional and does not fall into regressive retreat to one of the basic assumption groups. Margaret Rioch describes the fight-flight basic assumption group as a group focused on preserving itself by fighting back against a perceived threat or running away from someone or something.[9] This call for immediate action invariably requires a leader who recognizes the threat and is willing to lead the group in battle or retreat. This leader is often charismatic and able to inspire courage and sacrifice from followers, accentuated by a paranoid element that ensures if there is no obvious enemy one will be located. To be noted Trump finds much of life to be filled with threats that, for example, require building walls to keep evil others out or deploying militarized officers in the service of seeking law and order relative to protesters (Lafayette Park, D.C. and Portland). An important aspect of the fight or flight group is that it is based on the development of primitive emotions and excessive anxiety that makes the group anti-intellectual in nature as well as a group that avoids self-reflection that would promote disquieting awareness of its group life and its actions. This lack of critical thinking and reflectivity forms the basis for blind and adoring followership where the leader who appears to be charismatic and authoritative although this leader may only exist in fantasy supported by psychological splitting, projection, and transference. Fight and flight basic assumptions will be further discussed as sentience groups in Chapter 12.

We now turn to a discussion of the Age of Trump using the concepts of splitting and projection that contribute to the formation of an idealized charismatic and powerful other whose "reality" promotes fear and anxiety in followers by continually locating threats to fear – paranoia.

Psychological Projection in the Age of Trump

Projection that is discussed here and in Chapter 2 is a defense mechanism that reduces anxiety and feelings of guilt and shame. Projection involves unconsciously splitting off parts of oneself (or group) that are distressing to be aware of and locating them usually in another in mind. The other is said to become a mental object that becomes the repository of the projections. These mindful unconscious dynamics inevitably leak out into the interpersonal world including some of the time with intentionality to encourage others to act in ways that are consistent with the projections (projective identification). When this occurs, it confirms his/our perception about how bad and dangerous the other individual or group is. The *other* becomes as the projector wishes.

Projection is helpful in terms of understanding how Donald Trump worked as businessman, as presidential candidate, and as president. The Age of Trump can be better understood when viewed through the lens of projection.[10]

The Age of Trump reminds us that words count. Trump has mastered the skills of insulting others and lying and manipulating the media. His words attract attention, promote fear, and encourage splitting and projection to create evil others everywhere – the list is almost limitless.

- Undocumented immigrants are described as animals and bad people, rapists, drug smugglers, gang members, and invaders.
- Hillary Clinton was crooked and should be locked up.
- James Comey was said to be a leaker and liar.
- Adam Schiff was sleazy.
- Kim Jong-un was Little Rocket Man.
- Barack Obama's legitimacy was questioned by birtherism and the assertion he was born in Kenya. Kamala Harris – ditto.
- The national and cable news channels and journalists were transformed into the "lame stream media," the "Fake News," and the enemy of the people when what is being reported does not fit with Trump's narrative.
- The Charlottesville, Virginia, white nationalist/neo-Nazi demonstrators shouted, "You will not replace us," were described by Trump as very fine people on both sides. Paradoxically Trump asserts the Democrats are anti-Jewish and anti-Israel.

- Robert Mueller's inquiry into Russian influence in the 2016 presidential election is said to have been a witch hunt and "hoax."
- The existence of a deep state in the federal government speaks to a massive conspiracy and secret cabal of Democrats, socialists, left-wing "progressive" liberals, and others that is supposedly sabotaging Trump as the elected American leader.
- It is also the case that many of our former allies are now viewed as suspicious and former enemy states as potential friends. The United Nations and the World Health Organization are said to be not aligned with Trump's interests leading to bullying and defunding.

This admittedly partial listing suggests there is much more going on than any one of the individual items.

What if we imagined these as a matrix of thought, emotion, and action toward *others* who become an imagined group of people. They or them are bad, sinister, malevolent, and dangerous and a threat to the good – us, United States. The polarized black and white us versus them world we live in is filled with an abundance of enemies which can become, as Thomas Hobbes suggests, a figurative war of all against all and life becomes short and brutish.

We experience these projected characteristics as if they are the property of those whom we despise, exclude, and protect ourselves from. We sense *them* as deeply menacing and poised to invade us or, worse, they already have invaded. In our minds, *they* are Bad, and We are Good. I, we, us, them becomes split apart into good versus bad parts where most often the good is retained and the bad projected outward onto others. What is not appreciated is that their despised attributes (noun) are characteristics that we have attributed (verb) to Them. In this confusion of self and other the other is well known since Them is our selves projected onto or into Them which can be said to create pathological certainty about Them and their bad intentions. Terrible things are inside Them, not Us. We also, in a sense, need Them to embody our own evil so that we will feel good about ourselves. Without You, I could not know myself to be good.

This process creates polarization between Us and Them that provided the emotional fuel for the Cold War and currently fuels the social and political polarization in the United States at the present and around the world. Today the motto "Make America Great Again" translates into such things as white supremacy in America and dominance of the rest of the world. This position is desirable on the right end of our political spectrum where international politics becomes a zero-sum game with the United States on the winning side.

The matrix of ideas, emotions, and ideology as characterized and that reside within The Age of Trump turns out to be at the unconscious level, Us-in-Them. Statements, nicknames, epithets supposedly about Them can be understood to be our own characteristics. For example, Trump's long history of affairs, misogyny, psychological abuse, and disrespect for women, is unconsciously linked to his accusing immigrants of his own misdeeds and violation of ethical behavior toward women. Trump accuses opponents of crookedness, press leaks, lies, sleaziness, fake information to the public, witch hunts, hoaxes, and of being enemies of the people. However, these assertions closely resemble Trump's own way of living life and doing business as we discussed in Chapter 3. He is, we suggest, describing himself after he splits these off and projects himself onto others who become recognizable as threats and enemies. He in a sense knows this beyond a reasonable doubt (he knows himself *in* others), and evidence to the contrary is placed in the fake news trash pile.

The question splitting and projection raises here is whether the courage and wisdom exists to reflect and begin to take back our projections and discover what they tell us *about ourselves* that may have to be forgiven since our individual humanity always contains the good and bad. From a geopolitical sense, the entire earth depends on it.

In Conclusion

Charismatic and paranoid leaders who identify threats everywhere promote fear and anger on the part of loyal followers who become dependent on the leader to protect them, even if the leader created the threats – a dynamic commonly found when an individual aspires to greatness and domination of a group, organization or country. These leaders are highly motivated and may take extreme risks to achieve domination and control, which include their own removal or demise (not being reelected) and the destruction of the social and economic well-being of "their people" with whom the leader becomes fused (compromising trust in election integrity). Hitler is said to have believed if he did not survive the war the German people would also not survive.[11]

These fight or flight dynamics and moving against others are energized by the paranoid features of the leader who intuitively understands the key to power, control, adoration, and even worship lies in promoting fear whether it takes the form of going to hell without being saved, being replaced by immigrants of color or overtaken by a left-wing ideology such as communism, socialism, or progressive liberalism. Understanding paranoid charismatic leadership, we believe does contribute to understanding the Age of Trump.

Chapter 7 further explores the relationship between the charismatic leader and his or her followers from whom unquestioning loyalty is expected, so much so that they lose their personal integrity and autonomy becoming sycophants.

Notes

1. STU Online. (2018). What is charismatic leadership? Leading through personal conviction. *STU Online*. Miami Gardens, FL: St. Thomas University. https://online.stu.edu/articles/education/what-is-charismatic-leadership.aspx.

2. Charismatic authority. (2021, May 7). In *Wikipedia*. https://en.wikipedia.org/wiki/Charismatic_authority.
3. Allcorn, S. (2003). *The dynamic workplace: Present structure and future redesign.* Westport, CN: Praeger.
4. Stein, H. & Allcorn, S. (2014). Good enough leadership. *Organisational & Social Dynamics*, 14(2), 342–366.
5. Costelloe, M. (2018). Paranoid-schizoid and reparative states: Mending the injury we have inflicted on others. *Psychology Today*. https://www.psychologytoday.com/us/blog/the-me-in-we/201806/paranoid-schizoid-and-reparative-states.
6. Paranoid-schizoid and depressive positions. (2021, April 18). In *Wikipedia*. https://en.wikipedia.org/wiki/Paranoid-schizoid_and_depressive_positions.
7. Allcorn, S. (1994). *Anger in the workplace: Understanding the causes of aggression and violence.* Westport, CT: Quorum Books.
8. Bion, W. (1961). *Experience in groups.* London: Tavistock.
9. Colman, A. & Bexton, W. (Eds.) (1975). *Group relations reader.* Sausalito, CA: Grex.
10. Stein, H. (2019). Howard F. Stein: Projection in the Age of Trump. *Tulsa World*. https://www.tulsaworld.com/opinion/columnists/howard-f-stein-projection-in-the-age-of-trump/article_9a894df4-5167-11e9-bc9e-f39235d28f93.html.
11. Beevor, A. (2003). *The fall of Berlin 1945.* London: Penguin Books.

7 Sycophants and Their Charismatic Leader

This chapter continues our exploration of the uncanny fit between the emotional needs of Donald Trump as a charismatic leader and his loyal followers many of whom are steadfastly committed to nurturing their leader so much so that they lose their personal integrity. Sycophants and sycophancy are terms that are pejorative in nature. The attributes of sycophants as they relate to powerful, autocratic, and charismatic leaders is usually attention-getting (discussed later in the chapter). There may, for example, develop a competition among these individuals for the attention, acceptance, and love of the leader who may reward them for this but also punish them for insufficient loyalty and subservience to "shape them up." Dynamics like this gradually create of a homogeneous group of highly committed supporters. Those who do not identify with the leader and the direction the leader is taking often find themselves labeled as not being team players (James in Chapter 2). They may then be undermined (back-stabbing) resulting in voluntarily leaving or being fired. This dynamic clears the way for selective recruitment of internal candidates who are known to seek this type of relationship with the leader or for outsiders (Fox News auditions aimed at being hired) who seem amendable to doing so during hiring interviews. One way to anchor sycophancy in everyday experience is to explore similar words that convey its meaning.

The Synonyms of Sycophancy

Many different synonyms for sycophants can be found with a quick inspection of the internet. The following exemplars anchor sycophancy in a reality that may be observed but also experienced by others that makes these individuals and their behavior "cringe worthy" if not ultimately repulsive.

- Apple-polishing
- Ass kissing
- Bootlicking
- Brown nosing

- Ego flatterer
- Fawning obsequiousness
- Flunky
- Groveling
- Hanger-on
- Kowtowing
- Self-seeking
- Servile
- Shameless self-promoters
- Submissive
- Subservient
- Sucking up
- Toady
- Yes man

This list accesses the distressing and problematic nature of this behavior when it comes to powerful, autocratic, and charismatic leaders. Along a range, submission, self-prostration (prostitution) and a near complete loss of personal integrity leaves these individuals hollowed out. They become dependent on the leader for a sense of self-worth. Loss of approval or favorite status can be devastating for these individuals. Many others, as observers, often stand back from these dynamics. The sycophants may be avoided as spies and shunned, which further isolates them from their colleagues and friends, making them more dependent on the leader to regulate their self-experience and perhaps even to protect them from critical, skeptical, and distanced others. There is then represented in this context the expression "having made a deal with the devil." In a metaphoric sense they sell their soul. They have sold themselves out which is mentioned relative to the Republicans in the senate and house of representatives as well as cabinet members and political appointees who submit to Trump's power and control discussed in Chapter 12. This dynamic is leading members of the anti-Trump Lincoln Project and other similar groups to the unfulfilled hope for a sweeping out of these people following the November 2020 elections. They are not considered to be suitable for the reconceived and rebranded Republican party going forward when the Age of Trump and Trumpism eventually ends.

The following conclusion seems reasonable to draw and it is in resonance with the mention of sycophancy in Chapter 5. Autocrats and authoritarians need loyal, admiring, and unquestioning followers who are excited to fully commit to this leader. Their close affiliation with a powerful and dominant leader who, in the case of Trump, demands loyalty to him and not the Constitution or America must not be questioned. It is clear Trump often seems to see the American people narcissistically fused with him – he is them; he is the country. There are many psychosocial dynamics to be considered to explain this unquestioning loyalty.

We explore in this chapter a process of how a charismatic leader ends up being created "in mind." The creative process is driven by what one sees, hears, and reads which is dominated by various forms of nationally broadcast television entertainment (*The Apprentice*), news along a range to near propaganda (Fox News, Newsmax, and *Wall Street Journal* Opinion), and news programing that resembles news but is closer to entertainment (Fox News opinion) to garner ratings to sell advertising time. This includes the ever popular "food fights" where two polar points of view are ostensibly argued out but also where one view may be so marginal as to create a false sense of equivalency when argued relative to a grounded, documented, and accepted perspective such as the argument about "global warming." To this, we add the powerful influence of "conservative" far-right regional television networks (Sinclair for example), talk radio programs (Rush Limbaugh, Sean Hannity) and the ever-changing and expanding world of internet-based social networking, blogs, and news sites (Breitbart, Facebook, Twitter, Parler).

The Creation of Loyal Followers and Sycophants

Most attempts to understand and explain Donald Trump have focused on his personal characteristics and traits. In this chapter, we explore the crucial role of Trump's loyal followers in the creation and sustaining of Donald Trump. The mirroring process between leader and these loyal and often submissive followers leads to understanding the role that projective and introjective identification play in this dynamic. The critical role of Fox News as a case in point in intensifying this mirroring and group polarization must also be considered. We once again rely on triangulation to explore the dynamics of the of Trump, Fox News, and Trump's loyal followers who staff and support his autocratic efforts to rule with their high voter approval.

The Election

The election of 2016 yielded an unexpected outcome with Donald Trump as the new leader of the most powerful nation on earth. This election of a leader who is a ruthless and self-serving executive, and a reality TV star of a program in which he was the focal point and judge and jury, has led to what some would say is a predictably chaotic outcome for the United States.[1] Considerable effort has been expended to understand Trump and his followers. Diagnostic questions have been posed. Does he have some combination of personality disorders such as narcissistic, antisocial, paranoid, or some other clinical label such as sociopath?[2] In this chapter, we do not wish to plow this fertile ground of personality analysis any further, but rather look instead to understanding those who have embraced him and the fantasy of "draining the swamp," and making his followers and America Great Again.

The drain the swamp slogan refers to a potpourri of Trump promises, grievances, and tweets, some of which are: voter fraud, media companies biased against him and his followers, shortcomings in the fight against ISIS, Obama's and Clinton's foreign policy, Obamacare, liberal Supreme Court justices, the Hillary Clinton e-mail investigation, and the revolving door where government officials become highly paid consultants and lobbyists for special interests and foreign governments.[3]

The Make America Great Again (MAGA) slogan is adapted from Ronald Reagan's and George H.W. Bush's "Let's Make America Great Again" that they used in their 1980 campaign but did not trademark it as Trump has.[4] Reagan and Bush spoke of American exceptionalism, consistent with Trump's 2011 book *Time to Get Tough: Making America #1 Again*, where he framed his agenda as a defense of American exceptionalism.[5]

MAGA is like all good slogans, a phrase that can mean whatever the hearer wants to it mean.[6] In particular, the slogan encourages thoughts and feelings associated with past utopian nostalgia (things were better back then) when a loyal and devoted workforce was rewarded with a decent middle-class lifestyle based on readily available and well-paying jobs, and a larger social sense that everyone was realizing the American Dream.[7,8,9] Terry Gardiner, a former CEO, captures much of the latent meaning of the slogan by writing:

> However, for core Republican voters this has a pretty specific meaning. This group deeply believes that President Obama, beyond being illegitimate, has not only been bad for America, but he has been purposefully bad for America, weakening the military, filling the country with illegal immigrants and Muslim refugees, giving favorable treatment to African Americans, apologizing all over the world, encouraging Muslim terrorists, oppressing Christians, and generally dissing and hurting white people, especially white men.[8]

Gardiner points out the slogan, while being a fill in the blank for audiences, does appeal to the 70% of voters who believe America was going in the wrong direction. It is a dog whistle for opposition to gay marriage, the expansion of women's roles including in the military, inter-racial marriage, rising immigration, losses of manufacturing jobs, an increasing population of people of color, and the growth of cities at the expense of developing rural areas.[8]

To gain understanding of this larger psychosocial milieu, we place this political context between two metaphoric mirrors. One reflects the admiration of the voters for the leader. The other reflects the devotion of the leader back to his followers. It is also the case that neither the subject nor the audience in this dynamic can be understood without appreciating the larger societal and historical context of the creation of a fight or flight polarized society during the last two decades.[10] To be explored here is the role of projective and introjective identification in understanding Trump as an "empty vessel" that is filled by followers' projections. This psychodynamic process that contributes to the current political and social polarization is fueled as mentioned by news organizations that *profit by promoting the polarization*.

News as a Driver of Social Polarization: A History

A brief historical overview provides insight into the evolution of the "news," from what was at one time a public service that did not make the networks money, to news as entertainment or "infotainment" that does make money depending on program ratings (How big is the crowd?). Marc Gunther notes, "Twenty years ago [early 80s], there was no network news 'business'. The Big Three broadcast television networks—ABC, CBS and NBC—all covered news, but none generally made money doing so."[11] The now for-profit news and the polarized societal context that locks in a loyal viewership reinforces the mirroring between leader and followers, which can become so unconsciously reinforcing as to create unquestioning loyalty and admiration for the leader – Trump. The same holds true for the leader being devoted to his followers where they are loved and admired by him regardless of their actions such as racist white supremacy demonstrations that become violent.[2,12,13,14]

The transformation of the news may be understood to have gradually happened as the large corporations that owned the networks sought to break even on the cost of the news – a necessity for a for-profit corporation.[11] There was a point in time when a phase shift occurred and the search for network profit was faced with growing competition from 24-hour cable news. The 1978 advent of Ted Turner's CNN 24-hour news that was largely objective news (just the facts), presented in informative but not entertaining segments, set a new standard, and created a transformative news format. The networks also discovered the money-making potential of news as entertainment – *60 Minutes*, *Dateline*, and *Nightline* are examples. Today, TV personalities star in segments that discuss recent events, including relying on the classic "food fight" format where opposing operatives from the left and right duke it out. The news sometimes resembles reality TV programs. These "shows" must maintain their ratings that drive corporate profitability through the sale of advertising – the more viewers the more profit. The historical evolution of the "news" to focus on profitability is worth exploring.[11]

Daniel Halin underscores in 1990 there are changes in news and news formats.

> Most of today's growth, meanwhile, has been at the "low end" in a proliferation of shows that practice what might be called "para-journalism." The most important new form is the "tabloid" news magazine, including

such shows as A Current Affair, Inside Edition, Hard Copy and The Reporters.

In a way, these shows represent something very new. They are not news shows that borrow conventions from entertainment television, but the other way around: entertainment programs that borrow the aura of news. The forms and the "look" are news – the opening sequences frequently feature typewriter keys and newsroom-like sets with monitors in the background. The content, however, has little of the substance of journalism; above all, little about public affairs.[15]

The year 1996 was a key year in the transformation of TV news to entertainment.

• Fox News Channel was founded in 1996 to fulfill the wished-for realization of a conservative TV news channel, envisioned by Richard Nixon and his aide Roger Ailes. Mr. Ailes (resigned in 2016 and deceased in 2017) eventually joined with Ruppert Murdock to create the Fox News channel with its distinctive, and it should be added, effective presentation of news spun to the right.[16,17]

• CNN, founded in 1978, merged with Time Warner in 1996, leading to format changes that were focused on ratings and competing with the success of Fox News. There was a gradual focus on liberal political opinion, creating distrust by viewers who consistently identified themselves as conservative.[18,19]

• MSNBC news was founded in 1996 and by 2000 had also shifted toward a heavy dose of political opinion distrusted by conservatives.[18,20,21]

CNN and MSNBC have similar formats to Fox News to compete with Fox News. In general, during the last decade a comparison of these two news sources to Fox News and Opinion reveals that Fox News was more effective at creating an integrated theme throughout the day (an echo chamber). Fox News had noticeable news and opinion threads picked up from one hosted program to another, whereas CNN and MSNBC achieve this to a lesser extent. More recently it appears the two networks are catching up to Fox in terms of formats, hosts, sets, and guests.

The channels now, in general, and Fox News in particular, can be thought of as effectively reinforcing the political and social biases (confirmation bias) and beliefs of their audiences, creating a loyal audience that improves competitive ratings, increasing the value of an advertising minute. Telling one's audience what they want to hear works, while also shaping what the audience knows and believes to be true works.[22,23] This is underscored by the following observation by Mathew Yglesias: "Long story short, if party leaders say ridiculous things, your party's rank and file will believe ridiculous things. If they say that news outlets that try to puncture the bubble of ridiculousness are exhibiting 'liberal bias,' your party's rank and file will learn to dismiss credible sources of information."[24]

The dominance of TV news is noteworthy. According to a 2016 Pew Research survey, approximately 60% of Americans get their news from TV, followed by 40% reading news on the internet.[25] In a second 2014 Pew Research report on political polarization, the researchers found that for those who are consistently conservative, 47% obtain their news from the Fox News channel as compared with those who are consistently liberal, who obtain their news in the range of 10%–15% from CNN, MSNBC, NPR, and NYT.[18] Fox News channel clearly has a large and loyal audience.

It may be concluded in 2020 that during the last two decades the major TV news sources, combined with the internet news sources and social media, talk radio hosts such as Rush Limbaugh and Sean Hannity, and other right-leaning publications and editorials, have come to dominate conservative political awareness, contributing to the current state of political polarization now and during the 2016 election. Although facts have also fallen victim to the rightward slant, these changes in the news media, combined with programming that promotes polarization, are a critically important element of understanding the leader and follower dynamics, so clearly visible today on the conservative side of the political equation.[26]

In sum, during the mid-90's the nature of TV news changed, especially with the creation of Fox News, which began to build an audience of like-minded people who are the "right" in the United States. They did this by reinforcing preexisting biases in this conservatively based large group, which created loyal followers half of whom get most if not all their news from Fox News. The other two networks gradually adopted Fox News' successful methods to compete but leaning left politically. Given the large audience organized around Fox News, Trump has successfully used it to his advantage, including monitoring some of the content of shows and phoning in. Trump as a fight/flight leader is focused on saying and doing things that excite this audience. He relies on the content on Fox News as a key indicator of what to say and do. This has created a triangulation between Trump/Fox News/and their "red state" audience. This outcome is contributed to and more importantly sustained by psychological splitting that creates a simplified black and white world – we are good, and the left is evil. This psychodynamically informed perspective contributes insight and sets the stage for exploring the triangulation and mirrors.

The Images of the Mirrors

Ever since he became a candidate for the U.S. Presidency, Donald Trump has been the subject of numerous journalistic and academic accounts of his personality traits and their consequences for his political actions. Most recently, mental health professionals have felt a public responsibility to warn the American public against Trump's danger to the country, and even to the world.[2]

A constellation of news and public discourse has been fueled by many observable behaviors and statements that reflect his misogyny, racism, and white supremacist ideology. His trafficking with neo-Nazis and the Alt Right, his anti-immigrant and anti-refugee beliefs, his chauvinism, his nationalism, his exclusivist (as opposed to inclusivist) vision of America, his inability to accept criticism, his surrounding himself with fierce loyalists, and his hatred of President Obama and everything associated with him, underscore his toxic nature and leadership. What all these behaviors, statements, and analyses share is that they encourage Americans to focus their attention on him and his psychological propensities and moving against others. In keeping with American individualistic popular psychology, the focus has been on the "inside" of Trump, and how these psychological propensities affect his beliefs, ideologies, words, and actions.

Although this approach has value in helping to explain Trump, it uniformly neglects a crucial dimension – the *uncanny psychological fit* between Trump and his ardent supporters in his administration, Congress, and the country. Trump is a group-transference target, an embodiment of idealizing projections that have led those around him to uncritically endorse his statements and actions (a cult leader or chosen one). They identify with him because they created him in their likeness in mind. This dynamic of mindful creation suggests one way to comprehend Donald Trump is as an empty vessel that his followers fill by projecting onto him as well as encouraging him to incorporate these idealizing projections (projective identification). His sycophants steadily pressure him (Stephen Miller is an example) to fit their image of him. This pressure is aided by regulating their approval of him that provides him much sought-after narcissistic supplies. Trump as well as many other leaders may, by incorporating the projections, become to a large extent the sum of all the projections onto and into him or her – a projective vessel.

Our understanding of the group psychology of Trumpism shares much with Sigmund Freud's formulation of the psychodynamic relationship between leader and large group. In *Group Psychology and the Analysis of the Ego*, Freud argues that in the large group (which he calls masses) the individual acts in ways that he or she never would as a single individual.[27] Impulses, emotions, and narcissism are given free rein. Libido is diverted from the original object (person) and given to the leader. Members of the group suspend their individual ego ideal and individuality and replace it with the leader as they identify with each other and idealize the leader. Members of the group are thus bound to each other in their shared idealization of the leader.

The experience in organizations of CEOs and other executives, who become transference targets of employees, makes clear that projection onto and projection into executives by the employees is an omnipresent psychodynamic force. The reverse is true as well. Trump projects parts of himself onto his followers. The followers have projected many elements of their admirable abilities onto the leader, thereby magnifying the leader's abilities, while diminishing themselves. The leader joins in this dynamic by projecting his weakness, narcissistic injuries, and his less admirable features onto his followers (stupid and incompetent), who now feel deficient and feel only he can save them.[13,28,29,30]

The Psychodynamics of the Mirroring

Group Relations perspectives and object relations theory help us to understand the intrapersonal, interpersonal, and group dynamics of the relationship between Donald Trump and his followers.[12,13,14,31] Donald Trump, when viewed as an empty vessel that takes in the sum of all his supporters' idealizing projections and adoration (narcissistic supplies), can be understood to become a co-created political brand focused on his crowd size (ratings). If this is so, then the personal attributes of Trump should be in large part a mirror image of the attributes of the people who project their inner world onto and into him. To be noted is that the psychodynamics of the fight/ flight basic assumption group, that seeks a powerful leader, is the creation of an unconscious shared willingness to move toward the leader and against threatening others. The mirroring results in a list of Trump's attributes should also be a list of the attributes of those people who are his enthusiasts. He is in large measure the creation and embodiment of his followers: a brand, reality TV personality, and politician. There are several psychodynamics that contribute to this co-creative process, where the leader and followers become mirrored images of each other. Explored here is the unconscious nature of confirmation bias informed by object relations theory.

Wehner, discusses confirmation bias as a largely unconscious process.

> We're also learning that there is a physiological basis to confirmation bias, processing information that supports our belief system triggers a dopamine rush, and that our brains are hard-wired to embrace information that confirms our pre-existing attitudes and rejects challenges. Our beliefs are also often tied up with our ideas about who we are individually and our group identity. The result is that changing our beliefs in light of new evidence can cause us to be rejected by our political community.
>
> To say that we all struggle with confirmation bias is not to say that some individuals don't overcome it better than others or that some aren't closer to seeing the truth of things better than others. Objective reality exists, truth matters, and we have to pursue them with purpose and without fear. But in our present moment, truth, including truth that unsettles us, has far too often become subordinate to justifying and defending at all costs our own, often unsound, preconceptions.[32]

Confirmation bias helps us to understand how audiences select one TV news channel over another and one leader over another. Kelly Swanson, reporting for Vox.com on a new Politico/Morning Consult poll, notes: "Attacks on the 'fake news' media have become a staple of the Trump administration — and nearly half of voters, including the vast majority of Republicans, believe the president when he claims that the media is making up stories about him."[33]

About half to three-fourths of Republican voters believe that major news organizations fabricate stories about Trump. In contrast 20% of Democrats believe the media creates fake stories about Trump.

Confirmation bias involves listening only to what reinforces one's existing beliefs, but also not listening to information that is not consistent with the biases, or otherwise ignoring, disregarding, or dismissing the contrary information as fake. Terms such as denial, splitting, and projection, transference, projective identification, result in the surreal interpersonal space described by the metaphor of mirrors.

We often seem to "know" someone else, a leader, even if we have never met the person. The person is good or bad, dominating, or submissive, effective at leading or not. In part we may selectively attend to the person as leader and his or her behavior, reconfirming pre-existing biases based on an array of unconscious associations relative to the person, who might, for example, look or act like one's punishing father or loving mother, or other caretakers, siblings, relatives, or acquaintances. Appearance, the sound of the voice, mannerism, language used, and actions taken become seamlessly woven into the leader as a self-created image familiar to one's self. Of course, this may seem and feel foreign to the other person who is the target.

This unconscious process of constructing the leader in one's mind, yields thoughts and feelings toward the leader consistent with this construction. In some instances as with Trump, the leader may be fantasized to be a powerful, highly effective individual (a new sheriff in town) who takes no prisoners and who has as a trademark (brand) disregard for social conventions and civility (anti-PC). Trump is seen to be someone who will aggressively attack those who have created narcissistic injuries relative to himself and his followers. People who are unemployed may blame Obama, Congress, corporations, other countries, or immigrants for their predicament.[2] There is then a process in which a leader is created as a fight/flight leader who promises to right all wrongs, and to liberate the disadvantaged and oppressed from their suffering. The leader becomes all-powerful and avenging (moving against others), fueled by the absorption of all these largely unconsciously communicated desires. The leader, as an empty vessel, becomes filled to overflowing with the group's narcissistic rage that resonates with his own inner narcissistic injuries and grievances.

Consider the ideological constellation of racism, ethnocentrism, white supremacy, anti-immigrant, and anti-refugee beliefs. Early in his presidential candidacy, Trump characterized immigrants from Mexico and Central America as "rapists" and "criminals," noting as an after-thought perhaps some are good. He promised that a wall would be built to separate the two countries and "us" from "them." Further, he vowed to expel all those immigrants who entered illegally, and more recently their children who arrived with them and without them and who know no other life than in America (DACA – The Dreamers). His ideas were met by his supporters with ardent enthusiasm. Build the wall!

Projection, Projective Identification, and the Empty Vessel

The dictum that power corrupts applies to the leader who elicits these projections and identifications from followers. The wishes of the followers who want to control the leader may become more coercive, creating demands on the leader to "walk the talk" and act on their behalf by vanquishing the evil others who have injured their collective narcissism. There is then a two-edged sword that is fashioned by the followers in creating their fantasized leader. The leader basks in the many strong positive feelings of followers who are loving and admiring him, while at the same time feels oppressed by follower demands that require acting on their behalf to maintain their adoration and loyalty. This is the nature of the political contract between voters and those they elect. As a result, the followers, who may be thought of as inferior to this grand leader, may become the focal point of leader's rage and aggression (movement against) for holding such high behavioral expectations.

Leadership is rife with projective identification. In fact, projective identification, originally thought of as an individual, intrapsychic defense, also binds relationships for couples, families, large groups, and between groups. As a kind of relationship defense as well as an individual defense projective identification binds leaders and followers to each other.

Often projective identification (in mind) includes introjective identification, where the leader embodies, identifies with, and enacts the projections, a kind of reciprocal them-in-leader and leader-in-them process. The leader carries out the delegated "assignment" of the group. In sum, the long-held but simplistic notion that the leader leads (directs) the group, and the group follows, requires a much more nuanced understanding of the unconscious dance between them. Examining family psychological dynamics contributes additional insight.

Family Leadership Dynamics in Depth

The work of Helm Stierlin on "delegation" of obligations and roles in families, and of Maurice Apprey on unconscious "errands" in families (including intergeneration transmission of trauma among African Americans) is relevant in terms of understanding leadership from a depth psychological perspective.[34,35,36,37,38,39,40] For Stierlin, the child who becomes a family-delegate is treated as a narcissistic extension of his or her parents. Similarly, for Apprey, a child is chosen to embody and enact unconscious "urgent voluntary errands" that are first mandated and then unconsciously appropriated.

These dynamics suggest that idealized leaders of large groups, organizations and nations do consciously and unconsciously assume delegated obligations from followers who share projections arising from shared childhood fantasies and conflicts, intergenerationally transmitted group trauma, and unconscious family obligations. Followers invest in their leader the hope to reverse their narcissistic injuries and make them feel great again about themselves. The group thus delegates its "urgent voluntary errands" upon its leader, who in turn enacts the group fantasy on the public stage. Also, to be considered is that leaders may project and displace personal and familial conflicts, crises, and traumas (often multi-generational) onto public issues, decisions, and events. In sum, the family is also a contributor to creating the leader, the followers, and the larger psychosocial context.

The Filling of the Empty Vessels

President Trump is a distinct person bounded by his skin, but he may also be understood psychodynamically to be an "empty vessel" who is filled with the electorate's idealizing projections and assignments. He welcomes this to promote feelings of being loved and admired and powerful and in control, all of which compensate for his own narcissistic deficits. Even though Trump embodies his follower's fantasies, he can also quickly become emotionally deflated unless he is continually reaffirmed. He constantly requires refueling from his followers (holding rallies, Fox News approval) in order not to feel empty and desolate inside. His rage and desire to take revenge against anyone who fails to admire him and demonstrate loyalty can increase to the point of obliterating them (You're fired!). His pursuit of narcissistic supplies leads him to say and do whatever is necessary to acquire these supplies. This, in turn, reinforces his expansive sense of himself, which is paradoxically fragile and easily injured.[2]

The Empty Vessel as Brand

The notion of an individual becoming a brand, not unlike a company, product, or an entertainer, elevates the image of filling of the empty vessel with projections and adoration to a new level of consideration. The empty vessel as brand metaphor is supported by the observations of many who believe Trump has no or few ideological preferences. He is seemingly only interested in how good he looks, his ratings and crowd size, and being reelected.

However, he also has a long history of believing some things – such as Obama not being born in the United States, and the Central Park 5 (Antron McCray, Raymond Santana, Kevin Richardson, Yusef Salaam, and Korey Wise) being guilty despite DNA and a confession from the actual rapist.[41]

The empty vessel as brand speaks to Trump's paying close attention to his ratings and audience preferences, negotiating a script with them that works for him and excites them. He identifies with them as they do with him – mutual imaging or mirroring. This dynamic is aided by his tuning into Fox News, where nearly half of his voters get their news and indoctrination.[18] Once again, there is the apparent interaction or interdependence (triangulation) between him, Fox News, and his followers, where there is continual mutual adjustment to locate the script or narrative of the moment to keep the bonds between the three parties of the triad strong. The empty vessel also speaks to self-esteem. Trump seeks love, admiration, and preferably adoration from others and from Fox News. Trump is concerned about the size of the crowd and his approval ratings because they are essential to his feeling good about himself. If criticized he seeks what Karen Horney refers to as vindictive triumph by striking out at, moving against, those who injured him.[42] A bit harder to understand is the constant very public lying about many things which are readily debunked, which would seem to undermine the view that he is the smartest guy in the room worthy of unquestioning admiration. The lying appears to be edited out by his followers via denial, rationalization and selective attention which is also a form of psychological investment in their mindful image of their leader.

In Conclusion

This chapter has explored the triangulation of Trump, Fox News, and Trump's followers. While most analyses have focused on Donald Trump's personality traits, we have focused attention on how Trump is created, amplified, and sustained by Fox News and his loyal followers. Appreciating the role of the mirroring process – projection and projective identification – that fills an empty vessel in mind and in the other adds important perspective to understanding leader and follower dynamics.

Chapter 8 explores yet another aspect of the Age of Trump – chaos. Trump epitomizes how confusing and dominating a powerful leader can become when unpredictable and erratic actions and decisions that impact the lives of many are simply doled out via stream of consciousness in tweets.

Notes

1. Buettner, R. & Baglijune, C. (2016). How Donald Trump bankrupted his Atlantic City casinos, but still earned millions. *The New York Times*. https://www.nytimes.com/2016/06/12/nyregion/donald-trump-atlantic-city.html
2. Lee, B. (2017). *The dangerous case of Donald Trump: 27 psychiatrists and mental health experts assess a president*. New York: NY, Thomas Dunne Books.

3. Arnsdorf, I., Dawsey, J. & Lippman, D. (2016). Will 'drain the swamp' be Trump's first broken promise? *Politico*. https://www.politico.com/story/2016/12/trump-drain-swamp-promise-232938.

4. Tumulty, K. (2017). How Donald Trump came up with 'Make America Great Again'. *Washington Post*. https://www.washingtonpost.com/politics/how-donald-trump-came-up-with-make-america-great-again/2017/01/17/fb6acf5e-dbf7-11e6-ad42-f3375f271c9c_story.html.

5. Jouet, M. (2017). Trump didn't invent "Make America Great Again" How conservatives hijacked the idea of American exceptionalism. *Mother Jones*. https://www.motherjones.com/politics/2017/01/american-exceptionalism-maga-trump-obama/

6. Simonoff, J. (2016). What does 'make America great again' even mean? *Quora.com*. https://www.quora.com/What-does-%E2%80%9Cmake-America-great-again-mean.

7. Barry, A. (2016). What made Trump's 'Make America Great Again' slogan so powerful? *The Journal*. https://www.thejournal.ie/trump-slogan-make-america-great-again-3071552-Nov2016/.

8. Gardiner, T. (2016). What is "Make America Great Again"? *Quara.com*. https://www.quora.com/What-is-%E2%80%9CMake-America-Great-Again%E2%80%9D?no_redirect=1.

9. Smith, K. (2016). What "Make America Great Again" means. *Psychology Today*. https://www.psychologytoday.com/blog/full-living/201608/what-make-america-great-again-means.

10. Cohn, N. (2014). Polarization is dividing American society, not just politics. *The New York Times*. https://www.nytimes.com/2014/06/12/upshot/polarization-is-dividing-american-society-not-just-politics.html.

11. Gunther, M. (1999). The transformation of network news: How profitability has moved networks out of hard news. *Nieman Reports*. http://niemanreports.org/articles/the-transformation-of-network-news/.

12. Greenberg, J. & Mitchell, S. (1983). *Object relations in psychoanalytic theory*. Cambridge, MA: Harvard University Press.

13. Grotstein, J. (1993). *Splitting and projective identification*. Northvale, NJ: Jason Aronson.

14. Hamilton, N. (1990). *Self & others: Object relations theory in practice*. Northvale, NJ: Jason Aronson.

15. Halin, D. (1990). When hard news goes soft, entertainment takes over. *Center for Media Literacy*. https://www.medialit.org/reading-room/whatever-happened-news

16. Oster, P. (2017). Roger Ailes, founder of Murdoch's Fox News, dies at 77. *Bloomberg*. https://www.bloomberg.com/news/articles/2017-05-18/roger-ailes-founder-of-murdoch-s-fox-news-channel-dies.

17. Fox News. (2021, May 27). In *Wikipedia*. https://en.wikipedia.org/wiki/Fox_News.

18. Mitchell, A., Gottfried, J., Kiley, J. and Matsa, K. (2014). Political polarization & media habits. *Pew Research Center*. http://www.journalism.org/2014/10/21/political-polarization-media-habits/.

19. Ted Turner. (2021, May 13). In *Wikipedia*. https://en.wikipedia.org/wiki/Ted_Turner.

20. Postman, N. (1985). *Amusing ourselves to death: Public discourse in the age of show business*. New York, NY: Penguin Books.

21. MSNBC. (2021, May 26). In *Wikipedia*. https://en.wikipedia.org/wiki/MSNBC.

22. Martin, G. &Yurukoglu, A. (2017). *Bias in cable news: Persuasion and polarization*. https://web.stanford.edu/~ayurukog/cable_news.pdf.

23. Lowry, B. (2011). Wallace admits Fox News' agenda: Host lets slip the other side of the cabler's story. *Variety*. http://variety.com/2011/tv/columns/wallace-admits-fox-news-agenda-1118039115/.

24. Yglesias, M. (2017). Establishment Republicans mystified by their base should look at Ed Gillespie's campaign. *Vox.com.* https://www.vox.com/policy-and-politics/2017/10/12/16439948/ed-gillespie-ms-13.

25. Mitchell, A., Gottfried, J., Barthel, M. & Shearer, E. (2016). The modern news consumer. *Pew Research Center.* http://www.journalism.org/2016/07/07/pathways-to-news/.

26. Allcorn, S. & Stein, H. (2017). The post-factual world of the 2016 American presidential election: The good, the bad, and the deplorable. *The Journal of Psychohistory,* 44(4), 310–318.

27. Freud, S. (1921/1955). Group psychology and the analysis of the ego. *In: The standard edition of the complete psychological works of Sigmund Freud.* Volume 18. London: Hogarth Press, 69–143.

28. Allcorn, S. & Stein, H. (2015). *The dysfunctional workplace: Theory, stories, and practice.* Columbia, MO: University of Missouri Press.

29. Czander, W. (1993). *The psychodynamics of work and organizations: Theory and application.* New York, NY: Guilford Press.

30. Kets de Vries, M. F. (2006). *The leader on the couch: A clinical approach to changing people and organizations.* San Francisco, CA: John Wiley & Sons.

31. Bion, W. (1961). *Experiences in groups.* London: Tavistock.

32. Wehner, P. (2017). Seeing Trump through a glass, darkly. *The New York Times.* https://www.nytimes.com/2017/10/07/opinion/sunday/trump-republicans-confirmation-bias.html?action=click&pgtype=Homepage&click-Source=story-heading&module=opinion-c-col-left-region&region=opinion-c-col-left-region&WT.nav=opinion-c-col-left-region.

33. Swanson, K. (2017). Poll: 46% of Americans believe major news outlets make up stories about Trump. *Vox.com.* https://www.vox.com/policy-and-politics/2017/10/18/16495544/poll-americans-news-outlets-fake-stories-trump.

34. Stierlin, H. (1973). The adolescent as delegate of his parents. *Australian and New Zealand Journal of Psychiatry,* 7, 249–256.

35. Stierlin, H. (1976). *Adolf Hitler: A family perspective.* New York, NY: Psychohistory Press.

36. Stierlin, H., Rücker-Embden, I., Wetzel, N. and Wirsching, M. (1980). *The first family interview.* New York, NY: Brunner/Mazel.

37. Stierlin, H. (1982). *Delegation und familie: Beiträge zum Heidelberger familiendynamischen konzept.* Frankfurt am Main: Suhrkamp.

38. Apprey, M. (1999). Reinventing the self in the face of received transgenerational hatred in The African American community. *Journal of Applied Psychoanalytic Studies,* 1(2), 131–143.

39. Apprey, M. (2014). A pluperfect errand: A turbulent return to beginnings in the transgenerational transmission of destructive aggression. *Free Associations: Psychoanalysis and Culture, Media, Groups, Politics.* http://freeassociations.org.uk/FA_New/OJS/index.php/fa/article/view/102/137.

40. Apprey, M. (ND). (2015). Urgent voluntary errands. *Psychoanalysis today.* http://www.psychoanalysis.today/en-GB/PT-Articles/Urgent-voluntary-errands.aspx.

41. Burns, S. (2016). Why Trump doubled down on the central park five. *The New York Times.* https://www.nytimes.com/2016/10/18/opinion/why-trump-doubled-down-on-the-central-park-five.html.

42. Horney, K. (1950). *Neurosis and human growth: The struggle toward self-realization.* New York, NY: Norton.

8 The Reality of Chaotic Leadership

The United States, its federal government, and some state governments introduce chaos into everyone's lives. Will the mail arrive or not? Will face masks be worn or not? Chaos is made all the more common by a leader who acts and governs autocratically, and is surrounded by loyalists and sycophants who no longer provide the guard rails that were discussed when senior military and other experienced officials did their best to keep the Trump train on its tracks. This is, during 2020, accentuated by the failed impeachment that made Trump immune to accountability, regulation, or containment by the House and Senate. This is the Age of Trump.

Trump is described as erratic, unpredictable, making sudden decisions with limited to no consultation, and drawing lines on weather forecasts to justify what he said that was not true or accurate. Actions like these have also created confusion about America's relationship with its allies around the world.

A familiar approach Trump uses to infuse confusion is to first side with "his administration" regarding what may be considered a reasonable policy such as wearing masks but then later criticize the policy and disown it. When questioned he may then again endorse the policy and but again reject it later in a tweet. He is then for and against the same policy at the same time speaking in a sense "out of both sides of his mouth."

This dynamic is underscored by his loyalists in powerful positions who may speak for a position one day, then be criticized and retreat from what they had just said the next day. And to be noted those who hold press conferences on his behalf are willing to lie to the media (crowd size) and distort, dissemble, and use "alternate" facts to defend and explain away his pronouncements.

Trying to understand the chaos of the Age of Trump necessitates providing background information drawn from credible recent sources on the internet. It underscores there are convergent points of view regarding Trump "living off chaos." Trump's actions indicate a willingness to win at any cost to business partners, groups, and individuals and the United States – apparently acceptable collateral damage.

Chaos and Converging Points of View

Chaos as a concept in a social sense includes such words as disorder, confusion, disarray, disorganization, confusion, and turmoil. A human stampede away from danger that leaves many people killed and injured is one example where any sense of order and regularity is lost. And, as discussed here, a powerful, charismatic, paranoid, autocratic leader who follows his gut feelings may well provide no clear or consistent direction or appear to follow an accepted ideology or philosophical position. Trump, unencumbered by tradition, the Constitution, and supported by sycophants may, often opportunistically, decide to change direction at a whim with no discussion.

Jonathan Rauch noted that Paul Ryan, as he assumed the role of House speaker, complained that Americans view Washington as chaotic and that the two parties and their members cannot agree on much, creating a leadership vacuum.[1] Jeb Bush described Donald Trump as the chaos candidate who would become the chaos president, although Trump's followers themselves appear to be advocates of chaos, nihilism, and destruction of "business as usual" in Washington. Political correctness and compromise are out.

Rauch suggests one way to understand these dynamics is the Chaos Syndrome which is an inability for a political system to self-organize.[1] It arises when political parties and congressional leaders fail to hold politicians accountable for pursuing their self-interests to the exclusion of considering what may benefit the country. The political system becomes fragmented and chaos becomes the norm. Extremism is unleashed and moderate positions become a rarity, accentuated by single issue group voters and those who feel alienated from the "system," discussed in Chapter 13. These well-organized and motivated extremist groups predominate when less than 20% of Republican voters vote in primaries, which led to Donald Trump winning the primaries by a small but highly motivated fraction of the electorate.

Rauch writes: "In March, a Trump supporter told *The New York Times*, 'I want to see Trump go up there and do damage to the Republican Party.' Another said, 'We know who Donald Trump is, and we're going to use Donald Trump to either take over the G.O.P. or blow it up.'" Rauch continues: "That kind of anti-establishment nihilism deserves no respect or accommodation in American public life. Populism, individualism, and a skeptical attitude toward politics are all healthy up to a point, but America has passed that point."[1] The outcome is a self-mutilating embrace of anti-establishment rhetoric, yielding polarization, rejection of compromises, a pursuit of ideological purity (tribalism), and chaos.

Thomas Edsall points out, "As the 2018 election demonstrated, Trump's personally chaotic approach to governance, his record of undermining relations with allies and strengthening ties to autocrats; his use of trade policy to heighten market insecurity; his aggression, his recklessness, his incessant lying; and his sneering contemptuous, bullying style, together worked against him and the Republican Party."[2] Edsall concludes that Trump's embrace of chaos, disorder, and his guiding principle of narcissistic self-interest will, he correctly predicted, lead to Trump's intolerable defeat.

John Wagner and Abby Phillip note president-elect Trump has via Twitter sowed confusion about his ban on foreign Muslims, attacked China for seizing an underwater drone, and suggested the United States should enhance its nuclear capability which he doubled down on after his staff attempted to water down the statement.[3] His staff are on the record saying that his social media and public statements should be largely dismissed in favor of paying attention to what he actually does regarding public and foreign policy. Even so, it is worth noting that his nuclear policy is unclear and there are multiple explanations he and others have provided regarding his confusing December 2016 nuclear weapons tweet about strengthening and expanding our nuclear capability.

Russ Buettner and Maggie Haberman write that Trump, consistent with his personal history in business dating back to the 1980s, continues to insult adversaries, undermined subordinates, frequently change his direction, and brag about his deal making ability supposedly enabled by using chaos as a strategy in the service of disorganizing his opposition.[4] Largely lacking conscience, he disregards the collateral damage he creates by aggressing others. His continual free flowing lies make fact checking and rebutting them an effort approaching a fool's errand.

Bobby Jindal offers similar insights about Trump. His critics are alarmed by his impetuous, narcissistic, crude, and unfocused manner of managing. His loyal followers overlook these "minor" flaws as compared to his willingness to hammer the mainstream media, party elites, and the establishment in Washington on their behalf because they feel ignored and defeated by them.[5] The best defense is often said to be a good offense – a strategy Trump seems of have mastered.

Missy Ryan, Paul Sonne, and Josh Dawsey report for *The Washington Post* that Trump complains that his defense secretaries have been insufficiently aligned with his foreign policy goals. He has accused Pentagon officials of undermining him.[6] His response has been to become more assertive regarding personnel matters. Disloyalty is not to be tolerated. Pressure continues throughout his administration to replace officers, staff, and employees with loyalists as compared to filling positions with qualified people who may wish to do their own thinking.

Paul Krugman offers one additional perspective to the chaos creation by pointing out that the modern right in the United States, in addition to supporting unfettered capitalism, are committed to the belief that we all are better off when individuals engage in the untrammeled pursuit of self-interest.[7] The notion of a common good such as everyone wearing facemasks is lost to a misplaced sense of individual freedoms untrammeled by government in any form – federal, state, county, and local.

Admiral McRaven offers a fitting conclusion. "And if Americans stop believing in the system of institutions, then what is left but chaos and who can bring order out of chaos: only Trump. It is the theme of every autocrat who ever seized power or tried to hold onto it."[8]

Chaos and Convergence: In Sum

Trump thrives on the chaos and being unpredictable in part because it makes for compelling TV coverage (political theater) and ratings (crowd size) this former reality TV star pays close attention to. He so far has survived one crisis after another that would normally cripple other politicians. His status as someone taking on the system on the part of his base voters metaphorically allows him to shoot someone in the middle of the street with impunity. Negative news coverage, "fake news," continually affirms for his supporters he is taking on the establishment confirming the media's bias against him and them and simultaneously creating media coverage. This dynamic is accentuated by those in opposition and Democrats engaging him in battles (movement against, fight/flight) that are distracting and usually fulfill the assertion everyone is out to get him (victimization). This creates a stance of his being perpetually aggrieved while he is steadfastly doing battle for "his people."

In 2020 chaos fatigue may have set in. Voters, turned off by all the turmoil, preferred a steadier hand (Biden) during times of a true crisis period (COVID-19, recession, and Black Lives Matter) as compared to one that is "trumped up" to irritate the opposition and excite his followers. During stressful times, Trump's chaos-inducing management strategies have created excessive stress and anxiety about the nation's handling of Black Lives Matter, the spread of COVID-19, and the yet to be fully comprehended COVID-19 recession.

We have tried in a few words to convey the sense of the chaos Trump creates which, as noted, irritates those on the left. These commentators seek a more logical and science-based approach, in contrast to as decisions informed by right-wing ideology and the rejection of experts in favor of loyalists. Chaos, in fact, appears to be a strategy aimed at consuming all the "airtime," by attracting desirable criticism from the media and those on the left in Washington, to the enjoyment of his followers who feel he is doing what they desire – essentially giving the "middle finger" to the Washington elites and the "establishment" that has looked down on them and not fulfilled their political agendas.

The ability to fulfill this agenda is enhanced by the unilateral power wielded by a powerful charismatic autocratic fight/flight leader who finds there are enemies and threats everywhere. The wielding of this power inflicts collateral damage on others and other countries limited only by those instances that his actions begin to negatively affect his ratings. And to be noted this is not a new dynamic. Trump's business career also relies on creating chaos for success. Nationally it seems reasonably clear that the chaos is distracting. It leaves critics wandering in a wasteland of lies and leaves even close associates in the dark. Add to this that the Age of Trump is filled with avoidable problems, harm, and threats that are first inflicted on others (cities, immigrants, allies) that then only he can save them from. This methodology, when used as a negotiating strategy, has clear limitations. Well documented are the failure of tariffs on China to yield changes in trade or sanctions on North Korea and Iran to curb their nuclear ambitions, or threats to defund the United Nations and World Health Organization to change their policies. In sum, there is then resident within all this chaos toxicity, dysfunction, and harm.

A paranoid, charismatic fight/flight leader who seemingly intentionally pursues chaos for success raises many psychodynamic questions. We now turn our attention to a psychodynamically informed inspection of paranoia, charisma, chaos, and autocratic leadership.

The Expansive Self-Conception that Fuels the Paranoid Charismatic Leader's Chaos

Chapters 6 and 7 have highlighted the role of object relations theory and Bion's fight or flight basic assumption group. The co-creation of the charismatic leader in terms of splitting and projection both in mind and in life, when combined with the threats a paranoid leader identifies and puts forward to frighten followers into becoming loyal and submissive followers, is a powerful interpersonal dynamic. The presence of enemies and threats is stressful for many individuals and groups that, in turn, leads to excessive anxiety and the need to locate a powerful leader to lead them in fighting back against enemies or fleeing. Karen Horney's theoretical perspective also contributes to understanding these leader and follower dynamics.

Karen Horney's theoretical perspectives, discussed in Chapter 2, offer considerable insight to understanding the paranoid, charismatic leadership style. The expansive solution to anxiety that includes three basic elements, *perfectionism, narcissism, and arrogant-vindictive triumph,* is an insightful way to understand why paranoia is often a prominent feature of charismatic autocratic leaders who locate enemies everywhere. This creates fear and anxiety on the part of followers who are motivated to follow the leader who promises to save them.

Perfection

The charismatic leader may wield perfection like a sword. Only the leader knows what to do. Trump's claim of omniscience is all empowering. It is understood that the problem at hand was created by imperfect others and has not thus far been remediated because they are imperfect. The leader magically knows the right, just and correct direction to take and how to proceed down the path to a powerful and strong victory over imperfect and resistant others. Followers who are not loyal enough are castigated as fools, dumb, stupid, and arrogantly labeled with pejorative nick names, like Attorney General Jeff Sessions was labeled as Mr. Magoo – a hapless, bumbling, nearsighted elderly cartoon character. Enemies are also pejoratively labeled, such as Sleepy Joe Biden, Pocahontas for Elizabeth Warren, Crooked Hillary (Clinton), and Rocket Man for North Korea's Kim Jong-un.

Perfection requires never admitting a problem, a poor decision or error which also seems to be a common characteristic of the Republicans such as George W. Bush not being able to recall a single misjudgment on his part save one – a poor hiring decision. For Trump admission of error is a sign of abhorred weakness. Identification with images of strong and powerful leadership and slogans such as Mission Accomplished, are, it seems, critically important to the far-right culture and self-envisionment. This dynamic requires substantial use of psychological defense mechanisms, such as denial, rationalization, and selective attention/inattention which is supported by Fox News and an abundance of other programing such as radio and social media. It is much easier in the twenty-first century to avoid accurate reality testing and embrace an alternate reality. This dynamic is also supported, as has been discussed, by splitting and projection, where "I" is "known" to be perfect and all others are imperfect thereby requiring the leader to lead them.

Narcissism

Chapter 4 discussed in-depth narcissism and how it informs understanding Trump. Here we focus attention on the relationship between a self-consuming sense of a self with few limits (expansive) that is vulnerable to being threatened by others and events. There is a sense that "only I" matters and everyone else and everything else are secondary. John Bolton underscores this by saying that the only thing that truly matters to Trump is being reelected, and he will use all the instruments of the federal government to achieve this including calling into question the 2020 election results.

Given this self-consuming sense of self, there are only those who are loyal, unquestioning, enabling supporters and, along a range, many others who are less supportive and possibly enemies who are openly critical or defiant who must be defeated and destroyed (fired). In a sense the "self" expands to embrace everything around this leader who must control as much as possible to avoid harm to what many observers refer to as a delicate ego and being thin-skinned. At the same time, he thinks nothing of harming and destroying others. Empathy and sensitivity are lacking or, if present, only in service to his wish to be seen this way. It is not unreasonable to consider that everything a narcissist says and does is almost entirely done to fuel the narcissism, garnish love and admiration and loyalty, and to fend off harmful others who may inflict narcissistic injuries.

Paranoia, it may then be appreciated, is paired with narcissism, as there are always threats that narcissistic injury may be incurred. This expansive sense of self that tries to control and encompass everything around the leader is ultimately doomed to fail fulfilling the urgency of feeling paranoid. There is a self-fulfilling prophecy at work. Efforts to stem the paranoia by trying to control everything as well as vanquishing those who created narcissistic injuries may generate a long list of enemies for "pay back." This cycle of control combined with attacking others only serves to encourage more resistance, fighting back against this aggressor, and fending off the leader's efforts to control everyone's thoughts, feelings, and actions. There is then a sense of delusional power and control combined with close attention to any disloyalty and threat to the expansive sense of self. This leads to an endless cycle of the pursuit of power and control to stave off a paranoid sense that others are out to get you.

Arrogance and Vindictiveness

Narcissism represents a view of one's self as all important and preferably the center of everyone's attention. Being loved and admired, or failing that, feared are the goals. This is ultimately imperfectly achieved and narcissistic injuries are unavoidable. These injuries when combined with arrogance (knowing more than everyone else) leads to the necessity of vindicating injuries to the narcissism and arrogant self-pride system, sometimes by any means available. Mutual harm and even self-destruction may be risked. Winning is all that counts. Trump is a leader who is willing to try to take out and destroy anyone or any group or organization that resists his power and control including harming the essence of American democracy – voting. Injures to his narcissism and expansive self are arrogantly vindicated and social norms and conventions are no inhibitor. He can do anything he wants. Vindication is for Trump a way of life. He pays back offenders many times over the original perceived injury. His wealth, business, all the instruments of government are potentially of use. This includes firing all those who presume to investigate him, his actions, the actions of those in support of him (Inspectors General, for example – Michael Atkinson, Mitch Behm, Glenn Fine, Christi Grimm, and Steve Linick). He is also willing to pardon and commute sentences for loyal supporters and protectors who are convicted of crimes (for example, Roger Stone and General Flynn).

Here again paranoia is a companion to the arrogant pride-system, where threats to the arrogant sense of self abound and must be carefully monitored. They seem to be everywhere – the Fake News, Nancy Pelosi, and Chuck Schumer, and of course accurate reality testing where the spread of COVID-19 is a "hoax" and is not happening.

The Expansive Solution to Anxiety – In Sum

The three elements of this solution *perfectionism, narcissism, and arrogant-vindictive triumph* are mutually reinforcing attributes of the paranoid and charismatic leader who is dependent on others to be loyal, admiring, and subservient. These three elements can arise individually, serially, or all at once. The narcissist's self-importance is often accompanied by arrogant pride such as, "Only I can save you." And Trump and his followers, when they identify others who are not loyal or dare act in opposition, are willing to attack without conscience. Offending others are imperfect, fools, and disposable human beings. There is present in this appreciation also chaos in that any one at any time may be subjected vindictive triumph or rewarded for obedience and submission and this may even occur in one tweet. The expansive solution, therefore, is one of unlimited self-efficacy without consideration of others (low empathy) paired with an ever-present sense of paranoia that there are enemies everywhere.

Understanding this sense of paranoia within the charismatic leader can be contributed to by object relations theory and the paranoid-schizoid position.

Paranoid–schizoid Position

Chapter 6 explained the paranoid-schizoid position. We here provide a brief reminder how it contributes to understanding the origin of chaos relative to paranoid charismatic leaders' thoughts, feeling, and behavior – in particular, Trump's.

The paranoid-schizoid position is a state of mind that emphasizes the relational nature of life, where part objects are created in mind that we omnipotently control and where the "other" lacks a separate identity and autonomy. Paranoid anxiety is represented by a fear of invasive malevolence from outside that threatens imminent annihilation. Schizoid refers to the splitting of the good object from the bad object that is the source of the persecutory anxiety and paranoia. Splitting is useful because it protects the good from being destroyed by the bad. These intrapsychic processes also involve projection, where the good may be retained and the bad projected onto others or not infrequently the opposite. Badness, when projected, may become the basis of racism, homophobia, or any other irrational hatred of another group (liberals, conservatives, Northerners, Southerners). Goodness when projected diminishes the self and serves to create an idealized object – the paranoid charismatic leader.

Given these intrapsychic dynamics the presence of paranoid feelings within the charismatic leader leads to his or her bad self-experience and qualities being located in others. This creates the basis for finding reasons to be anxious, paranoid, and persecuted by others, groups, and events that, while seemingly impersonal, are invariably personalized. Events are always about this leader. Given that these dynamics arise in the mind of this leader, others cannot be entirely sure why the paranoia exists or understand why specific others are targeted, which leads to a sense of chaotic uncertainty. This uncertainty when combined with an overly anxious process on the part of the leader can lead to locating enemies everywhere all the time, creating a very real sense of chaos in the minds of followers who do not know who to trust other than their leader.

There is one additional perspective borrowed from group relations theorizing that contributes insight into leaders who see threats everywhere and who promote fear and anxiety in followers, thereby creating the basis for strong motivations to fight back against or flee from the threats.

The Paranoia of Fight or Flight Leaders

Although we covered the paranoid fight or flight leaders in Chapter 6, we once again briefly mention this relative to the chaos these leaders such as Trump can create.

Fight or flight are driven by fear, anger, and rage and may be considered a basic assumption group whose members are focused on preserving the group by fighting back against a perceived threat or running away from it.[9] There is a sense of immediacy that requires a leader who makes clear that there is a threat and is willing to lead the group in battle or retreat. Charismatic leaders are especially able to inspire followers to act when enemies and threats are spotted everywhere by the paranoid leader. Fight and flight responses that arise within individuals and groups are anchored in primitive emotions where the power and immediacy of the fear and anxiety overwhelm thinking and self-reflection, leading to blind and adoring followership such as during the Age of Trump.

In Conclusion

This chapter has furthered our understanding of a leader like Trump who, as a charismatic and autocratic leader, sees enemies, resistance, and disloyalty everywhere. These threats must then be weeded out (fired), forced out, removed to a less threatening position, or brought under control by a loyal subordinate who is superior to the offending and threatening individual. Everyone in the executive branch of the U.S. government, the military, and the media are at risk as are all the employees in his privately owned companies. The more challenging the times, the more complexity encountered, the more unintended consequences of rash decisions and actions thereafter the greater the anxiety experienced. This experience must be mastered to stave off a collapse of what amounts to an expansive sense of self that needs nurturing with narcissistic supplies. The intensity generated by the anxiety (conscious and unconscious) can generate excessive energy invested in at times frantic pursuits of command and control (lawsuits over election results) and the marginalization or elimination of enemies, where offenders and offenses are never forgotten.

We now cross a boundary into Part III of this book where we explore the role unquestioned ideologies play in creating power and control, and less desirable outcomes. Each U.S. political party as well as many around the world possess ideological approaches to governing. Unfortunately, resident in these ideologies is – chaos and polarization. When the party on the left passes legislation and issues presidential edicts that are progressive, the party on the right tears them all back out when they have power. This is historically the case and may be understood to be a form of compulsive repetition driven by unconscious group dynamics where doing the same thing over and over is expected to create a different outcome is the definition of insanity.

Notes

1. Rauch, J. (2016). How American politics went insane: It happened gradually – and until the U.S. figures out how to treat the problem, it will only get worse. *The Atlantic*. https://www.theatlantic.com/magazine/archive/2016/07/how-american-politics-went-insane/485570/.
2. Edsall, T. B. (2019). The Trump voters whose 'need for chaos' obliterates everything else: Political nihilism is one of the president's strongest weapons. *The New York Times*. https://www.nytimes.com/2019/09/04/opinion/trump-voters-chaos.html.
3. Wagner, J. & Phillip, A. (2016). The chaos theory of Donald Trump: Sowing confusion through tweets. *Washington Post*. https://www.washingtonpost.com/politics/the-chaos-theory-of-donald-trump-sowing-confusion-through-tweets/2016/12/23/11e1315c-c928-11e6-85b5-76616a33048d_story.html.
4. Buettner, R. & Haberman, M. (2019). In business and governing, Trump seeks victory in chaos. *The New York Times*. https://www.nytimes.com/2019/01/20/us/donald-trump-leadership-style.html.
5. Jindal, B. (2019). Embracing chaos in the Trump era. *National Review*. https://www.nationalreview.com/2019/12/embracing-chaos-in-the-trump-era/.
6. Ryan, M., Sonne, P. & Dawsey, J. (2020). White House intensifies effort to install Pentagon personnel seen as loyal to Trump. *Washington Post*. https://www.washingtonpost.com/national-security/white-house-intensifies-effort-to-install-pentagon-personnel-seen-as-loyal-to-trump/2020/06/25/1bfeee3a-9f86-11ea-9d96-c3f7c755fd6e_story.html?hpid=hp_politics1-8-12_pentagon-300pm%3Ahomepage%2Fstory-ans.
7. Krugman, P. (2020). The cult of selfishness is killing America: The right has made irresponsible behavior a key principle. *The New York Times*. https://www.nytimes.com/2020/07/27/opinion/us-republicans-coronavirus.html?action=click&module=Opinion&pgtype=Homepage.
8. William H. McRaven, R. (2020). Trump is actively working to undermine the Postal Service – and every major U.S. institution. *Washington Post*. https://www.washingtonpost.com/opinions/the-countrys-future-could-hinge-on-postal-workers/2020/08/16/c0f7b97e-dfca-11ea-8dd2-d07812bf00f7_story.html?hpid=hp_save-opinions-float-right-4-0_opinion-card-a-right%3Ahomepage%2Fstory-ans&itid=hp_save-opinions-float-right-4-0_opinion-card-a-right%3Ahomepage%2Fstory-ans.
9. Bion, W. (1961). *Experience in groups*. London: Tavistock Publications.

Part III

The Power of Ideologies

Understanding the power and omnipresence of ideologies in our daily lives and their influence on national and international politics and relationships is an essential and sobering exercise in learning. We provide in this section a systematic approach to understanding the complex links between ideology, public policy, groups that are often singular in their interests and advocacy, and psychodynamic perspectives. The psychoanalytic links between ideology and action are explored to provide deeper insights into the creation of ideologies, their persistence, and the actions by their followers that they lead.

Ideologies are often rigidly adhered to by followers as they simplify thinking and feeling by telling "you" what to think and feel and how to act. Ideologies in the United States are a driving force for the "right" in local, state, and national politics where libertarianism and economics often seem to be more important than a concept such as social justice. Ideologies provide a simplistic black and white world view that lacks complexity. This is anxiety reducing and soothing especially for those who identify as conservative and far-right voters and politicians. The economic focus on the right makes it important to look beyond the fantasies of a rational, self-regulating marketplace that has made the pursuit of shareholder value paramount. These beliefs have compromised, at times, morality, business ethics, and consideration of creating a social good for all. A better understanding of ideologies on the right is then critical we believe in terms of creating a prosperous, fairer, and just society and world community. We contribute to this here by exploring "ideology" from a psychodynamically informed point of view.

Part III

The Power of Ideology

9   Introduction to Ideology

An understanding of ideology and its relationship to bureaucracies that are organizational hierarchies filled with humanity is important for better understanding the complexities and dynamics of the conceptual "public square." Explored in this chapter is this relationship and what becomes a recurring historical spiral of repetitive ideologically-driven cycles in society and culture that lead to some good outcomes and too often to undesirable outcomes such as polarization and the Age of Trump.[1,2,3,4,5,6] Exploring this interactive nature helps to explain "why history repeats itself" in what may be thought of as a form of repetition driven by often undiscussable and out of awareness social dynamics.

The world around us is complex and confusing, whether it is viewed from the perspective of atomic structure (individual psychodynamics) or meta-analyses (societal dynamics) that encompass global considerations such as transnational terrorism, wars, and immigration. The perspective used here is to explore how ideologies that, when operationalized, become controlling bureaucracies, that in turn at a molecular level are constructed based on organizational hierarchies, that then, at an atomic structural level, are filled with human nature. Human nature as we use it here includes our thoughts, feelings, and actions that arise from our natural propensities, from learning throughout life and from the presence of rationality and irrationality and the conscious and unconscious aspects of our daily lives.

Ideology

Ideology constitutes much of what we understand to dominate contemporary life. Its many forms and conceptions permeate society to such an extent that it essentially disappears from awareness and simply becomes the way things are. At the same time, adherents of these ideologies often wage endless intellectual warfare if not actual war, creating today what seems like irreconcilable, opposing realities and "red" state versus "blue" state political and social polarization.

Christopher Bollas notes that at the individual and group level, ideologies maintain certainty by psychological mechanisms aimed at eliminating all opposition.[7] A state of mind such as this, where leaders and followers prefer to hold unquestionable and self-evident beliefs, requires reliance on psychological mechanisms that expel other points of view, such as selectively attending to information, that supports one's point of view, combined with rationalization and denial. This simplifies the psychic landscape. "Into this void where critical thinking once existed are placed slogans, sound bites, ideological maxims, and management fads."[8] We become ideologically certain, thereby creating a black and white world where I or we are right, and you are wrong. Ideology with its rigid thought and belief systems leads to the righteous elimination in one's mind or in the physical world of others who hold opposing views. Any means of elimination may eventually be considered appropriate. Dehumanization and objectification aid elimination. Human beings may be turned into evil others, vermin, gooks, ragheads, invaders, and rapists.

"The cleansing of the self suggests the possible birth of a new, forever empty self to be born with no contact with others, with no past (which is severed), and with a future entirely of its own creation."[7] "The individual is 'born again'. The 'other' is known to have taken a form consistent with corrupting projected content that then permits denigrating and destructive characterizations and the use of words to label, define, or categorize the other (those that threaten us)."[8] These "others" become targets for projections and the aggression of projective identification (taking over another) when the projections are incorporated/integrated by the target, and when, in turn, the target's self becomes consistent with the projected content.[9,10] As a result, "... a state of mind becomes an act of violence."[7] The other individual(s), group, or nation is changed in the mind of the holder of the ideology. Perhaps also in a violent takeover of the mind of the targets, the targets become like the projections (introjection of the projections).

The embrace of ideology, therefore, eliminates opposing points of view and allows the maintenance of certainty that the ideological perspective is righteous and correct. "You are either with us or against us" is sometimes heard in the political realm – as President George W. Bush declared shortly after the terrorist attacks on New York and Washington D.C., on September 11, 2001. "Ideological thinking becomes independent of all experience from which it cannot learn anything new even if it is a question of something that has just come to pass."[8] Arendt points out that ideological thinking can become an alternate reality based on projection detached from what we perceive with our five senses that replaces reality.[11]

As is or has become self-evident in the United States, perpetual warfare is being conducted against accurate reality testing. "This outcome is a sign of simplicity triumphing over complexity and regressive withdrawal into the safety of dedifferentiation, oneness, and homogeneity."[8]

With time, ideologies as belief systems become formalized, growing in rigor, comprehensiveness, rigidity, and exclusivity, as they progress in their evolution. In order to be embraced by groups, organizations, and nations, ideological perspectives must be articulated in terms that break down the often abstract nature of the ideology into concrete understandable and implementable terms, such as Chairman Mao Tse-tung's *Red Book* of quotations distributed to the masses in China; and the use by Bolsheviks of Political Commissars to purify Communism in Russia. Sufficient understanding of the appeal of an ideology is a prerequisite for imposing it onto those who are to be subjected to it and are then "policed" to be certain of compliance. The disbeliever must be cast out or destroyed, as is sometimes the case, both figuratively and literally, to achieve ideological purity.

The translation and transformation of an ideological belief system into the political mobilization of a "movement" that can be embraced by many is a challenge. Those ideological systems that achieve societal status such as various religions, or more darkly Nazism, Fascism, or white supremacy/nationalism, do so by creating and communicating a clear, concise, understandable, and emotionally appealing message, such as Adolf Hitler's *Mein Kampf*, or in the present, internet websites. The outcome is a gradual regimentation of thought and messaging combined with actionable and implementable strategies to realize the ideology in practice that take the form of bureaucratic structures.

Ideologies Are Operationalized through the Creation of Bureaucracies

Bureaucracies are an omnipresent aspect of contemporary life. This form of organization with its many branching specialized layers dominates government, regardless of ideology or nation, at all levels from national, state, county, and city in the United States and similar multilevel governing arrangements are prevalent internationally. It is essential to fully appreciate the abundance of bureaucratic organization structures. A number of thought leaders have written enlightening books on the subject. We examine a few of these now.

Henry Jacoby – Bureaucratization of the World

Jacoby points out how pervasive bureaucracy is in terms of daily life being inescapably directed and controlled by governments organized as bureaucracies.[12] Their impersonal and impenetrable power and control promote fear and discontent and introduce significant social costs when bureaucracy turns its functionaries into representatives of an "it" that manipulates everyone. This outcome dehumanizes everyone who is subjected to it creating alienation from one's larger society.

Ralph Hummel – The Bureaucratic Experience

Hummel, like Jacoby, points out modern bureaucracy harnesses power that makes it possible the control of literally millions of people.[13] The triumph of bureaucracy is its success at acquiring, maintaining, and directing power in both the private business and corporate sector and the public political sector. The power to create control at all levels of organizations is important to recognize in societies but also within organizations as indicated by a hierarchy of positions titles that infantilizes those lower in the structure.

This control most often is associated with checking that procedures are adhered to where the procedures may detail every action that may be taken, making the accomplishment of useful organizational and social tasks of secondary consideration – do it by the book! The work people perform is most often divided into specialties and subspecialties that make these experts dependent on top-down management control to coordinate their many actions. This disconnection between employees' personal morals, ethics, creativity, free will, and their *work selves* "... is the precondition to functionaries' willingness and need to carry out commands. This willingness deprives functionaries of personal power to act, of knowledge of ends values, of existence as a private personality apart from bureaucratic identity, and of the ability to trust other speakers."[13]

This outcome is also described by Howard Schwartz as the "organizational ideal" and Michael Diamond as "organizational identity."[14,15] Hummel, consistent with Schwartz and Diamond, offers this dark observation and conclusion:

> Bureaucracy becomes an instrument of power without compare because it is able to remove the human spirit that is the obstacle to power. In doing so it also removes the only valid human purpose for the exercise of power – the affirmation of the human form of life. From its very beginning, bureaucracy has claimed it must destroy man to save him.[13]

Robert Merton, Ailsa Gray, Barbara Hockey, and Hanan Selvin – Reader in Bureaucracy

Merton and his colleagues further echo Hummel's dark assessment of the role of bureaucracy in society and the world, including its applicability to all forms of implemented ideology:

> The primary source of the superiority of bureaucratic administration lies in the role of technical knowledge which, through the development of modern technology and business methods in the production of goods, has become completely indispensable. In this respect, it makes no difference whether the economic system is organized on a capitalistic or socialistic basis.[16]

We once again observe that specialization is associated with efficiency and rationally structured processes, systems, and organizations. However, also to be noted is that the presence of efficiency does not necessarily lead to the conclusion that high levels of efficiency are necessarily effective. Bureaucracy can become dysfunctional when efficient work is not consistent with achieving a larger mission. The notion of "red tape" is used to describe the impact that the pursuit of control and efficiency via specialization and policies and procedures may have on getting the job done, which is especially so under time pressure.

This leads to an appreciation that, "When those subject to bureaucratic control seek to escape the influence of the existing bureaucratic apparatus, this is normally possible only by creating an organization of their own which is equally subject to the process of bureaucratization."[16] Escape from bureaucracy usually proves to be problematic, with the possible exception of a powerful leader who presumes to know all, and who commands and controls unilaterally all those under him or her, where bureaucracy becomes an inhibitor to wielding power (deep state resistance). Trump is clearly such a powerful leader who presumes to know all. However, also to be appreciated there are size limitations to this idea where the leader of a large organization cannot know all or presume to decide all aspects of the workplace, leading inevitably, we suggest, to dependence on hierarchical bureaucratic structure to "drill down" control with all the power residing in the topmost position(s).

Anthony Downs – Inside Bureaucracy

The growth of and dependence on bureaucratic hierarchies is correlated with the growth of size and complexity over time. Downs writes:

> As bureaus grow older, they tend to develop more normalized rules systems covering more and more of the possible situations they are likely to encounter. The passage of time exposes the bureau to a wide variety of situations, and it learns how to deal with most of them more effectively than it did in its youth. The desire for organizational memory of this experience causes the bureau's officials to develop more and more elaborate rules.[17]

It is often the case that, to avoid adverse consequences, the level of detail in terms of policies and procedures that everyone is expected to follow exactly, can become oppressive. Downs continues by noting:

> These rules have three main effects. First, they markedly improve the performance of the bureau regarding situations previously encountered, and make the behavior of each of its parts both more stable and more predictable to its other parts. Second, they tend to divert attention of officials from achieving the social functions of the bureau

to conforming to its rules – the "goal displacement" described by sociologists. Third, they increase the bureau's structural complexity, which in turn strengthens its inertia because of greater sunk cost in current procedures. The resulting resistance to change further reduces the bureau's ability to adjust to new circumstances.[17]

As noted, these considerations can adversely affect the pursuit of efficiency and effectiveness in the service of avoiding errors, by creating the proverbial red tape that slows down problem-solving, innovation, and decision making. And to be noted is that a notion like goal displacement helps to explain why an efficient organization is not necessarily effective at carrying out its mission. This, as Peter Blau notes, becomes important when an ideology like free market capitalism is considered.

Peter Blau and Marshall Meyer – Bureaucracy in Modern Society

To fulfill their "destiny," ideologies are dependent on a stable and predictable operating environment. The pursuit of capitalism, communism, or socialism is advanced by creating a predictable bureaucratic context. Blau and Meyer note:

> The rational estimation of economic risks, which is presupposed in capitalism, requires that the regular process of the competitive market not be interrupted by external forces in unpredictable ways. Arbitrary actions of political tyrants interfere with the rational calculation of gain or loss, and so do banditry, piracy, and social upheavals.[18]

They continue:

> Capitalism then promotes effective and extensive operations of the government. It also leads to bureaucratization in other spheres. The expansion of business firms and the consequent removal of most employees from activities directly governed by the profit principle make it increasingly necessary to introduce bureaucratic methods of administration for the sake of efficiency.[18]

Efficiency, and preferably effectiveness, for large corporations require bureaucratic structure that assures some measure of control over thousands of specialized employees who are sometimes scattered around nations and the world to produce profit and stockholder value. Blau and Meyer, however, also underscore the importance of bureaucratically designed organizational structures for society and government in terms of achieving objectives that might not otherwise be achievable. We once again appreciate that bureaucracy appears to be essential to operate large organizational and political entities and impose ideologies in the form of "isms" on society.

Bureaucracy in Sum

Bureaucratic organizational structure is an omnipresent aspect of contemporary life. Organizations of all kinds that are staffed by large numbers of people who endeavor to fulfill a stated, explicit mission – whether it is to generate stockholder value, deliver a social good, or govern – rely on structured bureaucratic hierarchies. Those at the top of the organizational structure control people and operations via detailed sets of policies and procedures, and, by the careful structuring of specialized workers and work groups. This omnipresence is in large part accounted for by the notion that leaders and people, in general, tend to locate and keep what works and discard that which does not work.

Edgar Schein describes this dynamic as organizational culture:

> The connection between culture and leadership is clearest in organizational cultures and microcultures. What we end up calling a culture in such systems is usually the result of the embedding of what a founder or leader has imposed on a group that has *worked out* [emphasis added]. In this sense, culture is ultimately created, embedded, evolved, and ultimately manipulated by leaders. At the same time, with group maturity, culture comes to constrain, stabilize, and provide structure and meaning to the group members even to the point of ultimately specifying what kind of leadership will be acceptable in the future.[19]

Schein, in few words, recasts our understanding of the nature of hierarchal bureaucratic organizations as created by a leader or leaders over time, based on what seems like a logical and rational process. These leaders intentionally or often less so locate what works to create profit, deliver a service, manufacture a product, or govern at the level of a city, county, state, or nation. All organizations public or private struggle for survival and cannot afford to remain maladaptive for long. Stated simply, Schein speaks to an adaptive process of trial and error which has been a standard method for millennia. Stated more abstractly, he speaks to the evolution of complex systems based on feedback loops driven by the necessity to adapt to changes in task environments. Schein also underscores the controlling, constraining, and regulating nature of bureaucracies that directly or indirectly designate what leaders may do and may not do (routinized leadership). Nonetheless, in any given period an authoritarian charismatic leader may be disruptive, as is clearly in evidence in the United States during the Age of Trump.

We now turn to considering the underlying embedded hierarchical nature of bureaucratic organizations that empowers the leader or a very few at the top of the hierarchy, often to the exclusion of all other organization members. At the same time, managers and employees have the power to make things not happen, including passive or overt resistance to what the leader orders (Trump's deep state). This latter exemplifies the constraining nature of bureaucracies that Schein notes earlier in this chapter.

Bureaucracies Operate as Hierarchies of Power and Control

Bureaucracies are omnipresent administrative agents of power and control created via the use of hierarchical organization structures that amass most if not all formal power and control for the leader and his or her immediate group of followers, who often blindly support the leader and follow every dictate.

> The bureaucratized group controls the action of its members by creating rigid routines, impersonal professional interactions, carefully defined authority and routinized leadership. Working relations are preferably role-to-role interactions. Communication, interactions, and decision making must follow prescribed protocols that maintain the integrity of the chain of command where progressively more decision-making authority lies with the ever-higher positions within the management hierarchy. Many layers of command and control exist, as well as specialized departments and divisions that may not be allowed to interact directly across organizational boundaries.[20]

The hierarchical nature of bureaucracy places into the hands of a leader(s) power and control preferably impersonally deployed. Organizations that are a hierarchical bureaucracy have been discussed by many, using such terms as organizational charts, scalar organization, and scalar or positional authority that is said to arise from the position (role, status) held as compared to the person in the position (not charismatic in nature). However, upon closer inspection, this outcome is often more of a convenient rationalization that conceals the use of the presumably *impersonal* power and control and the rational pursuit of organizational performance and success, from the often-distressing reality that the power and control are wielded for deeply *personal* and *irrational* reasons (discussed below). The only constraint is by organizational culture and the routinization of leadership.

Everyone in modern society either explicitly or intuitively understands this fundamental outcome of relying on hierarchical bureaucratic organizations that amass disproportionate power at the top of the pyramid-like organizational structure. This creates a profound sense of alienation, disempowerment, marginalization, infantile-like subordination of all organization members and, in the case of government, disenfranchisement of voters by unelected officials who are presumably expected to serve them. As noted, escaping this outcome is challenging and perhaps not possible. We now turn to explore the unstated obvious – organizations are created by people who bring the organization to life everyday they come to work.

Bureaucratic Hierarchies Are Operated by People, Thereby Introducing Irrationality into the Workplace

There is a growing knowledge base that examines from a psychodynamically informed perspective bureaucratic hierarchical organizations and their roots in the darker irrational side of human nature that reside in leaders as well as in groups and in organizational and national political dynamics.[1,15] This body of knowledge explores the irrational side of the workplace where stress and anxiety that are commonplace may readily induce psychologically defensive responses in leaders, groups, and throughout an organization or even a nation. These defenses distort accurate reality testing, introduce confusing interpersonal dynamics, and regrettably often introduce toxicity that disrupts the leader's and group, organization, or nation's ability to effectively respond to problems and threats.

The light and dark sides of human nature that, on the one hand, may yield industrialized genocides of people, animals, and the destruction of nature, but, on the other hand, also humanitarianism that extends to others, animals, and the caretaking of the earth, are important facets of organizational dynamics. People bring bureaucratic hierarchies to life for better or all too often for worse. It is important to better understand the darker side of human nature that does get expressed in bureaucratic hierarchies and its implications for gaining insight into the Age of Trump.

The reality of an omnipresent sense of bureaucratic power and control, and its tendency to unleash irrationality on the part of those operating its mechanisms, has been appreciated by others who study hierarchical bureaucracy. Here we highlight the work of the authors of four books.

Henry Jacoby notes that people who have learned to rationally embrace bureaucracy may also be willing to act irrationally and follow a charismatic leader into harm's way.[12] They often do so if the leader offers a reward to compensate for the resentment arising from feelings of impotence relative to the powerful and controlling bureaucracy and leader that subordinate and infantilize everyone.

> Although control of our complicated technological existence requires rational thought and action, in the final analysis things do not remain rational .... But what characterizes our age is precisely the forceful transformation of rational administration into the irrational exercise of power, the lack of clearly defined limits to coercion, and increasing competence of a state which arrogates independence to itself.[12]

This irrational exercise of power, combined with the powerful, all-encompassing presence of bureaucratic hierarchies in governance and in non-governmental organizations, has also been explored by Yiannis Gabriel:

> Organizational hierarchies represent hierarchies of both authority and accountability. Within such hierarchies, superiors hold certain rights

over the subordinates, which include the right to issue particular types of command, to reward and to discipline. At the same time, superiors are accountable both for their own actions and those of their subordinates to their own superiors. Subordinates, for their part, are obligated to carry out the commands of their superiors, provided that they accord with the organization's impersonal system of rules and regulations. Thus, authority and accountability, from the organization's point of view, are not attached to individuals but invested in the positions within the hierarchy.[21]

We, however, suggest that this hygienic description of how bureaucracies operate is largely a fantasy. The myth of rational management control is largely an anxiety reducing illusion that cannot be fulfilled in reality. There is never enough control especially for those who are easily made to feel anxious. For some leaders control can become a grandiose dream that subordinates, people, groups, and organizations allowing them to be treated like machines. Followers, in contrast, have their anxieties minimized by having their dependency needs met by someone who is in charge, in control, even if the leader is feared and despised. Bureaucracies also tend to create anxiety for employees and those who interact with them. Baum highlights this by noting employees of bureaucracies are often anxious about being shamed by superiors for poor performance. To avoid shame employees may avoid taking potentially blamable action in addition to trying to confuse others about their responsibilities including resorting to reciting bureaucratic rules and regulations, indicating they were only following orders.[22]

Bureaucratic hierarchies are then a unique combination of potentially anxiety creating and alienating features. The workers within bureaucracies often have insufficient authority to carry out their responsibilities, and superiors, who control work and evaluate performance, are not particularly visible and accessible.[22] Under-authorized organization members may readily feel vulnerable by having to submit to these remote authority figures often compromising along a range their personal integrity and autonomy. As a result, workers often do not feel satisfied with their jobs or themselves perform marginal work and introduce performance robbing interpersonal conflicts into the workplace. These outcomes waste organizational resources and detract from serving constituents and customers.

Also, to be considered is that organizational hierarchies tend to introduce rivalry among members who compete for promotion in a hierarchy that can be manipulated to create layers of positions and status markers to give individuals a sense of upward mobility. Harry Levinson similarly notes much the same outcome as a result of hierarchal pyramid-shaped organizations, having ever fewer higher-level positions as one approaches the top.[23] This is sometimes described as promotion by death or retirement. We also observe that the nature of hierarchical pyramids of power and control promote the emergence of the dark side of human nature in the form of authoritarianism and autocracy.

A Note on Authoritarianism and Autocracy in the Context of Hierarchic Irrationality

Levinson suggests, consistent with Kernberg,[24] that, while personality may contribute to authoritarianism, it may also stem from features of hierarchical organizational structure and not necessarily from personality. The hierarchical organization model, that invests power in positions, may well contribute to (pull) behavior that is authoritarian – the power is there why not use it? To be noted these powerful and controlling positions are especially desirable to have for individuals who have narcissistic tendencies such as Trump who demands loyalty or else "You're fired."

> Because of the way that the hierarchical model distributes authority, people may find themselves in positions of power without having had any training in the use of authority. Well-trained in other areas, for other tasks, they are nevertheless ill-prepared for managing the people whom they supervise.[23]

This is particularly true in government and professional organizations where elected or appointed officials may have little experience working within and managing a large complex organization. The same holds true for professionals who have outstanding technical skills and knowledge but no experience in management.

Given these likely shortfalls in preparation to manage, incumbents of higher-level positions may find themselves so ill-prepared that they intentionally and unintentionally create operating problems and promote interpersonal conflict. The leaders can readily come to feel anxious, psychologically defensive, and rely on coping strategies aimed at controlling events and people in the hope more control will reduce the stress and anxiety. Leaders' efforts at achieving ever greater control often accentuate the stress and anxiety because of resistance on the part of organization members to being over-controlled and micro-managed. This creates an ever-greater reliance on the pursuit of control (a self-fulfilling prophecy). Learning does not take place.[25] The leader(s), organization, and employees find themselves in what seems to be inexorable dysfunctional downward spiral of compulsive repetitions.

In Sum – Human Nature Within Bureaucratic Hierarchies

Bureaucracies are based on hierarchies of power and control. They are filled with rational and irrational pursuits of power and control that unavoidably lead to organizational dysfunction and toxicity.[1,26] The fusion of hierarchy with bureaucratic organizational structure compounds these negative tendencies by introducing the deeply embedded aspects of human nature that arise when organization members are confronted with powerful and remote authority figures. Their distance and unavailability open the door to fantasy about their malevolence. Bureaucratic leaders may act rationally much of the time, but they may also more darkly and irrationally strike terror into the hearts of employees, and sometimes into the public and the organization's customers. Those in powerful positions may also act to advance their careers, avoid taking risks and blame others for problems leading to the organization lacking the consistency, predictability, and efficiency of a bureaucracy.

We now turn to considering the implications of introducing human nature into a context where ideologies are formalized by creating bureaucratic organizations to promulgate them. These bureaucracies, as noted, are hierarchies of power and control that are often driven by the unconscious and irrational aspects of human nature.

Human Nature at Work: The Irrational Side of Organizations

Any discussion of organizational dynamics where the organization takes the form of a bureaucratic hierarchy must include, as already discussed, the darker unconscious and irrational side of human nature that is evoked when positions of power and authority are sought after, and the power that resides in these scalar positions is used for less than rational organizational purposes. This evokes psychological defensive responses on the part of organization members and organizational social structure may become shaped by hard to comprehend and dysfunctional unconscious dynamics.

Bureaucratized groups "control their anxieties by creating what is a socially defensive system aimed at eliminating adverse group experience and containing anxiety."[20] Hierarchical organizational structure, with its accompanying policies and procedures, rules, and regulations ends up not only controlling member interactions, but also the leader's uses of power and authority that becomes circumscribed culturally (routinized).[20] From a psychodynamic perspective bureaucratic hierarchical organizations contain elements that are present because of psychologically defensive tendencies to achieve control over anxiety ridden inner experience that is fueled by splitting and projection. A black and white world filled with threatening others is an outcome making ever better control important. However, achieving enough control to allay this experience is, as already noted, problematic for leaders in that being excessively controlling encourages anxiety on the part of those who must submit to the control leading to splitting and projection and resistance to being controlled.[27]

In sum, these organizational dynamics can result in some unintended consequences. Organization members may find themselves not particularly responsible for organizational events and outcomes, and perhaps even responsible for their own workplace thoughts, feelings, and actions because they are defending themselves against the distressing experience of submission to remote and sometimes less than fully rational authority figures and distressing losses of self-integrity. Manfred Kets de Vries and Danny Miller write: "The controlling top executive is not willing to relinquish sufficient control over operations to allow for a participative mode of decision making. Instead, company policies are the manifestation of compulsive features [of the leader] rather than objective, adaptive requirements."[28] During the Age of Trump losses of control by Trump lead to narcissistic fits and tweeted criticism and terminations.

Narcissistic Needs for Power and Control

A narcissistic leader may experience the loss of control of others as an anxiety-ridden threat to his or her sense of grandiosity. In turn, this creates a narcissistic crisis and unconsciously driven over-determined responses aggravated by the eventuality that many in leadership roles have sought out those roles to fulfill narcissistic needs. This underscores the deep sense of personal threat that an out-of-control context poses to these leaders who prefer to see themselves as powerful, strong, loved and admired and in control. During the Age of Trump almost anything may be said, contemplated or done to bond conservative voters to Trump including Republicans in Congress.

Over-determined narcissism on the part of Trump and autocratic leaders, in general, leads to a corresponding commitment on the part of those who blindly follow their idealized charismatic leader to "hold the leader together" while their leader pursues grand visions however conceived and evolving over time. The difference between the leader and the mission may not be apparent, as may be the case between the leader and the group, organization, or nation as a whole. They are co-identified. Trump presumes to speak for all Americans. We, then, suggest recognizing this leads us to understand that the creation of ideologies and accompanying bureaucratic hierarchies may be driven by toxic charismatic leaders, irrationality, and more broadly human nature and its many reality-bending psychologically defensive elements that lead to dysfunctional group dynamics.

A Note on Basic Assumption Groups and Directions of Movement

The insights of Wilfred Bion and later Pierre Turquet, suggest that we may *think* that we are performing workplace tasks, thinking rationally, and adapting our organizations to an ever-changing reality.[29,30] However, to be considered is that some if not much of the time in hierarchical, bureaucratic organizations, organization members are sabotaging organizational performance by defending themselves against anxiety by relying on unconscious group "basic assumptions" such as dependency upon an imagined-omnipotent leader, fight-flight relative to a group enemy, magical rescue by creation of a savior (pairing), and renouncing individuality permitting fusion into homogeneous oneness. Contrary to what "we" are certain we are doing in hierarchical bureaucratic organizations; some of the time we are acting defensively to contain our anxiety about working within a bureaucratic organization. Movements toward and against organizational leaders are all too common as is just simply moving away and wishing to be left alone to work. The more stressful the organizational context, culture, and leadership are, the more often psychologically defensive group and organizational dynamics are found to be at work.

Coming Full Circle: Conclusions and Implications

This chapter has addressed four social and behavioral science concepts – ideology, bureaucracy, hierarchy, and human nature that we suggest contain a circularity arising from psychosocial dynamics. Human nature is influenced by and in turn influences ideology, bureaucracies, and hierarchies. These concepts are a complex interactive whole that contains rationality and irrationality, and feelings and actions that include psychological defensiveness. The presence of the dark side of human nature raises for examination the seemingly endless repetitions of destructive societal events where *social, organizational, and individual learning* seem to not apply as is the case during the Age of Trump and its threat of American democracy. This appreciation is especially relevant when it comes to paranoid charismatic leaders like Trump who continuously arise in organizations and countries throughout history (Poland, Hungry, Egypt, Russia). In sum, the juxtaposition of human nature and unconscious psychological defensiveness to fend off anxiety arising from dependence on ideology, bureaucracy, and hierarchy contributes to what becomes dysfunctional historical repetitions.

Chapter 10 extends our exploration of how ideological systems of thought are translated into social structures. It provides an operationalized discussion of ideologies where their presence and adherence to them have direct effects on the governance of the United States, its states, counties, and cities in the Age of Trump.

Notes

1. Allcorn, S. & Stein, H. (2015). *The dysfunctional workplace: Theory, stories, and practice.* Columbia, MO: University of Missouri Press.
2. Allcorn, S. & Stein, H. (2017a). The post-factual world of the 2016 American presidential election: The good, the bad, and the deplorable. *Journal of Psychohistory*, 44(4), 310–318.
3. Allcorn, S. & Stein, H. (2017b). The politics of shame. *Journal of Psychohistory*, 45(2), 78–93.
4. Allcorn, S. & Stein, H. (2018). Donald Trump: Empty vessel and sum of all projections. *Journal of Psychohistory*, 44(1), 3–16.

5. Stein, H. & Allcorn, S. (2010). The unreality of American deregulation. *Journal of Psychohistory*, 38(1), 27–48.
6. Stein, H. & Allcorn, S. (2018). A fateful convergence: Animosity toward Obamacare, hatred of Obama, the rise of Donald Trump, and overt racism in America. *Journal of Psychohistory*, 45(4), 234–242.
7. Bollas, C. (1992) *Being a character.* New York, NY: Hill and Wang, 203.
8. Allcorn, S. (2007). The psychological nature of oppression in an American workplace. *Organisational and Social Dynamics*, 7(1), 39–60, 48–49.
9. Grotstein, J. (1985). *Splitting and projective identification.* Northvale, NJ: Jason Aronson.
10. Scharff, J. (1992). *Projective and introjective identification and the use of the therapist's self.* Northvale, NJ: Jason Aronson.
11. Arendt, H. (1951) *The origins of totalitarianism.* New York, NY: Meridian.
12. Jacoby, H. (1973). *The bureaucratization of the world.* Berkeley, CA: University of California Press, 2.
13. Hummel, R. (1982). *The bureaucratic experience.* New York, NY: St. Martin's Press, 220–222.
14. Schwartz, H. (1990). *Narcissistic process and corporate decay: The theory of organizational ideal.* New York, NY: New York University Press.
15. Diamond, M. (2017). *Discovering organizational identity: Dynamics of relational attachment.* Columbia, MO: University of Missouri Press.
16. Merton, R., Gray, A., Hockey, B. & Selvin, H. (1952). *Reader in bureaucracy.* New York, NY: The Free Press, 25.
17. Downs, A. (1967). *Inside bureaucracy.* Boston, MA: Little, Brown and Company, 28–29.
18. Blau, P. and Meyer, M. (1971). *Bureaucracy in modern society.* New York, NY: Random House, 27–28.
19. Schein, E. (2010). *Organizational culture and leadership.* San Francisco, CA: Jossey-Bass, 3.
20. Allcorn, S. (2003). *The dynamic workplace.* Westport, CN: Praeger, 26.
21. Gabriel, Y. (1999). *Organizations in depth.* Thousand Oaks, CA: Safe Publications, 85.
22. Baum, H. (1987). *The invisible bureaucracy: The unconscious in organizational problem solving.* New York, NY: Oxford University Press, vii.
23. Levinson, H. (1981). *Executive.* Cambridge, MA: Harvard University Press, 84.
24. Kernberg, O. (1979). Regression in organizational leadership. *Psychiatry*, 1(42), 24–39.
25. Argyris, C. & Schon, D. (1978). *Organizational learning: A theory of action perspective.* Reading, Boston, MA: Addison-Wesley.
26. Allcorn, S. & Diamond, M. (1997). *Managing people during stressful times: The psychologically defensive workplace.* Westport, CN: Quorum Books.
27. Czander, W. (1993). *The psychodynamics of work and organizations.* New York, NY: Guilford Press.
28. Kets de Vries, M. & Associates. (1991). *Organizations on the couch.* San Francisco, CA: Jossey-Bass, 256–257.
29. Bion, W.R. (1961). *Experiences in groups.* London: Tavistock.
30. Turquet, P.M. (1974). *Leadership: The individual and the group.* In G.S. Gibbard, J.J. Hartman and R.D. Mann (Eds.) Analysis of Groups, San Francisco, CA: Jossey-Bass.

10 Contemporary Right-Wing Ideology and Its Relationship to Shame

The United States and how it is governed is highly influenced by well-organized and funded right and far-right groups and their ideological perspectives. These have been exploited to create social polarization that rallies voters to "conservative" causes as compared to progressive change-oriented "liberal" causes. This splitting apart of society along ideological lines is explored here and in Part IV. Deregulation as a specific dysfunctional ideology merits full discussion in Chapter 11. The focus here is to explore right-wing ideologies and their often-shameful societal consequences. We begin by briefly highlighting the points made in Chapter 9 regarding ideologies before more thoroughly exploring right wind ideology and the implicit shame resident within this worldview.

Ideology

Ideology constitutes a pervasive presence in societies. It often is underappreciated if not disappearing from awareness. The embrace of ideologies in all forms serves an important purpose for adherents by creating a sense of certainty about how life is and should be lived that reduces anxiety. These unquestionable and "self-evident" beliefs require avoiding exposure to contrary sets of beliefs (ideologies) others may hold. I or we are right, and you are wrong. This psychological simplification is supported by what amounts to purified information flows (right-wing news and conspiracies) and simplified communications from leaders such as tweets, slogans, and sound bites. Opposing points of view are preferably never read or heard – the fake news.

This process of purification is accompanied by splitting and projections, where one's corrupting thoughts are projected onto others (not us) who may then be denigrated and dehumanized. "You are either with us or against us." This simplification and creation of a black and white world experience must be continually reinforced and any challenge to it is avoided. Everyone must feel safe within the embrace of their group identity that as a political and social movement seeks to control government and society via bureaucratic hierarchies that promote their ideology.

Given this orientation to ideology, discussion of right-wing ideologies grounds the exploration of the current ideological polarization in the United States, the Age of Trump, in a historical and explanatory framework.

Right-wing Ideologies

Discussions on the internet, cable news, print media, and books provide many insights into a range of right of center and far-right thought, theory and values that fit beneath the umbrella term conservative. The term right-wing is associated with conservatives and reactionaries to liberalism, and the extreme right-wing is most often associated with fascism, Nazism, and white supremacy, and in the U.S. McCarthyism, the John Birch Society and of course the Age of Trump. The far-right may also advocate for absolutist government that is unencumbered in using the power of the state to support the dominant ethnic group or religion. And, at an extreme, far-right Libertarian principles may encompass all those opposed to state or federal authority.

Historically the concept of a left and right in politics has its origins in the French parliament where the right that sat on the right side was supportive of the past monarchical approach to governance and opposed to changing this approach. During the 1800s there developed an economic shift toward capitalism that the center-right supported. In the United States this shift came to embrace social conservativism. From a populist perspective those right of center also often include nationalists, nativists who oppose immigration, a strong military, and religious conservatives. From a governing and philosophical point of view the right opposes communism, socialism, and social democracy. An element fundamental to conservatism is that there is an opposition to progressive change that is thought to undermine traditional values including white patriarchy. The status quo is preferred which serves to lock in social disparities and biases to the advantage of those opposing change. This resistance to change is enabled by controlling bureaucratic hierarchies that include the executive (President), legislative (Congress), and the judiciary (appointment of conservatives).

Libertarianism is a prominent ideology in contemporary right-wing politics in the United States and merits additional discussion.

Libertarianism

Libertarianism has as its core belief political freedom and personal autonomy (individualism), which translates into a desire to limit federal and state power (anti-maskers, desegregation). The dominant form of libertarianism, that includes approximately 25% of the voters in the United States, advocates for civil liberties, natural law, free-market capitalism, and a reversal of the modern welfare state. The most recent manifestation of libertarianism is the rise of the Tea Party in 2009, although there were some differences with mainstream libertarianism. These points just made underscore that there is always diversity in every ideology no matter how strong the pursuit of purity is.

We now turn to a perspective that is, we believe, underappreciated when right-wing ideological perspectives are pursued. These pursuits lead to the taking of positions, the defense of positions, and the shifting of positions in the service of pursuing power and control by garnering voter approval. During the Age of Trump, we find almost anything can be said or done while pursuing power and shamelessly so. No shame it appears is being felt regardless of how non-traditional, anti-social, and corrupt the statements and actions are. These dynamics merit a more thorough discussion.

Shame

It is our observation that shame resides in the worldview, philosophy, and ideology of the current political right that underpinned the election of Donald Trump. Denial of shame to avoid appearing weak helps to explain the appeal and tenacity with which the right embraces its understanding and interpretation of the world. Consistent with this point of view much of what the right does politically may be viewed to be unethical, not consistent with generally accepted human values and, therefore, must be concealed or spun to sound less undesirable to others while staying consistent with their political beliefs and ideology. We underscore these appreciations by inspecting these dynamics using three perspectives: authoritarianism, cultural history, and object relations psychoanalytic theory. This approach offers a triangulation for locating the role of shame in the contemporary politics of the right.

Our discussion of shame begins by exploring the contribution authoritarianism makes to understanding the left and right in politics and society and the many paradoxical positions that are taken to justify political ideologies, beliefs, and actions on the right that have become so prominent during the Age of Trump. Recent reports of events are provided to ground the discussion in the news headlines, although what is factual today is problematic in that partisanship creates two realities. A cultural-historical perspective of shame in the United States provides insights, and when combined with psychoanalytic object theory the shameful adherence to right-wing ideologies is more fully revealed. Understanding shame using this theory informs understanding how Americans came to elect a leader who speaks to the discontent not only of his voters but also many other Americans who feel it is time to throw the rascals out – Drain the Swamp.

Shame and Its Meaning – A Psychodynamic Perspective

Shame is generally defined as feelings of having done something dishonorable, disrespectful, improper, or cowardly, including shaming by others that seems to be common in social networks. While this general statement seems relatively clear, there is more complexity to understanding shame and the allied concept of guilt.

Shame is a feeling of self-loathing that may or may not include how we expect or believe other people are experiencing us. Morrison notes that to feel shame we do not necessarily need the presence of an "other" who shames us or even a viewing audience. We only need a judgmental "other" in mind as an internalized figure who is a part of who we are.[1]

There may then exist a core sense of unworthiness and inferiority. We know ourselves to be wrong, weak, and inadequate as compared to Trump's frequent mention of "strong and powerful." This may be linked to how others view us or just as likely how we *believe* others see us. Shame may then be understood to be a self-driven dynamic we impose on ourselves and ultimately can only be avoided or eliminated by our own efforts. At a deeper level of the unconscious there exists a fear of abandonment (the walking away in disgust of the parent creating separation anxiety) and death by emotional starvation.[2] We feel unworthy of being loved and cared for. Gilligan underscores this appreciation by noting: "The word I use in this book to refer to the absence or deficiency of self-love is shame; its opposite is pride, by which I mean a healthy sense of self-esteem, self-respect and self-love."[3]

Shame can be differentiated from guilt. Put simply, guilt is a judgment about something I did; shame is a judgment about who I am. We feel guilt when we violate rules and taboos. We feel shame when we experience failures to measure up to our ideals. Morrison writes: "These failures are experienced as defects in the self-as-I-want-to-be (the ideal self, or the ego ideal of traditional psychoanalysis)."[4] If our ideals are harsh and exacting we may feel chronic shame. Shame therefore arises out of a tension between the Ego, and the Ego-Ideal whenever goals and images presented by the Ego-Ideal are not reached.[2] Guilt has different origins in the form of self-judgments compared to shame and our use of language also signals this. We may, for example, say that an action was shameful but not say we are guilty of violating a rule or taboo.

Shame, conscious and unconscious, contributes to understanding the political beliefs and worldviews on the right during the Age of Trump.

The Origins of Shame in Politics

Shame can be explored from the perspectives of the political right and far-right in the United States as represented by the Republican Party or the Party of Trump, and its fringe elements, the Libertarian and Tea parties, which are a dominant influence in the country. The resulting political dynamics have created a harsh, confusing, and even chaotic sense of direction for the country that leads to examining the contribution shame makes to understanding the metaphoric political swamp Trump was to drain.

We begin by making several distinctions that shame makes to understanding recent events and the toxic polarization in the country.

Hetherington and Weiler in their book *Authoritarianism and Polarization in American Politics* examine how to understand those on the political left and right in America and the polarization in our politics and society. They write: "We find persuasive the broad-based findings that show authoritarians to be more likely to feel threatened by, and dislike, outgroups; more likely to desire muscular responses to conflict; less politically well informed; and less likely to change their way of thinking when new information might challenge their deeply held beliefs."[5] They compare this to a non-authoritarian worldview that embraces a diversity of opinion, fairness, outgroups, and a striving for accuracy while avoiding prejudicial thinking – views most often associated with liberalism.

These descriptions may be reframed as absolutist versus relativist worldviews. The political right may be described as preferring a black and white world where good and evil are clearly designated, and there is little doubt what is good or bad, such as an "axis of evil." Compare this to relativism with its greater tolerance of ambiguity and a willingness to embrace a "grey zone" where good and bad are not so clearly demarcated. The absolute worldview, by its nature, must contain considerable rigidity combined with adherence to clearly defined perspectives, ideologies, and values. Hence the preoccupation with distinct boundaries, borders, and walls. The relative worldview, with its willingness to accept complexity that introduces uncertainty and a lack of reliance on clear and accepted principles for understanding the world, stands in stark contrast to absolutism. There is then in the concept of authoritarianism an important comparative basis for understanding contemporary social and political polarization in the United States and around the world.

Polarization, based on these worldviews, forms a hard-to-overcome social division based on unconscious splitting and projection and the pursuit of self-interest as represented in the politically oriented right's willingness to support a notion like self-regulating markets (maximizing self-interest and corporate profit). Compare this to a liberal willingness to support wealth redistribution and social justice on the left.

This is underscored by Alan Greenspan's (former Chairman of the Federal Reserve) and Paul Ryan's (former Speaker of the House) attachment to novelist Ayn Rand and the harsh societal reality of her book *Atlas Shrugged*.[6] Ms. Rand, a noteworthy figure in Hollywood, is sometimes said to provide a rationale that defends greed in America. Mr. Greenspan wrote a letter to *The New York Times* to counter a critic's comment that "the book was written out of hate."[7] Mr. Greenspan wrote: "'Atlas Shrugged' is a celebration of life and happiness. Justice is unrelenting. Creative individuals and undeviating purpose and rationality achieve joy and fulfillment. Parasites who persistently avoid either purpose or reason perish as they should."[7] Mr. Greenspan, as chairman of the Federal Reserve, adhered to a considerable extent to notions like free markets and deregulation, although there was and remains a self-confessed "flaw" in his ideology that led to the great recession of 2008.[8]

Rand, in her book, *The Virtue of Selfishness* argues for an ethics of rational selfishness that rejects sacrifice.[9] Selfishness, however, does not mean "doing whatever you please." Moral principles are not a matter of opinion – they are based in the facts of reality, in man's nature as a rational being, who must think and act successfully to live and be happy. Morality's task is to identify the kinds of action that in fact benefit oneself. These virtues (productivity, independence, integrity, honesty, justice, pride) are all applications of the basic virtue, rationality. Rand's moral ideal is a life of reason, purpose, and self-esteem.[10]

We note here that the heavy reliance on rationality is ultimately not justifiable. This perspective is further explained by Rand:

> Poverty, ignorance, illness and other problems of that kind are not metaphysical emergencies. By the metaphysical nature of man and of existence, man has to maintain his life by his own effort; the values he needs—such as wealth or knowledge—are not given to him automatically, as a gift of nature, but have to be discovered and achieved by his own thinking and work.[11]

These perspectives translate into an economic perspective that advocates for adherence to laissez-faire capitalism. "When I say 'capitalism,' I mean a full, pure, uncontrolled, unregulated laissez-faire capitalism—with a separation of state and economics, in the same way and for the same reasons as the separation of state and church."[11]

These considerations lead to the appreciation that a society run on these principles, as represented in *Atlas Shrugged,* creates a society lacking compassion. American conservatism does indeed have a hard edge as expressed in images of Reagan's racist "welfare queens," presidential candidate Mitt Romney's 47% who are takers, and limiting the notion of social safety nets such as continually reducing the commitment to help unemployed workers. "Get a job," was an expression often heard during the great recession starting in 2008 and beyond when there were in fact approximately four workers for every available job. We suggest that continually cutting back on the safety net as a concept that ranges from food for families and children, healthcare, housing, and jobs leads to the experience of conservatism as having a hard edge that is unsympathetic to those in need and therefore lacking compassion. Perhaps the parasites are simply pariahs and outcasts, as Greenspan notes above. We are also reminded of George W. Bush's effort to rebrand conservatism as "compassionate conservatism." This took the form of supporting charitable organizations as compared to "government handouts." We do not wish to belabor these insights. We are continually reminded of this compassionless presence. The efforts to end Obamacare in court cases pending in 2020, creating the loss of health coverage by millions of citizens is an ongoing example.

The combining of an appreciation of authoritarianism on the right with conservative political ideologies that lack compassion is a basis for exploring the contribution that shame makes to understanding the Age of Trump. In fact, right-wing ideology cannot be understood without recognizing that it is rooted in shame. Shame is an underlying presence in this compassionless worldview – rebranding or not. The presence of deeply felt shame must be denied and rationalized away to believe in and advocate for public policies that either hurt people (races, ethnic groups, religious groups) or are not particularly supportive of them. Is there no notion of a *helping hand* without a price tag attached to it – higher taxes on the wealthy? Must the 47% perish? To be explored here is the nature of the politicians who reside in the human "swamp" that *Make America Great Again* has become to the detriment of many seeking to live their lives in peace and prosperity. And to be noted the right is not particularly interested in protecting the natural environment – another harsh reality underscored by many actions such as allowing oil and gas drilling in Alaska's fragile Arctic refuge.

A prominent feature of modern-day politics that contributes to creating the swamp is the willingness of Republican politicians as well as many politicians around the world to distort, misrepresent and fabricate falsity without hesitation – the ends are said to justify the means (Orwell).[12] This leads to an observer's likely sense that this willingness is shameless, although whether the politicians in question feel shame or not is open to question.

Is There No Shame? The Metaphor of the Swamp

The 2016 U.S. presidential election results mean as many different things as everyone's conscious and unconscious motivations are for voting for one presidential candidate or one political party over the others. There are, however, themes and images that resonate in many ways across a broad spectrum of American citizens. Chosen here is one of these – the "swamp" – to explore one facet of this dysfunction that affects everyone who is aware of the many daily and weekly pronouncements by politicians and political leaders. The question is, how in the world could politicians, their spokespersons, and the talking heads say and do things that are so contradictory? How can they pursue public investigations of opponents so relentlessly for months or years and then disregard many of the same issues for politicians within their own party? These contradictions are dismissed by a handful of polished, implausible, and obfuscating talking points and "go to" excuses and explanations, leading to the conclusion this is just simply politics as usual. What do you expect of politicians anyway? If they are moving their lips they are lying.

Understanding these often false and contradictory pronouncements and actions is helped along by considering the perspective of what shame can contribute to understanding these dynamics that are attention-getting and alienate many in the country. There are times in the political realm that many might think what took place or was said is shameful – even deplorable. Shame offers insights into individual and group behavior that are underappreciated in understanding not so much the politicians and political parties but rather how the public senses something is seriously wrong inside the beltway. Shame contributes to understanding our current state of political affairs in the Age of Trump.

Reporting on Shameful Contradictions and Self-serving Positions

Before proceeding it must be noted that reporting on anything in the political sector must necessarily be considered to be partisan. In a post-factual world, anything may be said to be true. The following information is provided as concrete examples of contradictory and self-serving positions and actions. The two news articles cited below are from *Politico* and *The New York Times*, both considered to be left-leaning. We also note that these reports have been overtaken by the rapid flow of events since 2016, becoming "old news." These articles are provided to illustrate the points being made here as compared with documenting a point of view. Also, to be noted is that even though these reports have become old news, the new news is much the same if not outrageously worse. Wright reports for *Politico*:

> Congressional Republicans spent years investigating Hillary Clinton's emails and launched a special committee to get to the bottom of the Benghazi attacks. But when it comes to alleged Russian interference in the presidential election, the GOP appears to be taking a more restrained approach. Senate Majority Leader Mitch McConnell (R-Ky.) and House Speaker Paul Ryan (R-Wis.) are rejecting growing calls for a wide-ranging special congressional panel to investigate the issue, instead pointing to the narrower oversight work already being performed by the House and Senate intelligence committees. This approach offers no guarantee that final investigative reports will ever be released to the public — and potentially shields President-elect Donald Trump from a deeper congressional investigation looking into Russia's motives.
>
> On Monday, McConnell told reporters that the Senate Intelligence Committee "is more than capable of conducting a complete review of this matter." It quickly became clear the Kentucky Republican was not necessarily ordering any kind of formal review aimed at producing a final report — like the one that resulted in the committee's 2014

investigation of the Benghazi attacks — but was simply calling on the committee to continue its ongoing probe on the issue.

"The committee's ongoing oversight captures exactly what the leader described," McConnell spokesman Don Stewart said in a follow-up email. Also reported is, "It's clear the Russians interfered," McCain said on CBS's "Face the Nation." "Now, whether they intended to interfere to the degree that they were trying to elect a certain candidate, I think that's a subject of investigation."[13]

Reading a report like this leads to the conclusion that there seems to be an important contradiction. Add to that Trump's public call for Russia to release hacked emails and it is hard to deny the Russians might have the missing emails. How can the Republicans, after years of investigating the likely Democratic presidential candidate, Hillary Clinton, not be willing to investigate this Russian interference in our election? Senator McCain's quoted comment points out the contradiction.

The Republicans have remained steadfast in resisting efforts to investigate Trump despite an impeachment and Mueller's investigation and report. Avoidance of information surfacing that might compromise their party and Trump's legitimacy appears to be of the highest priority. Is the pursuit of power all that matters in U.S. politics? Must everything be shamelessly self-serving when it comes to politicians and political parties? Is winning and defeating the other party by any means available all that matters? Must it always seem that it is the politician and his or her political career and party that come first and the county second? Unfortunately, with only a few exceptions when there is authentic compromise to create legislation, there seems to be no shame at all attached to the spin, distortions, lying (propaganda) to advance one's political interests and using the government to further Trump's reelection.

The following second report covers another important topic that must be denied, dismissed, and possibly removed from the public record by the Republicans. The Editorial Board of *The New York Times* offers the following insights on declassifying the Senate report on torture.

> In late 2014, Senate Democrats delivered to a handful of federal agencies copies of a 6,700-page classified report about the secret prison network the Central Intelligence Agency established after the Sept. 11 attacks. The report offered a comprehensive and unvarnished account of the torture several detainees endured as American intelligence agencies scrambled to find out if there were other plots in the works.
>
> Senator Dianne Feinstein of California, who oversaw the report, hoped it would become a seminal document for national security professionals for generations to come, a reminder of a dark and shameful period during which the American government succumbed to fear.

Now the report, and the instructive history it contains, is at risk of remaining under wraps for more than a decade.

At the Justice Department's direction, officials at the C.I.A., State Department, Pentagon and Office of the Director of National Intelligence placed their copies in safes, unread. When Republicans regained control of the Senate in January 2015, Senator Richard Burr, the new chairman of the Senate Select Committee on Intelligence and an outspoken critic of the report, wrote to President Obama demanding that all copies be returned to the Senate. He also instructed the administration not to enter the report into the executive branch's system of records, since doing so would make it subject to retention. It would also mean that the report could at some point see the light of day.

On Friday, the White House informed Ms. Feinstein that it intended to preserve the report under the Presidential Records Act. That step bars the incoming administration from destroying all copies of the report, a scenario Senate Democrats feared. But President Obama did not heed their calls to declassify the study, which means that the report would remain secret for at least 12 years.

"We can't erase our mistakes by destroying the history books," said Ms. Feinstein, who released a partly redacted summary of the report in December 2014. "While this report isn't easy to read, it offers a vital lesson on what happens when we ignore our values."[14]

Here once again there is revealed the exceptionally combative relationship the two political parties have relative to truth and knowing. We are left to imagine what might be written in these thousands of pages. However, we have some idea based on leaks and releases of the seven major sections of content as reported by *The New York Times*.[15] A few of the sections can be briefly summarized. The CIA's interrogations were more brutal and extensive than reported. The program was mismanaged and the CIA misled Congress and the White House about how effective the brutal interrogations techniques were. And last some interrogators in the field who tried to stop the brutal techniques were repeatedly overruled by senior C.I.A. officials.

It is reasonable to draw the conclusion that, rather than embrace these findings, the Republican response, since it does not fit the Republican pro-torture and enhanced interrogation worldview, is to erase what happened from history and continue to block it from being entered into the Congressional record. Once again, it is striking how contradictory actions like these are since they are not consistent with a standard of ethics and transparency the public would like to see.

There are ample grounds to conclude actions like these and many others are shameful. Why conceal or eliminate them just because you do not like them? Nonetheless suppressing and removing this knowledge from the public record, and most preferably from public consciousness, is a goal to pursue by any means available. Denial and rationalization are core defenses against feeling a sense of shame. To noted other "inconvenient truths" are also threatened with "erasure" from the public record, such as climate science information. Erasure is not inevitable. Many of the findings regarding Russia's intrusion into our election have been strategically saved by the Obama administration to avoid erasure.

We now turn to a developing a historical perspective to inform our psychodynamic understanding of the shameful performance of our government – federal, state, and local. Not only may a worldview contain elements that promote shame; a national history may as well.

Historical Perspectives on Shame: The Journey from Shame to Shamelessness

The flaunting of shameless insolence and pride characterizes much of the popular culture and the Age of Trump. Donald Trump boasted of his sexual prowess and crass objectification of women; of his contempt for Latinos, Muslims, Blacks, and LGBT people; of his delight that the Russians hacked the democrats with the aim of favoring his election; and much more. Recent events in the Age of Trump can be characterized as a reversal of chronic shame.

Open racism, sexism, virulent nationalism, anti-Semitism, and anti–Muslim hatred all can be seen to exemplify efforts to undo shame. For white nationalists, many insist that, far from being an embattled, diminishing majority, they are in fact the essence of America. The Ku Klux Klan and the insurgent white supremacy movement have openly asserted themselves. White America is attempting to restore the boundaries of pride and supremacy by walling off and expelling Latinos, and by surveilling and excluding Muslims and banning immigration from many parts of the non–white world. Hate crimes directed at minorities have become more frequent. Hate also helps to displace for awareness a sense of shame that one's group is losing ground.

Shame, denial, rationalization, and shame reversal can be visualized on a longitudinal timeline and as a series of historical convergences meeting in the present. Consider the following framing of this psychosocial dynamic.

The national sense of inferiority felt by many Americans and collective shame, led to an attempt at reversal of this shame by replacing it with shameless pride and the slogan "Make American Great Again." The slogan attests to the widespread feeling that America is no longer "great." Barack Obama's presidency and the Hillary Clinton's political career are seen as part of the cause of American decline. Symbolized by Trump's open sexual brazenness, Trump vows to restore America's macho and potency at home and in the world. His frequent mention of "strong and powerful" speaks to his desire to be perceived as America's Strong Man following in the footsteps of Vladimir Putin of Russia and Hungary's Viktor Orban. He personifies the denial and undoing the shame of having a black American President by seeking to restore the national self-image of American white supremacy. The slogan "Make America Great Again" is sometimes understood to say, "Make America White Again." This deeply felt shame has historical roots.

There are noteworthy indicators of America's shame-filled declining efficacy abroad and at home. The long Vietnam War of the 1960s and early 1970s led to the defeat of the United States and the humiliating evacuation of U.S. personnel from the top of a building. It was the first modern day war that the United States lost becoming a historical trauma the nation has tried to live down. It was a shame-filled national convulsion, most conveniently assigned to those who fought the war, creating yet another enduring national shame.

Beginning in the early 1980s, an era of relentless downsizing, restructuring, reengineering, and outsourcing together with the massive layoffs occurred along with the decline of many American major industries. These dynamics and the decline are another source of widespread shame. Workers and employees internalized the cause of their suffering rather than locate it in brutal and ineffective leadership. Many who lost their jobs and who could not find comparable employment blamed themselves. They thought that something was wrong with them that had led to their job loss and being left behind. Many men felt a sense of humiliation at having to tell their wives and children that they had been fired. Some did not tell their families at all.

The attack on the United States on 9/11 2001, was yet another source of shame. How could the greatest military power on earth be so defenseless, so vulnerable? There were more lives lost on September 11th than at Pearl Harbor, an earlier "Chosen Trauma" that was a blight on the American self-image.[16] The ensuing protracted wars in Iraq and Afghanistan, intended to exact revenge and reverse and undo national humiliation, appear to be without end or success – yet another shameful loss of national efficacy. The wars against Al-Qaeda and ISIS are equally problematic.

The Great Recession of 2008 was yet another blow to American sense of pride in being the most vital economy in the world. Many asked, how could this happen to us? Millions became unemployed and found that their skills were unmarketable and their age too advanced. If they found jobs, they were often less meaningful jobs, and at a lower wage and without benefits. This was yet another source of humiliation – having to seek unemployment compensation, or even refusing to seek it because it would feel shameful to admit that they had lost an honorable and well-paying job.

In American history there is perhaps an Ur-shame, or original shame, that set the stage for later cumulative shame and responses to undo it. That original shame is the ethnic cleansing of Native Americans from their lands and the enslavement of sub-Saharan Africans forcibly brought to the United States beginning in 1619 and continuing long after European countries banned slavery. The slavery of Blacks in the United States is, in the American conscience, a greater emotional weight than the slaughter and forced movement of American Indians from their original homes. This shame–filled history of white supremacy lives on in the twenty-first century. The Civil War was fought as an attempt to preserve slavery and not primarily to hold onto "cultural values and identity," as many white Southerners insist today.[17] For many white Southerners, the loss of the Civil War was a shame-filled loss of southern pride and honor compounded by Reconstruction. And to be noted, groups like the Tea Party have been referred to as a neo-confederate response to Obama's election.

Many vow to reverse the shame and restore the grandeur that was the Plantation South. The slogan, "The South Shall Rise Again," attests to the inability to acknowledge and mourn loss. In Vamik Volkan's phrase, the loss of the Civil War is a "Chosen Trauma" that is passed on from generation to generation, with a vow to avenge it.[16] If we "fast forward" to the twenty-first century and the Age of Trump, many white Southerners likely saw in Trump the opportunity to reverse this shameful loss and restore their white social and cultural identity. The return of open racism, white supremacy, and ethno-nationalism in American culture and politics can be understood as an attempt to heal ancient injuries with defiance and violent shootings in a black church and a Walmart. This provides interpretive perspective for the shame reversing current ethnocentrism and pursuit of historical national identity based on white superiority that now includes inferior and dangerous "others" – Hispanic immigrants and supposed Islamic terrorists.

Shame is then an important aspect of our awareness both in terms of cumulative shame, and in how we experience our political process that continually generates shameful outcomes – destructive *repetitions* driven by ideologies and human nature. Our right-wing political leaders, their operatives, and the voters who support them, exhibit a lot of shameless behavior partially concealed by political double-speak and the embrace of propagandized news and conspiracy theories. These shameful national and social dynamics can be better understood using object relations theory concepts to explore this sense of shame psychodynamically.

Applying Object Relations Theory to Understanding Shame and the New Political Reality

Authoritarianism on the political right that is sometimes described as Trumpism with its "me" first approach to life contains an underlying compassionless element that lends itself to being explored from a psychodynamically informed perspective. Understanding the steadfast adherence to a selfish if not interpersonally punishing worldview and the unacknowledged but ever-present sense of shame that accompanies it is important. Political and social polarization invites inspection from an object relations perspective that helps to explain what creates a black and white world with self-created-and-perpetuated evil others – liberals and immigrants. Consider the phrase, "Take my country back." as has been used by the left and the right. This speaks to the polarization of a deeply split-apart society, holding opposing worldviews amplified by television's quasi-news/propaganda and the vastness of the internet that is now heavily relied on by the right for knowing about and understanding the world around us. In this context, the opposing side of the polarization is constantly held up for contempt and condemnation as a threat to one's very identity. Evil others lurk everywhere, including in the immigrant communities that we until recently welcomed in our midst. Fear is being continually promoted using black and white and good versus bad imagery that promotes splitting and projection and transference of past traumas and anxieties onto the present context.

It is also the case that splitting and projection have driven much of our national history. There are many fundamental splits in our society, such as black versus white, north versus south, rural versus urban, old versus young, poor versus rich, and middle class versus the poor and the rich. These splits have been exploited by politicians and political parties for profit and political gain since the founding of the country. Politicians invariably tell supporters what they want to hear. These splits are palpable. They feel "natural." They are filled with unconscious dynamics that promote and maintain them.

The populist ethnocentrism and economic national centrism that have arisen not only in the United States but also around the world are exploited by political leaders who induce fear and then promise to rescue everyone from it. It is a world of us versus them and good versus bad. This splitting and the accompanying transference help to explain authoritarianism on the right. The "me first" worldview, contains shame, and it is shame that must be coped with via denial – suppression from awareness – and reversal of shame into fierce pride. Hillary Clinton's "deplorables" embrace this pejorative label with pride as a slogan on T-shirts. Shame may also be split off and projected onto supposedly worthless, incompetent, and shameful others who should feel ashamed for calling us "deplorable."

In sum, object relations theory contributes to understanding the creation and maintaining of the polarization and the undoing of shame in our cultural history. The us versus them and the good versus bad dichotomies are best understood by using object relations theory and the concept of shame. This contributes to understanding much deeper conscious and unconscious psychodynamics that make those on the right feel set upon, rejected, and viewed as holding unacceptable values that are anti-social in nature, selfish, and lacking compassion for others.

These psychodynamic insights also echo group relations basic assumption group dynamics such as fight/flight and dependency groups that depend on a "strong and powerful" leader to save their members from threats identified by their leader. The far-right must defend its less than compassionate ideologies from liberal attacks that are sometimes ignored as though they never happened (flight) or during the Age of Trump often brutally attacked if the attacks appear to be garnering much media attention. Dependency is clearly an element of the Republican politicians since they fear being attacked by Trump for any display of disloyalty leading many to "sign on" to attacking the 2020 election results.

Horney's three directions of movement also contribute insights. The polarization is filled with movements toward like-minded ideologically pure believers and against all those who believe otherwise. Social trends that include moving to locations where the residents are all of the same mind is gradually furthering the development of social and political polarization that also accounts for rejecting and excluding others who do not embrace the familiar ideologies of the right. And to be noted, these stressful group and social dynamics may well alienate many who prefer to ignore and move away from those who embrace the opposing ideologies and the destressing psychosocial polarization that they create.

In Conclusion

In this chapter, the psychodynamics underlying the Age of Trump have been explored. We have argued that the worldview of pursuing one's self-interest under the banner of rationalized selfishness and a political ideology of "government is the problem" espoused by political leaders on the right, introduces deeply felt shame that has to be denied to exist, split off and projected in order to maintain self-comforting thoughts. The omnipresence of continuous lying, distorting, and misleading voters about the outcomes such as reinventing the health care system that may disenfranchise many millions of citizens from receiving healthcare considered by conservatives to be a privilege and not a right can be observed to be a shameless pursuit of ideology. When viewed from a historical perspective it is reasonable to embrace the notion of a culture of shame on the right. Unless these social and psychological dynamics are acknowledged and held up for inspection, reflection, and discussion they will likely remain a constant presence, continuing to create social and political polarization.

Chapter 11 explores the power of ideologies by highlighting deregulation as a not infrequently destructive ideological perspective that is, across time, continually adhered to regardless of the negative outcomes. Deregulation is the companion in a form of action to Reagan's considering government to be the problem.

Notes

1. Morrison, A. (1970). *The culture of shame.* Northvale, NJ: Jason Aronson, 16.
2. Piers, G. & Singer, M. (2015). *Shame and guilt: A psychoanalytic and a cultural study.* Mansfield Centre, CT: Martino Publishing, 16.

3. Gilligan, J. (1996). *Violence: Our deadly epidemic and its causes.* New York, NY: G.P. Putnam's Sons, 47.
4. Morrison, A. (1970). *The culture of shame.* Northvale, NJ: Jason Aronson, 73.
5. Hetherington, M. & Weiler, J. (2009). *Authoritarianism & polarization in American politics.* New York, NY: Cambridge University Press.
6. Rand, A. (1957). *Atlas shrugged.* New York, NY: Random House.
7. Rubin, H. (2007). Ayn Rand's literature of capitalism. *The New York Times.* http://www.nytimes.com/2007/09/15/business/15atlas.html.
8. Stein, H. & Allcorn, S. (2010). The unreality principle and deregulation: A psychocultural exploration. *The Journal of Psychohistory*, 38(1), 27–48.
9. Rand, A. (1964). *The virtue of selfishness.* New York: NY: Signet.
10. Ayn Rand Institute. *The virtue of selfishness – Themes.* https://www.aynrand.org/novels/virtue-of-selfishness.
11. Ayn Rand. *In Wikiqoutes.* https://en.wikiquote.org/wiki/Ayn Rand.
12. Orwell, G. (1949). *Nineteen eighty-four: A novel.* London: Secker & Warburg.
13. Wright, A. (2016). GOP leaders shield Trump from expanded Russia probe. *Politico.* http://www.politico.com/story/2016/12/republicans-russia-donald-trump-232528.
14. Editorial Board. (2016). Declassify the senate torture report. *The New York Times.* http://www.nytimes.com/2016/12/12/opinion/preserve-the-senate-torture-report-dianne-feinstein.html?action=click&pgtype=Homepage&-clickSource=story-heading&module=opinion-c-col-left-region&region=opinion-c-col-left-region&WT.nav=opinion-c-col-left-region&_r=0.
15. Ashkenas, J., Fairfield, H., Keller J. & Volpe, P. (2014). 7 Key points from the C.I.A. torture report. *The New York Times.* https://www.nytimes.com/interactive/2014/12/09/world/cia-torture-report-key-points.html.
16. Volkan, V. (1998). *Transgenerational transmissions and chosen traumas.* XIII International Congress International Association of Group Psychotherapy, http://www.vamikvolkan.com/Transgenerational-Transmissions-and-Chosen-Traumas.php.
17. Baptist, E. (2014). *The half has never been told: Slavery and the making of American capitalism.* New York, NY: Basic Books.

11 Deregulation as a Right-Wing Ideology

The Age of Trump is yet another episode of the over 50-year-old legacy of the Republican ideology and practice of deregulation. We have failed to learn from the repeated failures of this history. Deregulation is one of the more prominent right-wing ideologies that is, in addition to tax cuts, offered as a cure-all for all forms of economic and social problems. Deregulation is said to reduce operating costs, thereby increasing profits and jobs, even though the environment may be damaged, people poisoned, corporate corruption allowed, and financial disaster to occur. Thomas Friedman, in an aptly titled opinion piece, "How We Broke the World," describes banks and other financial institutions that, when deregulated, recklessly invested in bundled together subprime mortgages that received less risky ratings from corrupted financial rating organizations.[1] Common sense turned out to be not so common and banks were "too big to fail." They were bailed out by the Republicans who ironically advocate for moral hazard.

In large measure, the 2008 economic crisis was a crisis of economic decision-making. It has long been contended that economic policy and market behavior are rational and based on enlightened self-interest. The economic crisis revealed how *irrational* much of economic policymaking and market behavior really is.[2] This appreciation leads to exploring the irrational *unreality* behind the policy of deregulation as a right-wing ideology in recent American culture and history. We also note that this irrationality includes the belief that self-interest and rationality are economic governing principles. Alan Greenspan's mention of "irrational exuberance" and the "flaw," in his Congressional testimony that attested to irrationality on the part of executives that led to the harming of their organizations disproves this belief. Understanding the unreality behind ideologies like deregulation requires a psychodynamically informed approach.

Exploring the psychodynamic dimensions of a widespread flight from a reality that continually demonstrates that deregulation as an ideology produces unacceptable outcomes, adds new insights. Also, to be noted, in addition to accurate reality testing being stressful and to be avoided, anxiety also arises over the fear of violating the ideology and being attacked or cast out of the "tribe" by loyalists. Non-compliance may also lead to anxiety over losing political power and the votes of loyal right-wing voters, and support from a funding base that approves of deregulation. Unquestioning and rigid adherence to an ideology like deregulation that produces less than desirable outcomes becomes essential in terms of managing a distressing reality that inevitably leaks in. Managing the dissonance gap created by accurate reality testing becomes a challenge that relies on psychological defenses such as denial and rationalization, the psychodynamics to be discussed – and a thoughtless and uncritical but comforting embrace of the ideology.

In sum, the unconscious dimension behind the adherence to the ideology of deregulation can be illuminated by psychodynamically informed analysis. This approach to understanding the complex links between ideology, public policy, and individuals and group dynamics permits looking beyond the fantasies of the unreality of a self-regulating "rational" marketplace with its invisible guiding hand of profit and self-interest. The triangulated psychodynamically informed perspectives used here, combined with a few additional perspectives offer insights into how reasonable people can do unreasonable things. We begin by exploring unreality in America since the 1980s.

The Idea of Unreality

There are several thought leaders who are informative and contribute to understanding the emergence of unreality in American society. We briefly highlight here the work of a few of these authors who provide different insights about unreality.

- In his psychoanalytic critique, *New Age Thinking*, English literature scholar Melvin Faber explores how the supposedly New Age science and religion of the late 20th century is anchored in psychological regression, magical thinking, and unreality.[3]
- In *The Unreality Industry: The Deliberate Manufacturing of Falsehood and What It Is Doing to Our Lives*, Ian Mitroff and Warren Bennis argue how American mass media have created a fantasy industry that turns all of life and news into entertainment (Fox News).[4] Designed to provide escape from the uncertainty, complexity, and anxiety of modern life, the media magically blur the boundary ("boundary warping") between fantasy and fact and oversimplify complex reality, boiling it down into mottos and sound bites. Political "spin" and outright lies become reality, and rational thought is replaced by an alternate world of quick, easy answers (talking points and sound bites) that are prominent in the Age of Trump.
- In *Communicating Unreality: Modern Media and the Reconstruction of Reality*, Gabriel Weimann comes to similar conclusions about the

manufacture of unreality in a post-factual world created by the media and its uncritical acceptance by mass society.[5]

- In *Fatal Illusions: Shredding a Dozen Unrealities That Can Keep Your Organization from Success*, James Lucas explores widely held wish-fulfilling myths about business: "Everybody knows what quality is" and "We don't need passion if we have a good plan."[6] However, the reality is that many products lack good quality, and rational objective "strategic planning" and "mission statements" are undermined by the irrationality of "human factors." Fondly held wish-driven unreality is only sustainable by diligently pursued psychological defense mechanisms.

- Chris Hedges wrote *Empire of Illusion: The End of Literacy and the Triumph of Spectacle*.[7] He notes that cultures die if they cannot distinguish between reality and illusion. Those who cling to fantasy in stressful times often turn to cult-like demagogues and entertainers like Trump to reassure them. This opens the door to charismatic "con artists" who autocratically seize control and say *only they can save us*.

In sum, these authors have recognized that American society on the right has come to embrace a self-destructive unreality. Trump's preferred narratives of 2020 that he has the Covid-19 virus under control, and that everyone can get tested, stands in stark contrast to an ever-rising infection rate and death toll. It will magically go away – eventually. Unreality can be further "unpacked" by using psychoanalytic theory to understand it.

The Psychodynamics of Unreality in Politics and Society

American society's ability to adapt to reality is in question. This can be better appreciated if several different theoretical perspectives are considered, in addition to the three theories in Chapter 2. We once again briefly highlight some of these perspectives that speak to conservative America's flight from reality.

John Ralston Saul writes that "Equilibrium is dependent upon our recognition of reality, which is the acceptance of permanent psychic discomfort. And the acceptance of psychic discomfort is the acceptance of consciousness."[8] The opposite – deregulation for example – lies in the delusional refusal to recognize a reality that does not support the unreality that deregulation creates economic and social problems. Fantasy, wish, and desire distort awareness and understanding and make it hard to "learn from experience."[9,10,11,12]

Gordon Lawrence writes that psychosis in general is "the process whereby humans defend themselves from understanding the meaning and significance of reality, because they regard such knowledge as painful. To do this, they use aspects of their mental functioning to destroy, in various degrees, the very process of thinking that would put them in touch with reality."[13] Not only do individuals do this but also organizations and whole cultures do it. The flight from distressing experience that arises from accurate reality testing into unreality comes to be preferred if not required when it comes to ideologies. In groups, this finds expression in an unconsciously driven retreat from reality-oriented "work" and toward the psychologically defensive enactment of basic assumptions such as fight/flight, dependency, pairing, and fusion into oneness.[10,14]

Unreality can, we suggest, influence cultural ideology, religious dogma, political propaganda, economic policy, and is often the subject of literature and movies. Unreality resides in literature and the surreal worlds created in novels such as Franz Kafka's *The Trial*[15], Lewis Carroll's *Through the Looking Glass, and What Alice Found There*[16], and George Orwell's *Nineteen Eighty-Four*.[17] Orwell's novel famously elucidated the political control of thought, known as "doublethink," and the control of thought through language (euphemism), known as "Newspeak," both of which ring true today on the political right and for example on Fox News. Unreality, it may be appreciated, is an omnipresent influence in our daily lives and society.

In sum, individuals and groups may not be interested in maintaining accurate reality testing but rather impose their conception of reality on the present moment becoming convinced this is reality. Indeed, boundary warping fantasy may magically win out over accurate reality testing thereby creating a shared "unreality" for individuals and groups.

Unreality and Individual and Group Experience

The psychodynamic world of group ideologies warps reality and may replace it with unreality. There is a concealing of the experience of painful reality behind a protective cognitive-affective mask of ideology. Much of group life can be understood to be "regulated" by psychologically defensive unconscious group dynamics and basic assumptions such as fight and flight that are attempts to deal with a threatening and distressing experience of reality.[18,19,20,21] Groups (organizations, ethnic groups, religions, nation–states) can often "successfully" impose their alternate reality on the world, at least for a time. Perhaps the loss of jobs to immigrants who do work that no one else wants to do (meat packing, migratory field work) can "reasonably" become the reality for their exclusion and being walled out.

From a psychodynamic perspective the unreality of a "successful" group "psychosis" is, at least to a degree, usually grounded in reality and is somewhat effective in mobilizing reality to support and actualize the group ideology.[22] From an object relations perspective perception is grounded in projection outward of an internal reality that is then re-internalized as a well-known reality – unreality. In a sense, the projected reality "confirms" the ideology, at least in the perception and experience of the individual and group. Such imaginary "adaptations" can persist a long time – unless or until some environmental challenge or inner conflict pokes a hole in the delusional system and forces contact with reality. And to be noted, groups can also be self-destructive and provoke the threats they fear, such as financial sector deregulation followed by economic collapse followed by the imposition of bail outs and more regulation.

In sum, irrational attachments to ideologies mediate anxiety-ridden experience but also produce dysfunctional, anti-adaptive outcomes (realities) that cannot be acknowledged. The ideology must not be questioned to avoid anxiety. Ideology, when attacked by others, triggers defending it as well as retreating further into the ideology behind walls of unreality. When this happens, it is much harder to learn from experience, since any doubt is forbidden and punished by others loyal to the ideology. The only acceptable knowledge is what the group members already know.

Unreality and Political Ideologies

James Glass' book, *Psychosis and Power*, links psychosis, ideology, and public life. He writes that, "Power driven by delusion is vicious and sadistic, and delusion is no stranger to political actors and movements."[23] He argues that, while individuals and groups may contain reality-oriented elements, under the pressure of the experience of distressing reality testing, there may arise anxiety that initiates psychological regression toward rigid, black and white polarized thinking that does not tolerate ambiguity. This in turn combines with paranoia to create a very real sense of threat reinforcing the regressive dynamic that fight/flight leaders mobilize to create a regressive basic assumption group dynamic.

Glass situates ideology as a cognitive-affective solution to regression, inner emptiness and barrenness, and flight from reality. A political ideology that "finds itself mired in closed systems of thought, in cult like behavior, in racist and unyielding concepts of reality replays what on an infantile-development level might be understood as the paranoid/schizoid position and its immersion in omnipotent power."[24]

Political/ideological formulations based on these dynamics lack the capacity to tolerate the external world with its competing demands. "A psychotic political program and its tyrannical forms of power remakes reality according to its own closed systems of perception; it denies consent, just as a democratic politics encourages it."[24] Political and economic ideologies may then be understood to be sociocultural defense systems defending the unreality principle and allaying individual and group anxiety.

From Anxiety to Ideology as a Defense in Groups

We now turn to exploring how anxiety, unreality, and ideology are connected psychodynamically. Anxiety leads to psychological regression, the embrace of psychological defenses, and to ideology that promises to reduce the anxiety by creating a non-threatening context (unreality) that, to work, must be vigorously defended over time.

Freud proposed with respect to the defensive splitting of the ego that "the ego rejects the incompatible idea together with its affect and behaves as if the idea had never occurred to the ego at all."[25] There is regression to more primitive processes and defenses such as splitting, projection, depersonalization, and derealization. A new "reality" is experienced, "behind the looking glass."

This reality is at once protective and reassuring, but also disturbing in that it requires further defense against anxiety induced by reality that inevitably leaks in when there are less than adaptive outcomes. The distressing and anxiety ridden; subjectively experienced outer world necessitates a solution to anxiety. This is provided by greater dependence on a rigid, orderly set of ideological constructs that filter and redefine reality. For those who have embraced an ideology like deregulation, the source of anxiety becomes anything that contradicts the ideology. The group must protect its own protection – the ideology. The outcome is that the group "successfully" creates an alternate unreality of alternate facts.

To be noted, ideology does not emerge as a full-blown internally consistent and coherent system of thought. It is formulated and realized piecemeal and then constantly revised based on experience. This appreciation leads to considering that the process contains elements of trial and error and feedback loops that create change in the service of ideological adaptation. But also, to be considered are human needs and psychological defenses that introduce compulsive repetitions. These repetitions can be understood to be a form group madness that continuously enacts and reenacts the repetition compulsion, where the repetition makes it unlikely that the group consistently learns from experience.[26,27] There is then a continuous conflict within groups that embrace an ideology between making it more adaptive and maintaining it as is. In sum, these conflicts create anxiety arising from awareness of distressing non-adaptive outcomes and the compelling need to maintain an unreality to defend the ideology.

This image of repetition corresponds to what George Devereux referred to as the "vicious cycle of psychopathology," wherein anxiety generates an initial imperfect defense, which leads to the experience of further anxiety and greater reliance on psychologically defensive responses.[28] The distress and the anxiety that erupt are never completely mastered by these defenses. Adopting an ideology or belief system that attempts to explain why the cause of distress is there, what it means, and what action should be taken contributes to creating a less distressing unreality. However, the source(s) of distress is still present, and the experience of anxiety remains despite the protection accorded by the ideology. As a result, anxiety-driven psychological regression still arises leading to the greater use of psychological defenses such as denial, derealization, splitting, projection, projective identification, rationalization, intellectualization, and dissociation.

In this process, the group may enter what Lloyd deMause has called a "group trance," and a selective sensitivity and attention to one's surroundings. The rest is cognitively and emotionally "tuned out."[29] The individual and collective "gaze" is fixed or "frozen" on an ideology. The ideology must be kept pure and defended from corruption. The fear of loss, of emptiness and dissolution of boundaries underlies all defensive maneuvers to keep the ideology alive. The alternate reality of the ideology "becomes" synonymous with reality itself. Any opposition becomes an enemy to be ridiculed, excluded, walled out, or eliminated.

In sum, the connection between anxiety, regression, ideology, and unreality becomes fused. The expression "we have met reality and it is ours" speaks to the psychodynamic war being waged on reality. We now offer several informative concrete examples of how unreality and ideology play out on the cultural-historical stage that spans the presidencies of Ronald Reagan, George W. Bush, and the Age of Trump.

Ronald Reagan's Era of Deregulation

The late 1970s and early 1980s were in many ways experienced by Americans as a cultural nadir of morale. The highly ambivalent, even unpopular, Vietnam War was over, but for many, the sense of shame, guilt, grief, and betrayal cast a long shadow. We were mistrustful of government, feeling betrayed by President Richard Nixon and his zealots, and the Watergate scandal (1973–1974). The presidency of Jimmy Carter, having begun so relaxed and up-beat, became mired in the Iranian Revolution and in the humiliating holding of Americans hostages in Iran along with the embarrassment of a very public failed rescue effort. The 1970s were a decade of economic upheaval, characterized by demoralizing recession and "stagflation" when there arose depressed economic growth combined with inflation.

Ronald Reagan promised to make Americans feel good, strong, and proud (again). Nobody would "push us around." He promised to make the world "respect" America by building up the military, escalating the arms race with the Soviet Union, and initiating the militarization of space (termed Star Wars). The Cold War with the Soviet Union soon reached a feverish pitch. Reagan, as a leader, assumed the role of a charismatic fight/flight leader where the "enemy" was created in part by splitting and projection. The enemy had evil intent and "we" did not.

In such a threatening environment, Reagan was empowered to deregulate corporations and pursue union busting. Big government that suppressed our individual freedoms was being slain.[30] America, a land of opportunity, became a land of no-limits opportunism, and greed, echoed by Michael's Douglas's character Gordon Gekko in the 1987 movie *Wall Street*. Individualism ran unchecked. During Reagan's presidency, consistent with the black and white world of the far-right, the Soviet Union came to be known as the "Evil Empire." Ironically, there were two evil empires at that time, one outside the United States, the other inside. There was the Soviet "Evil Empire" but also the American government itself. Defeating both was essential, perhaps now reaching its zenith during the Age of Trump and the attack on the "deep state" which appears to have been a projection in that government hiring became focused on hiring people loyal to Trump.

Idealization of and identification with President Reagan underlay the embracing of his political and economic ideology that came to be called "Reaganomics." The doctrine of deregulation failed on its own.

Financial Deregulation – From Ronald Reagan to George W. Bush

In practice, the ideology of financial deregulation as a national policy has created major financial disasters. Before we explore in greater depth the social and national harm of embracing the ideology of deregulation as applied to financial institutions, we wish to note that eliminating and changing regulations is not "all bad." Thoughtful deregulation offers society benefits where over-regulation or misguided and out-of-date regulation restrict enterprise and personal freedoms. However, this unfortunately is not often the case when *ideology* drives the deregulation, where creating the massive world-wide financial meltdown and the 2007 "great recession" can be attributed to uncritical, ideologically driven deregulation, as was the case for the savings and loan crisis of the 1980s when over 1,000 deregulated institutions were closed or reorganized, and taxpayers lost billions to bail this out.

Ronald Reagan's declaration that government is the problem, illustrates the cultural cascade of ideology-driven-unreality.[31] As William Kleinknecht (2009) argues in his book, *The Man Who Sold the World: Ronald Reagan, and the Betrayal of Main Street America*, the Reagan Administration dismantled eight decades of social reform that had helped the American working class, and replaced protection of workers with protection of corporate leaders who sought deregulation of the economy.[32] In *The New York Times* essay, "Reagan Did It," Paul Krugman (2009), a Nobel winning economist, begins by quoting President Reagan:

> This bill is the most important legislation for financial institutions in the last 50 years. It provides a long-term solution for troubled thrift institutions. ... All in all, I think we hit the jackpot." So declared Ronald Reagan in 1982, as he signed the Garn-St. Germain Depository Institutions Act.

He was, as it happened, wrong about solving the problems of the thrifts. On the contrary, the bill turned the modest-sized troubles of savings-and-loan institutions into an utter catastrophe. But he was right about the legislation's significance. And as for that jackpot — well, it finally came more than 25 years later, in the form of the worst economic crisis since the Great Depression.[33]

Under George W. Bush restrictions on mortgage lending that limited the ability of families to buy homes without sufficient down payments and resources were removed and looser lending standards created an explosion of debt that propped up the economy post 9/11 with a housing bubble. The Financial Services Modernization Act of 1999 (Gramm-Leach-Bliley Act) allowed banks to use deposits to invest in derivatives that became involved with subprime mortgages. The 2000 Commodity Futures Modernization Act exempted derivatives from regulatory oversight including state regulations. These deregulation dynamics led to the creation of" toxic assets" (mortgage-backed securities, collateralized debt obligations (CDOs), and credit default swaps (CDS)) that had to be bailed out by the government's Troubled Asset Relief Program (TARP) program. Over-extended borrowers began to default in large numbers once the housing bubble burst and unemployment began to rise. These defaults in turn wreaked havoc with the financial system, drying up credit that is critical for consumption and for small and large business to thrive.

These insights are underscored by Alan Greenspan who, while Chairman of the Federal Reserve Board, offered the phrase "irrational exuberance" regarding what was thought to be unduly escalated asset values on Wall Street. Robert Shiller related economic, cultural, and psychological factors to an underlying "speculative fervor" in stock market behavior.[34] This once again underscores the false belief (unreality) that rationality and self-interest are governing principles for decision making.

The unreality of deregulation is clearly the root cause of these massive economic and social dislocations. Having not learned from experience and because common sense is not so common, it may be reasonable to assume that the embrace of the ideology of deregulation during the Age of Trump and beyond will continue, maximally defended from accurate reality testing.

In sum, to say that Reagan unleashed insatiable greed is at once true and too simplistic. Reagan and his administration exploited the anxiety, sense of loss, the wish to feel great again, and a sense of national shame over Vietnam by offering consumerism and the dream of homeownership as a solution to American domestic problems. George W. Bush did likewise after his 2000 election and this escalation of deregulation reached a logical extreme during the Age of Trump and Making America Great Again. Bush's deregulation opened the floodgate of consumerism and toxic home mortgages that fanned the flames of desire with "no limits" fueled by unlimited access to debt supplied by the deregulated financial industry. This dynamic was not only the basis for the savings and loan disaster under Reagan but also the source of the Great Recession beginning in 2007 with recovery only achieved around 2015. After 2016 Trump has also pursued deregulation and stripped the government of legitimacy and regulatory authority. He filled his administration with corporate lobbyists and ideologues hostile to government.

And to be noted, damage from deregulation is not limited to the financial systems. The Age of Trump witnessed a major effort to roll back many forms of regulation (more than one hundred Environmental Protection Agency regulations is an example) across a broad front said to reduce regulatory costs and unleash American industry to create jobs. Massive financial failures driven by deregulation are only one aspect of an ideology of deregulation. The following deregulation of building in easily identified floodplains is another concrete example where unreality seems to never yield to accurate reality testing.

Deregulation and Unreality: Perilous Building on the Central Texas Floodplain

In 2005 the Public Broadcast System aired a television program, *Flash Flood Alley*, which poignantly illustrates our unreality principle and its strong appeal.[35] In central Texas, real estate developers pressured cities to rewrite building codes that would allow them to build on river floodplains, which in New Braunfels meant the riverfront. Carefully selecting data that would support their supposed realism, they argued for the rarity of high water over the span of 100 or even 1,000 years. Not long after the developers had built on the floodplains, the homes were flooded.

The developers lured the city politicians with the imagery of city development, an increased tax base, and job creation. How could they pass up a deal like this? The city would be foolish to limit growth by regulation. It was a patent appeal to the politicians to suspend their normal reality-based judgment and to embrace unreality-based wish and grandiosity instead.

Despite the relatively recent as well as distant historical documentation of catastrophic flooding dating back to 1872, 1998, and 2002, the developers built the houses on the floodplain. Reality was replaced by a wish-and-ambition-driven alternate reality and supported by the unreality of an ideology of no regulation. A catastrophe in the making, based on the embrace of unreality, was the result. Hard evidence to the contrary was dismissed as portrayed in the documentary, where an old German brewery in New Braunfels had doors on which the flood levels of many major floods had long been marked (http://www.floodsafety.com/media/ffa/brewerydoors.htm).

One could argue that in this central Texas cultural narrative, not only did the pleasure principle completely override the reality principle, but also there was a widespread flight from (denial of) knowledge of earlier floods into an unreality of building where future devastating flooding would most certainly occur as documented by the television programing showing houses submerged up to their roofs.

Floodplain deregulation is a relatively common outcome of developers who pressure local state and federal government to change their regulations to allow for building in what becomes a situation no longer defined and regulated as a floodplain. Magically a floodplain was no longer a floodplain. Similarly, much the same can be said for all aspects of daily life where air and water are polluted, the food chain not carefully monitored, and dangerous products produced. Government regulation is often only called for after a catastrophe and mass illness and death.

Our triangulation of the three theoretical psychodynamically informed perspectives contributes to understanding the underlying psychodynamics and complexities of an ideology like deregulation of the financial industry or floodplains.

A Theoretical Triangulation: Object Relations, Group Relations, and Karen Horney's Model

The ideology of deregulation paired with the irrational belief that self-interest governed by rationality yields consistently good outcomes is not supported by accurate reality testing. This has led us to describe this dynamic as an unreality. The underlying psychodynamics have been touched upon and are now explored in a greater depth using our preferred triangulation of three complimentary psychodynamically informed perspectives.

Object Relations

President Reagan identified government and government regulation as the problem. This "diagnosis" is the foundation of the ideology of deregulation. How is it that government and regulation had become "bad" and must be eliminated? Splitting and projection offer an explanation grounded in infancy, childhood, and throughout life, when authority figures act to govern (control) the child and introduce rules and regulations the child (and adult) must follow that restrict personal freedom and play. "I can't be myself." We have all been subjected to this inevitability and share a resentment toward, distress about, and rejection of these experiences. This is natural but also makes us vulnerable to appeals of leaders and politicians who tap into this experience to reject being governed and regulated. Libertarianism is representative of this.

By identifying government and regulation as a threat, leaders become fight/flight leaders who encourage splitting and projection. Government and regulation become identified as a threat to personal freedom and autonomy and, therefore, as bad and must be stopped. Also, our self-experience of being controlling and of regulating others (children and supervisees for example) may be disowned and split off and projected onto the mental image of a remote government and its regulation of us. This dynamic is encouraged by political leaders who, by pointing out this threat, promote themselves as leaders who oppose this distressing self-experience. Government is the problem. Transference from our prior life experience onto this mindful creation invests the threat of government and regulation with strong negative emotions. Getting rid of the feelings of being limited and controlled becomes essential. This dynamic empowers leaders on the political right to deregulate most often their financial and political supporters (corporations, wealthy investors).

In sum, splitting off past oppressive life experience and one's own tendencies to be controlling, permits projecting them onto the "government" in mind, creating an entity to be avoided and defeated. This dynamic becomes more pronounced in groups.

Group Relations

Just mentioned is that those who lead the charge to eliminating government and regulation become fight/flight leaders. The group feels threatened and afraid and seizes upon a "strong and powerful" charismatic leader (often authoritarian) to save "us" from the evils of government and regulation.

Those who support this dynamic give over to the leader their willing submission to the leader who is expected to lead them to "the promised land." This is underscored by those who study authoritarianism in societies.[36] Perhaps as much as 40% of U.S. citizens have strong or moderate authoritarian leanings.[37] The fight/flight leader, as discussed, is most empowered when many threats are identified (paranoia) and the individual is sufficiently expansive and charismatic and able to evoke the splitting and projection that creates an "evil other" in everyone's mind that must be vanquished. Irrationality reigns supreme in these times and group members resort to thoughts, feelings, and behaviors that were inconceivable before the leader mobilized the fear, anxiety, and psychological regression of the fight/flight basic assumption group.

Karen Horney's Three Direction of Movement

We have thus far described the psychodynamics of creating a shared threatening government with its regulation that becomes invested with a lifetime of traumas of associated feelings. These are mobilized by leaders to attack government and regulation as a personal threat. The taking of action that follows elevates the threat to a cause (crusade) that requires moving against government and its regulation. This movement is fueled by perceived narcissistic injuries past and present that energize striking back, getting even, and vindictively destroying the "enemy." Expansive feelings of being perfect, all knowing and "absolutely right" (as compared to relativism) at least on the part of the leader, are accompanied by an expansive sense of self. This allows the paranoid leader and his or her followers who identify with their charismatic leader – who is invested via projection with perfection and strength – to feel empowered to proceed on a "crusade" to vanquish government and regulation.

These three psychodynamic perspectives may be observed to provide many cross-compatible insights creating a basis to understand a reality that continually ignores the major financial and social problems it creates – an unreality. Unreality (2016–2020) emerged as a strongly preferred psychosocial dynamic on the right that has split America almost evenly into strongly polarized groups that embrace different facts, truths, and realities. Compromise necessary for effective governance as a result is largely absent.

Conclusions: Reclaiming Reason and Reality

There is no simple, quick solution to unconsciously driven political and economic behavior based in the unreality of ideologies. At the level of political and economic culture, the beginning of the solution to an ideology like deregulation is to *recognize* the unconscious power it has over us in terms of allaying anxiety, but paradoxically making the defense of the ideology also anxiety-evoking. The beginning of a realistic solution is to give a name to and to understand the underlying process of what deregulation has been all along: namely, unreality. However, is an appreciation like this likely to emerge into public consciousness when the siren call of ideology is at work?

Alan Greenspan's testimony before Congress and his observation that everyone has an ideology that may well be flawed is a starting point. The flaw arises when the ideology is juxtaposed with the foibles resident in human nature – which are often exposed by stressful and anxiety-ridden fear, trauma, loss, and pain. A charismatic pied piper who offers a magic elixir (an ideology) that promises to restore national, group, or individual pride is all too often uncritically followed. Successes will be cheered, and failures overlooked or blamed on others. It is only when the failures create a cataclysmic outcome that the flaws in the ideology are grudgingly acknowledged, and then only for a time.

Given this dynamic, is there any reason to hope for a non-ideological world grounded as near as possible in reality? History tells us the answer is NOT LIKELY. History is filled with grand ideological visions (Marxism, socialism, communism, capitalism, and religious ideology and dogmas) that have wrought destruction upon the world.[21] The financial community in the United States continues to resist the very regulation that might forestall a future financial fiasco.

This dark assessment of the fusion of ideology with human nature and cultural history, however, also offers a challenge to leaders, politicians, and academics to promote critical thinking and the balanced inspection of new ideas and ideologies as they emerge. The voice in the wilderness must always be there to be heard should a listener be there to listen.

Part IV provides and examination of Trump and his *loyal followers* who share a common awareness and set of feelings that can be described as sharing a common sentience and culture. Our triangulation of psychoanalytic theoretical perspectives contributes to a better understanding of and appreciation of the many psychosocial complexities that have arisen between leaders and followers in the Age of Trump.

Notes

1. Friedman, T. (2020). How we broke the world: Greed and globalization set us up for disaster. *The New York Times*. https://www.nytimes.com/2020/05/30/opinion/sunday/coronavirus-globalization.html?algo=top_conversion&fellback=false&imp_id=918569813&action=click&module=Most%20Popular&pgtype=Homepage.
2. Krantz, J. (2009). *Psychoanalytic studies of organizations*. Sievers, B. (ed.). London: Karnac, xiii–ix.
3. Faber, M. (1996). *New age thinking*. Ottawa, ON: University of Ottawa Press.
4. Mitroff, I.I. and Bennis, W. (1993). *The unreality industry: The deliberate manufacturing of falsehood and what it is doing to our lives*. New York, NY: Oxford University Press.
5. Weimann, G. (2000). *Communicating unreality: Modern media and the reconstruction of reality*. Thousand Oaks, CA: Sage.
6. Lucas, J.R. (2001). *Fatal illusions: Shredding a dozen unrealities that can keep your organization from success*. Kansas City, MO: Quintessential Books.
7. Hedges, C. (2009). *Empire of illusion: The end of literacy and the triumph of spectacle*. New York, NY: Nation Books.
8. Saul, J.R. (1997). *The unconscious civilization*. New York, NY: Free Press, 190.
9. Bion, W.R. (1959). Attacks on Linking. *International Journal of Psycho-Analysis*, 40, 308–315.
10. Bion, W.R. (1959). *Experiences in groups*. New York, NY: Basic Books.
11. Bion, W.R. (1962). *Learning from experience*. London: William Heinemann.
12. Bion, W.R. (1967). *A theory of thinking. In second thoughts*. London: William Heinemann, 110–119.
13. Lawrence, W.G. (2000). *Thinking refracted. In tongued with fire: Groups in experience*. London: Karnac, 4–5.
14. Turquet, P. (1974). *Leadership: The individual and the group. In analysis of groups*. Gibbard, G. S., Hartman, J.J. and Mann, R.D. (eds). San Francisco, CA: Jossey-Bass, 349–371.
15. Kafka, F. (1995). *The trial (Der Prozess.)*. New York, NY: Schocken.
16. Carroll, L. (1871). *Through the looking glass, and what Alice found there*. Whitefish, MT: Kessinger Publishing, 2004 (original 1871).
17. Orwell, G. (1949). *Nineteen eighty-four*. New York, NY: Signet Classics, 1977 (original 1949).
18. Paul, R.A. (1987). The question of applied psychoanalysis and the interpretation of cultural symbolism. *Ethos*, 15(1), 82–103.
19. Stein, H.F. (1994). *The dream of culture*. New York, NY: Psyche Press.

20. La Barre, W. (1971). Materials for a history of studies of crisis cults: A bibliographic essay. *Current Anthropology*, 12(1), 3–44.
21. La Barre, W. (1972). *The ghost dance: The origins of religion*. New York, NY: Dell.
22. Sievers, B. (2006). The psychotic organization: A socio-analytic perspective. *Ephemera: Theory and Politics in Organization*, 6(2), 104–120.
23. Glass, J.M. (1995). *Psychosis and power: Threats to democracy in the self and the group*. Ithaca, NY: Cornell University Press, 14.
24. Glass, J.M. (1995). *Psychosis and power: Threats to democracy in the self and the group*. Ithaca, NY: Cornell University Press, 187.
25. Freud, S. (1894). *The neuro-psychoses of defence. In the standard edition of the complete psychological works of Sigmund Freud (SE)*. Vol III. London: Hogarth Press, 1961 (original 1894), 58.
26. Freud, S. (1914). *Remembering, repeating and working-through (further recommendations on the technique of psycho-analysis II)*. In SE. Vol. XII. London: Hogarth Press, 1958, 145–156.
27. Freud, S. (1920). *Beyond the pleasure principle*. In SE. Vol. XVIII. London: Hogarth Press, 1955, 7–64.
28. Devereux, G. (1955). Charismatic leadership and crisis. In Róheim, G. (ed.). *Psychoanalysis and the social sciences*. New York, NY: International Universities Press, 145–157.
29. deMause, L. (2002). *The emotional life of nations*. New York, NY: Karnac.
30. Levine, D.P. (2004). *Attack on government: Fear, distrust, & hatred in public life*. Charlottesville, VA: Pitchstone Publishing Co.
31. deMause, L. (1984). *Reagan's America*. New York, NY: Creative Roots.
32. Kleinknecht, W. (2009). *The man who sold the world: Ronald Reagan, and the betrayal of main street America*. New York, NY: Public Affairs.
33. Krugman, P. (2009). Reagan did it. *The New York Times*. http://www.nytimes.com/2009/06/01/opinion/01krugman.html?_r=1.
34. Shiller, R.J. (2005). *Irrational exuberance*. Second Edition. Princeton, NJ: Princeton University Press.
35. Flash Flood Alley (2005). (videorecording/DVD). PBS Movie. Produced by *FloodSafety.com*. Boulder, CO.
36. Heatherington, M. & Weiler, J. (2009). *Authoritarianism & polarization in American politics*. New York, NY: Cambridge University Press.
37. McWilliams, M, (2020). Trump is an authoritarian. So are millions of Americans. *Politico*. https://www.politico.com/news/magazine/2020/09/23/trump-america-authoritarianism-420681.

Part IV

The Followers of Trump

Thus far our inquiry in this book has explored a triangulation (Figure 1.1) that is a rigorous approach to understanding the United States as a political entity in the first quarter of the twenty-first century. Our focus has been on Trump, on charismatic leadership in general, on how these relate to Trump and those who may be labeled sycophants and enablers, and in turn, on the role ideologies play in politics and governance. Together, these have provided many insights.

This exploration still leaves open the question about why tens of millions of loyal Trump followers and voters, who may not approve of him as a person or of his morality and ethics, still steadfastly identify with his pursuit of their often single or few focused interests. As long as he is doing "their" work, they remain loyal. Understanding the psychodynamics of a charismatic leader and his followers is the focus of the next three chapters.

12 The Sentience of Followership

There is a clear psychodynamic link between the ideology and promotion of deregulation (Chapter 11) and the topic of sentience (emotion-based thought and action in groups) discussed here. We have established how emotion ladened ideology underlies the disastrous but repeated story of deregulation since the 1980's. The last two decades and the Age of Trump offer those trying to understand the American political scene a broad spectrum of dynamics that are being explored from many perspectives limited only by the imagination of historians, political analysts, and mental health professionals. A perspective that offers new and different insights is one grounded in an inspection of the role that sentience plays in understanding contemporary American politics. Sentience, as will be discussed, is the capacity to feel, perceive, or experience subjectively as compared to thinking and rationality.

To begin this inspection, it is necessary to touch upon an abbreviated overview of the development of conservative thought, complemented by the work of contemporary conservative thought leaders, and the realities of the right and far-right as represented, for example, by the Freedom Caucus and its parallels in state and local government. A review of the many conservative perspectives, ideologies, and positions yields a sense of dissonance and disagreement. Conservatism (or constitutional originalism in law) is not a monolithic, internally consistent philosophy or set of positions, but rather a fragmented and internally inconsistent set or values, positions, and ideologies that have changed over time to support political imperatives aimed at achieving power and control.

The Fragmented and Inconsistent
Nature of U.S. Conservatism

David Brooks, who is a noted conservative intellectual and columnist, notes, "As conservatism has become a propagandistic, partisan movement it has become less vibrant, less creative and less effective." He continues, "For years, middle- and working-class Americans have been suffering from stagnant wages, meager opportunity, social isolation, and household fragmentation. Shrouded in obsolete ideas from the Reagan years, conservatism had nothing to offer these people because it didn't believe in using government as a tool for social good. Trump demagogy filled the void."[1]

Brooks' perspective is supported by the research of Lupton, Meyers, and Thornton who hypothesize, "Perhaps Republican elites speak abstractly because the broad language of 'limited government' and 'freedom' that appeals to conservative sensibilities successfully unites actors who do not agree on policy." They wanted to test this possibility. "To test these theories, we used the Convention Delegate Study – surveys of delegates to the national party conventions in 2000 and 2004 – to examine party attitudes. We looked at convention delegates because they are party activists who shape party platforms and mass public opinion." They found that the Democrats are significantly more ideologically unified than the Republicans. "The results are stark. More than 80 percent of Democrats offered an ideologically 'correct' response to six or more of the 10 policy issues we examined; only 60 percent of Republicans responded in a way that was consistent with their party's ideology."[2]

Consistent with this research, Jonah Goldberg in an article in the *National Review* notes, "I think this is because conservatism isn't a single thing. Indeed, as I have argued before, I think it's a contradictory thing, a bundle of principles married to a prudential and humble appreciation of the complexity of life and the sanctity of successful human institutions."[3] Mike Lofgren offers additional insight, "All political movements display a degree of ideological inconsistency if they are to persuade different groups with varying interests to support them, but the conservative movement embodies so many seemingly impossible contradictions that it would appear unlikely to survive, let alone control three branches of the federal government and nearly two-thirds of state governorships and legislatures."[4]

Lofgren continues: "Let's unpack some of the contradictions. Donald Trump did not hijack American conservatism; in him it reached its logical culmination. The defining characteristics of post-1980 conservatism – its authoritarianism; denigration of reason and education; obsession with power at all costs; Manichean, black and white thinking; apocalyptic, religious fundamentalist mentality; paranoia and sense of being besieged even when in power; and gangsterish deceit, bad faith, and lack of principle, whether practiced by a transparent swindler like Trump or a supposed intellectual like Newt Gingrich – must lead to nihilism and mindless destruction."[4]

Recently considerations like those Lofgren expressed have led to some noteworthy desertions from the Republican Party, such as Joe Scarborough, George Will, and Steve Schmidt. There are many who are uncertain about their affiliation, such as David Brooks, Bill Kristol, Michael Steele, David Frum, Arnold Schwarzenegger, John Kasich, Jeff Flake, Max Boot (a Never Trumper), Jennifer Rubin, Charles Krauthammer before his death and of course the Bush family.[5] Polarization, it seems, has locked Trump supporters in and conservative thought leaders out.

Given the above assertions of a fragmented and internally inconsistent set of values, positions, and ideologies, the notion of shared feelings in the form of sentience groups – where what is valued, thought and believed is not per se the product of careful consideration but rather values, thoughts, and beliefs consistent with consciously and unconsciously shared feelings – sentience becomes the foundation for the various conservative political ideologies. Shared subjective and intersubjective experience can form a geographically distributed and strongly bonded but most often undiscussable political sentience group.[6] Sentience groups provide insights both into the polarized "us versus them" nature of recent politics on the right and the opposite end of the political spectrum, left or liberal sentience.

We now turn to an abbreviated overview of conservatism and far-right politics which draws upon the work of Roger Scruton, *Conservatism: An Invitation to the Great Tradition*,[7] the work of Russell Kirk as overviewed by McLeod and Adam Smith[8] as discussed by the Adam Smith Institute.[9]

Historical Perspective

Roger Scruton, in discussing conservative historical thought, writes:

> Liberals saw political order as issuing from individual liberty; conservatives saw individual liberty as issuing from political order. What makes a political order legitimate, in the conservative view, is not the free choices that create it, but the free choices that it creates. The question of which comes first, liberty or order, was to divide liberals from conservatives for the next two hundred years. But in due course new threats came to unite them, not the least of them being the growth of the modern state.[10]

Scruton maintains that: "Jefferson is important in the history of conservatism for his insistence on continuity and custom as necessary conditions for successful constitution building, and also for his warnings against the centralisation of political power."[11] He continues: "In particular consistent with Edwin Burke the organization of modern society is highly dependent on the continuity of religion and family as forms of collective wisdom where excessive belief in individualism arising from the chaos of the French Revolution is to be avoided in order to defend social inheritance."[11]

Conservatism is deeply rooted in the maintenance of traditional social norms embedded in religion, family, natural law, and maintenance of this "order." Its defense against encroachment by progressive change is essential to protect against chaotic change to the desired order. Some contemporary aspects of chaotic change are exemplified by fluid sexual identity (LGBTQ), social justice, racial equality, the embrace of the "alien others," and the orthodoxy of multiculturalism, where some Americans are said to no longer feel "at home in their own country," even though America was founded by immigrants from around the world. Chua and Rubenfeld write: "The causes of America's resurgent tribalism are many. They include seismic demographic change, which has led to predictions that whites will lose their majority status within a few decades; declining social mobility and a growing class divide; and media that reward expressions of outrage. All of this has contributed to a climate in which every group in America—minorities and whites; conservatives and liberals; the working class and elites—feels under attack, pitted against the others not just for jobs and spoils, but for the right to define the nation's identity. In these conditions, democracy devolves into a zero-sum competition, one in which parties succeed by stoking voters' fears and appealing to their ugliest us-versus-them instincts."[12] These considerations lead us to explore the notion of moral sentiments.

The Theory of Moral Sentiments

Eamonn Butler, co-founder and Director of the Adam Smith Institute and the author of *The Condensed Wealth of Nations* and *The Incredibly Condensed Theory of Moral Sentiments* provides an overview of Adam Smith's theory. Per the Adam Smith Institute website (www.adamsmith.org) the following briefly summarizes some of the cogent points of this theory.

> The Theory of Moral Sentiments was a real scientific breakthrough. It shows that our moral ideas and actions are a product of our very nature as social creatures. It argues that this social psychology is a better guide to moral action than is reason. It identifies the basic rules of prudence and justice that are needed for society to survive, and explains the additional, beneficent, actions that enable it to flourish.[9]

Regarding self-interest and sympathy, the site offers:

> As individuals, we have a natural tendency to look after ourselves. That is merely prudence. And yet as social creatures, explains Smith, we are also endowed with a natural sympathy – today we would say empathy – towards others. When we see others distressed or happy, we feel for them – albeit less strongly. Likewise, others seek our empathy and feel for us. When their feelings are particularly strong, empathy prompts them to restrain their emotions to bring them into line with our, less intense reactions. Gradually, as we grow from childhood to adulthood, we each learn what is and is not acceptable to other people. Morality stems from our social nature.[9]

Adam Smith's *Theory of Moral Sentiments*[9] as the foundation of human communities based in social psychology supports what is said to be conservatism however defined and operationalized over time. These shared moral sentiments that provide often out of awareness but strong bonds for members of the conservative way in politics must be further explored, beginning with a greater understanding of sentience.

Sentience

Sentience offers an important perspective in terms of understanding the conservative "mind" and individual and group identity. To begin with, sentience as a concept needs definition and clarification.

> Sentience is the capacity to feel, perceive or experience subjectively. Eighteenth-century philosophers used the concept to distinguish the ability to think (reason) from the ability to feel (sentience). In modern Western philosophy, sentience is the ability to experience sensations (known in philosophy of mind as "qualia"). This is distinct from other aspects of the mind and consciousness, such as creativity, intelligence, sapience, self-awareness, and intentionality (the ability to have thoughts about something).[13]

Malcolm Pines quotes Miller and Rice who discuss the concept of "sentient group." They write: "We shall therefore talk of sentient system and sentient group to refer to that system or group that demands and receives loyalty from its members; and we shall talk of sentient boundary to refer to the boundary round a sentient group or sentient system."[14,15]

Trist and Murray write:

> In the basic assumptions Bion (1961) describes the situation in which the sentience of the roles taken by the members of a group in the task system may or may not be stronger than other possible sentient systems. If the sentient systems of the individual members coalesce, that is, individual members find common group sentience, then the group can be said to be behaving as if it had made a basic assumption. If the common group sentience is opposed to task performance, that is, the control is not maintained by task leadership, other leaders will be found.[16,17]

This appreciation may in part contribute insight into Trump's election and his intensely loyal followers. An "other" leader has been found.

Yet another perspective is offered by Trist and Murray who write:

> In general, the larger the number of members of a group, the more members there are to find an outlet for their non-task related sentience,

and hence the more powerful can be its expression, and the more support can an alternative leader obtain. Equally, because of the large number, the more futile and useless can group behavior appear when there is no sentient unanimity among the membership either in support of or in opposition to, group task performance. In other words, *the larger the group the more opportunities members have to divest themselves of their unwanted or irrelevant sentience, by projecting it into or many others* (Emphasis added).[16]

Trump rallies filled with loyalists appear to be consistent with this as well as white supremacy (white power) gatherings such as occurred in Charlottesville, Virginia in 2017.

Colman and Bexton conceptualize group sentience as: "The existence of a group presupposes some emotional investment by its members in the identity of the group and hence in the preservation of the boundary round it. Groups vary on the extent to which they invest emotionally in their boundaries; in other words, some groups are more important to their members than others are, or to use a different terminology some groups have more sentience than others."[18]

Wilfred Bion was aware of the emotional and irrational side of groups. "The situation I have described was an emotional situation and is not easily conveyed by an account of the words used. It is this kind of episode that I am talking about when I speak of the group coming together as a group."[19] He also notes,

> To recapitulate: any group of individuals met together for work show work-group activity, that is, mental functioning designed to further the task in hand, occasionally furthered, by emotion drives of obscure origin. A certain cohesion is given to these anomalous mental activities if it is assumed that emotionally the group acts as if it had certain basic assumptions about it aims.[20]

Michael Diamond writes about organizational identity from the perspective of object relations theory. He describes organizational identity as "a psychodynamic concept for understanding the relational forces at work between individual members and their organizations."[21] He further notes that anyone wishing to understand group and organizational dynamics must:" … analyze cognitive, emotional, experiential, and associational patterns of networked relationships. These make up the structure and culture of and organizational systems, or what I call organizational identity."[22] And he notes, using an object relations theory perspective, that understanding organizational identity requires focusing on the intersubjective structure of self and other, subject and object. He continues, "Individual introjections and projections of self and others (external objects) shape how individual members come to identify themselves as belonging to a communal group or organization."[23]

This emphasis on organizational identity directs our attention to considering the underlying unconscious psychodynamics that leads to group and organizational dynamics, including the attraction of the underlying group sentience and shared conservative group bonds among conservatives. There are many possible conservative groups that this appreciation applies to where group members both consciously and unconsciously identify with the larger sense of what the group symbolizes, such as white power and supremacy including their underlying feeling states.

In Sum

Conservative thought emphasizes the need for historical continuity and social norms that must be defended from progressive social change, where the underlying "emotional energy" to steadfastly mount this cherished defense of a social fabric arises from the emotional bonding that arises from sentience groups. These insights provide important understanding to contemporary "tribal" identity politics that is fueled by splitting and projection and movements against the opposing groups and ideologies. There are many ways this understanding informs political dynamics in what some might say during the Age of Trump is the new GOP (Grand Old Party) or POT (Party of Trump). This perspective of group sentience and identity informs our understanding of our contemporary political scene. We now use a few concrete examples selected from among the many possibilities to illustrate this approach.

Fight or Flight Sentience Groups

Fight or flight in response to threatening signal anxiety is highly invested with emotions such as fear, anger, and rage. They are in their essence primitive responses to perceived threat.[24] Wilford Bion, as framed by Margaret Rioch, speaks of basic assumption groups. Rioch writes of the fight–flight basic assumption group:

The assumption is that the group has met to preserve itself and that this can be done only by fighting someone or something or by running away from someone or something. Action is essential whether for flight or for flight. The individual is of secondary importance to the preservation of the group. Both in battle and in flight the individual may be abandoned [sacrificed] for the sake of the survival of the group.[25]

Casualties and collateral damage are to be expected.

She continues,

A leader is even more important than in other basic assumption groups because the call for action requires a leader. The leader who is felt to be appropriate to this kind of group is one who can mobilize the group for attack or lead it in flight. He is expected to recognize danger and enemies. He should represent and spur on to courage and self-sacrifice. He should have a bit of a paranoid element in his makeup if he wishes to be successful, for this will ensure that if no enemy is obvious, the leader will surely find one.[25]

She concludes by noting that the fight or flight group is fundamentally anti-intellectual and steadfastly avoids self-reflection and the development of awareness of its group life. There is in this appreciation the basis for blind and adoring followership, where the leader and his or her decisions are preferably never questioned, out of fear of losing the leader or being destroyed by the powerful leader who largely exists in fantasy supported by psychological splitting, projection, and transference.

The conservative "mind" offers us in the present opportunities to anchor the shared fight/flight (fear, anger, and rage) sentience group in what is we hope accurate reality testing. The following outline list is offered both to anchor this sentience group in reality and to do so in what is an abbreviated but accessible manner.

Our contemporary political leadership (Trump, GOP, POT) fulfills these requirements of providing enemies to be feared (seemingly the rest of the world at the present) who must preferably be attacked at almost any social, moral, and ethical cost to the nation. The following list of fight or flight enemies illustrates the paranoid nature of current events.

- Anti-diversity such as relative to higher education or hiring, opposition to affirmative action
- Conservatives leaders being victimized by the "liberal" and fake news media
- An appeal to defending society in the form of law and order (police, ICE, FBI, CIA, military) to protect against the many forms that our enemies may take, including infants, children, mothers, race-based violence, and terrorists
- Sanctions and tariffs to protect against evil others and unfair trade
- Fear of loss of gun rights and guns
- Building a wall to keep out alien others who rape and pillage
- Shutting down legal immigration by severely limiting numbers and discrimination against countries who are said to harbor enemies
- Protection of religion and Christians from political correctness
- Protection from Muslim Sharia Law
- Protection of "right to life"
- Promotion of anger, rage, fear, and aggression such as was on display at the Nazi torch light parade in Charlottesville, VA (2017) – and with some frequency at Trump rallies
- Protecting the nation from kneeling football players who are protesting the lack of social justice for minorities

- Provision of work requirements for those receiving social safety net benefits to protect taxpayers from the "takers," including now blocking green card holders from accessing lawful services

These points highlight some of the many elements of the powerful forces resident in the pervasive presence of fight/flight fear and anger-driven political group dynamics contributed to by splitting and projection. These elements and the underlying fight or flight sentience group is heavily relied upon to motivate conservative voters. Only "I" can save you, as Trump said.

Fight or Flight Sentience Groups – In Sum

Fight or flight basic assumption sentience groups contain members who feel or can be made to feel threatened and fearful, leading to their quest to locate a paranoid charismatic leader who mobilizes their fear into fight or flight against one or many enemies. These directions of movement are like Karen Horney's three directions of psychologically defensive movement – toward a leader, against a threat and away as in flight from a threat. Our focus in this chapter is primarily on using basic assumption groups to examine group responses to threats and fear and their dependence on leaders who direct their attention to the threats promoting fear and dependence on the leader who can "save them."

These anti-intellectual non-reflective groups are fueled by strong emotional bonds that are manipulated by the leader. This "emotional energy" is released at the direction of this leader into all out and unrelenting attacks on the threatening other or political context invest with split off and projected disowned "bad" aspects of self and group experience. This then may be said to be a sentience group where the sentiment is rather clear. It may then also be contrasted with notions such as hope and thoughtful reflective leadership that promotes reasoned and measured responses, as modeled in large part by President Obama.

Other basic assumption sentience groups such as dependency and pairing may arise either serially of concurrently where, for example, the most motivated fight group still holds out hope for a leader who will meet their dependency needs. There are additional illustrative fight or flight sentience groups – left or right to be explored below.

Special Interest Group Sentience Based on Fight or Flight

Special interest groups can take many forms within the large, diverse, and complex societies of today. They are often filled with natural divisions such as race, age, sex-based differences, conflicting ideology, and religious perspectives to list but a few of the almost unlimited possibilities. We have selected five of these possibilities for brief inspection of their underlying sentiment-based nature.

Economic Sentient Groups

In the present the widespread economics of insecurity and scarcity (food, clothing, and shelter and more recently water and clean air) contrast with the top 10%, or 5% or 1% or even .01% at the top of the economic well-being pyramid. The sentience of being poor, disadvantaged and in harm's way is underscored by the rural and urban poverty so plainly visible as highlighted often by high crime rates, run down public housing, the presence of illegal drugs, homeless people and adult children still living at home, to list but some of the stereotypical categories of being poor and impoverished.

These many individuals share in common life experience that allows them, across all settings, to know each other's life experience, feeling empathy, and sharing insight and understanding. The feeling states that are often associated with these experiences are anger if not at times rage, fear, and vulnerability, and being discounted and discarded. These life experiences which naturally lead to a deeply felt sense of fight or flight are evoked by what often seems to be a humiliating socially imposed and reinforced dependency (Romney's 47% of takers discussed below). The sentiments of this large amorphous group of people are clear and most often unchanging across decades. Fighting to stay alive and raise families and fleeing from disparagement, rejection, and social discounting are the norms. Bion's remaining two basic assumption groups – dependency and pairing are discussed below as they also shed light on this sentience group.

In contrast the well off, wealthy, and super wealthy "want not." They have access to healthcare, education, expensive and safe living settings, unlimited nutrition and to a large extent non-threatening lives of leisure. For this group perhaps the main fear is loss of these many quality of life markers. From an ideological perspective avoiding taxation is a top priority. After all, wealth redistribution for this group is seen as inherently unfair. Flight into gated communities and fighting against redistributive taxation are well-established phenomena made possible by their wealth.

In sum, economically based special interest groups in a broad sense share in common fear, anger, and fight or flight dynamics that become the basis for their respective but quite different underlying sentient groups. And to be appreciated these different sentience groups often feel attacked by and fearful of the "other" opposing sentience group. Many of these same sentience dynamics are present in other special interest groups which we will now consider.

Social Change Sentience Groups

Immigration nationally and internationally has become a powerful organizing issue felt in the northern hemisphere where losses of white power and social supremacy are feared. White and national identity have become fused yielding anxiety, fear, and anger, provoking fight or flight sentiments of "us versus them." There lies within this a sense of existential anxiety. The presence of masses of immigrants threatens to flip the composition of the population of northern countries from white majority to not being majority white within a few decades in the United States. The highly energized response by the most threatened sentience groups (white nationalists for example) is to minimize and limit immigration, build border defenses, and enforce laws that limit the impact of immigration, and failing that to cause immigrants to adopt the ways of their host countries. France is an example. The burqa has been banned and the ban upheld by the European Courts.[26]

Immigrants in search of safe places to raise families, including some degree of economic wellbeing, experience themselves being unfairly discounted and discriminated against and redefined as violent threats and economic burdens. The sentiments that these victimized individuals share is clear.

In sum, we are once again left to consider the powerful role of fear and anger in forming sentience groups that resort to fight or flight group dynamics. Immigrants of non-white ethnic groups threaten white power and supremacy and must be defended against by striking back. Vulnerable immigrants including "boat people" from Vietnam or more recently from the Middle East and north Africa arriving in Greece and Italy are in flight from their dangerous native lands and must essentially attack borders (group boundaries) to gain access to safety and quality of life.

Law and Order Sentience Groups

"Law and order" as general precepts are in a sense prerequisite to civilization. However, in recent times on the "right" these notions and words are more likely be understood as racist "dog whistles" where the stereotypes are associated with people of color, who reside in drug and gang infested areas. For instance, Trump references Chicago as a city in need of law and order. More generally immigrants are lumped into the stereotypical catch-all for the use of the dog whistle. The MS-13 gang is often mentioned. Mara Salvatrucha (MS-13) is an international criminal gang that arose in Los Angeles, California, in the 1970s and 1980s to protect Salvadoran immigrants from other gangs. Fear is being promoted by a paranoid leader to mobilize this sentience group.

Law and order may then appeal to fearful and angry sentience groups who are made to feel more fearful, and politicians, usually on the right side of the political spectrum, mobilize these groups to vote for them as proponents of "law and order." Fear and anger and fight or flight sentience groups must, it seems, be continually reminded to feel angry and frightened, by politicians eager to keep this sentience group cohesive and motivated to vote. However, paradoxically the "right" that does not want to fund government is distressed at the cost of maintaining one of the world's largest prison populations. There is in this an appreciation for the confounding lack of internal consistency on the conservative right in terms of meeting the needs of the various sentience groups they rely on for votes. In contrast, those who are subjected to laws and their selective rigorous enforcement feel threatened, repressed, fearful, and angry about being hunted down and with some frequency, shot, killed, or deported.

In sum, once again fight or flight sentience groups are present, and once again with quite different sources for the sentiments held. Paradoxically law and order are not always compatible with a notion like social justice as revealed by the response to the kneeling football players who oppose police violence.

Religious Sentience Groups and the Culture Wars

Last to be considered are sentience groups that form the basis for the culture wars. Getting it "right" on right to life, and the correct sexual identity, and bathrooms are the basis of strongly motivated sentience groups that have members who know they are absolutely right on what are historically intensely individual and personal aspects of life. Once again resident in these religion-based perspectives is a sense of fear about social change that requires both ancient and newly public issues to be suppressed. Maintaining the historical sense of social order preferred by Thomas Jefferson is essential where social change is to be feared, opposed, and defended against. The fight for and against social change is contemporarily recast as the "culture wars."

Once again anxiety, fear, and anger form a basis for a fight or flight response to social change and all its new and unfamiliar anxiety-evoking elements such as fluid sexual identity and LGBTQ related issues. As discussed above the conservative worldview essentially requires maintaining an uninterrupted continuity from past to present to future. Many forms of change are felt to be threatening and must be fought against. At the same time those who seek change also feel under attack, fearful and must fight back. For this group flight and submission are not good options.

Fight or Flight Sentience Groups – In Sum

These five types of sentience groups based on anger (fight) and fear (flight) are common in the United States and world-wide and to be noted splitting and projection contribute by creation an "all good" self-experience and an "all bad" knowledge of the "other." At an extreme they yield fascist regimes and ethnic cleansing, and genocide.[27,28] We hope this discussion makes clear the relevance of sentience and basic assumption groups such as fight or flight that are the drivers of the culture wars on both sides of the divide. An overview of the liberal worldview as a basis of sentience groups is next explored from the perspective of the basic assumption sentience groups – dependency and pairing.

The Sentience of The Left/Liberal World View

If fight or flight seems to capture much of the essence of conservatism and far right politics then, in contrast, Obama's theme of HOPE in part captures the left side of the political sentience group divide. For many citizens the hope relative to the left/liberal political worldview is for some sense of empathy, caretaking, and support provided by a thoughtful leader and effective government that embraces the mission of furthering the wellbeing of all of its citizens all of the time. In contrast to this image, it is worth mentioning Ayn Rand's novel *Atlas Shrugged*. Ms. Rand is much admired by many on the right such as Alan Greenspan (the former Federal Reserve chairman) and Paul Ryan (Speaker of the House). Her novel embodies a worldview where a sense of compassion for others is lacking. It might reasonably be concluded that this is consistent with many of the positions conservatives have come to take, where the notion of economic justice on the right prevails (get a job) as compared to social justice on the left (a social safety net).[29]

An important question is posed by the false dichotomy put forward by Senator Mitt Romney that there are 47% who are the "taker class" who presumably victimize the "maker class" who have the resources to often bend government to their needs of building more wealth and paying fewer taxes. In his comments, Romney says: "these are people who pay no income tax," but they are people "who are dependent upon government, who believe that they are victims, who believe the government has a responsibility to care for them, who believe that they are entitled to health care, to food, to housing, to you-name-it."[29]

These paragraphs are worded not only to emphasize the differences between the stereotypical left/right split but also to emphasize the underlying valences of the sentience within the liberal world view. Given these valences, to be noted there are parallel elements to Bion's formulation of a second basic assumption group – the dependency group and the third basic assumption group pairing.

Margaret Rioch writes:

> The essential aim of the basic assumption dependency group is to attain security through and have its members protected by one individual. It assumes that this is why the group has met. The members act as if they know nothing, as if they are inadequate and immature creatures. Their behavior implies that the leader by contrast, is omnipotent and omniscient.[30]

There exists a shared fantasy that the leader can take care of everything for the group. Accompanying this fantasy is an idealization of the leader, who is encouraged to feel "god-like," which of course is seductive for the leader to buy into, although failure to meet all these expectations is inevitable. If the performance gap is too distressing a new leader may be sought out. There can be an overlap with fight or flight sentience groups in that, for example, being protected from alien others (immigrants, liberals), taxes and government regulation, also provides security, although fight or flight sentience is much more energized and usually the dominant sentience.

Regarding Bion's third basic assumption group Rioch writes, "The third basic assumption group is that of pairing. Here the assumption is that the group has met for the purpose of reproduction, to bring forth the Messiah, the Savior. Two people get together on behalf of the group to carry out the task of paring and creation."[31] She continues, "When this basic assumption is operative, the other group members are not bored. They listen eagerly and attentively to what is being said. *An atmosphere of hopefulness pervades the group* (Emphasizes added)."[31] There arises a pervasive hope that the creation or location of a new leader or thought will deliver the group from its past and present problems. The key element in this group is hopeful expectation, consistent with Obama's theme where the actual location of a leader willing to act is paradoxically not a particularly desirable outcome. Clearly Obama's theme was not fulfilled by the Republican Congress who blocked most of his efforts to improve the economy ironically to avoid deficits and provide healthcare for all citizens.

A proviso needs to be mentioned. All three sentient based basic assumption groups may be present at *both* ends of the political continuum – left or right. Members of a fight or flight group may also feel that it is the responsibility of government or society to care for many of their needs such as securing the food chain, creating jobs, or imposing steel tariffs to support local steel industry. Also, on the right there is clearly a sense of hope or wish for an authoritarian leader who will fulfill their ideological perspectives. And as discussed, the liberal-leaning citizens may wish to fight back against enemies foreign or domestic. In sum, typologies of any type should not suggest purity of the types or rule out fluidity in movement between the types, or the simultaneous embrace of opposing types. The world, society, and human nature are ultimately very messy, defying rigorous classification and insights.

This overview of the liberal left world view and its many sentience-based groups is admittedly brief but hopefully indicative. There is also in this discussion the basis for understanding both the dynamic collision of left and right sentience groups in the public sector, and private sector where families that gather for special occasions may now find that polarization creates too much tension for a peaceful gathering where tribal fight or flight may predominate.

In Conclusion

The argument made in this chapter is that sentience groups exist in many forms where the bonds are of an almost undiscussable emotional nature. Their sentient nature is often minimized by efforts to rationalize this shared experiential and affective reality by formulating compatible idealized ideological perspectives (backward engineering). These provide a more acceptable cognitive basis and action oriented (fight or flight) concealment and redirection of these emotion-based sentience groups. In the process much understanding is lost. The paranoid leader becomes especially important to conservative ideology. Enemies are everywhere and fighting them is better than fleeing. The leader who offers hope and caretaking seems to be consistent with the sentience on the left, to liberals, and to their political spectrum. These strong usually under recognized groups and their powerful social bonds have created a bimodal polarized distribution in societies that for the present, so long as they exist, will be exploited for acquisition of political power and control.

Chapter 13 provides important additional perspective in that Trump is often described as a "grievance leader" who symbolizes the grievances of his followers. This context of grievance is so pervasive that it may be called a *culture of grievance*.

Notes

1. Brooks, D. (2016). The conservative intellectual crisis. *The New York Times*. https://www.nytimes.com/2016/10/28/opinion/the-conservative-intellectual-crisis.html.
2. Lupton, R., Myers, W. & Thornton, J. (2017). Republicans are the party of ideological inconsistency. *Washington Post*. https://www.washingtonpost.com/news/monkey-cage/wp/2017/10/02/republicans-are-the-party-of-ideological-inconsistency/.
3. Goldberg, J. (2015). When we say 'Conservative,' we mean... *National Review*. https://www.nationalreview.com/g-file/conservatism-definition-difficult-produce/.
4. Lofgren, M. (2018). Will conservatism end in nihilism? Disaster lies not in Trump, but in the conservative dream fulfilled. *Washington Monthly*. https://washingtonmonthly.com/2018/01/03/will-conservatism-end-in-nihilism/.
5. Coren, M. (2016). Here's a running list of all the Republicans withdrawing their support for Donald Trump. *Quartz*. https://qz.com/804528/the-republican-leaders-who-no-longer-endorse-trump/.
6. Diamond, M.A. (2017). *Discovering organizational identity: Dynamics of relational attachment*. Columbia, MO: University of Missouri Press.
7. Scruton, R. (2018). *Conservatism: An invitation to the great tradition* [E-book]. New York, NY: All Points Books.
8. McLeod, A. (2005). *Great conservative minds: A condensation of Russell Kirk's "The conservative mind."* Birmingham, AL: Alabama Policy Institute.
9. Adam Smith Institute. (2011). *The incredibly condensed theory of moral sentiments*. Adamsmith.org.
10. Scruton, R. (2018). *Conservatism: An invitation to the great tradition* [E-book]. New York, NY: All Points Books, location 389.

11. Scruton, R. (2018). *Conservatism: An invitation to the great tradition* [E-book]. New York, NY: All Points Books, location 547.
12. Chua, A. & Rubenfeld, J. (2018). The threat of tribalism. *The Atlantic.* 322(3).
13. Sentience. (2021, May 21). In *Wikipedia.* https://en.wikipedia.org/wiki/Sentience.
14. Pines, M. (Ed.) (2000). *Bion and group psychotherapy.* London: Jessica Kingsley Publishers..
15. Miller, E.J., & Rice, A.K. (1967). *Systems of organization: The control of task and sentient boundaries.* London: Tavistock.
16. Trist, E. & Murray, H. (Eds). (1990). *The social engagement of social science: A Tavistock anthology.* Philadelphia, PA: The University of Pennsylvania Press, 277. https://books.google.com/books?id=QG8_CwAAQBAJ&pg=PA277&lpg=PA277&d-q=sentience+group+Bion&source=bl&ots=jD07zH5Ifq&sig=9P6xK7ds-4RKL7WMnX8IBan224Ms&hl=en&sa=X&ved=2ahUKEwjFsJaZqovdA-hUJZKwKHRlWAecQ6AEwBXoECAUQAQ#v=onepage&q=sentience%20group%20Bion&f=false.
17. Bion, W. (1961). *Experience in groups.* London: Tavistock.
18. Colman, A. & Bexton, W. (Eds.) (1975). *Group relations reader.* Sausalito, CA: Grex.
19. Bion, W. (1961). *Experience in groups.* London: Tavistock, 69.
20. Bion, W. (1961). *Experience in groups.* London: Tavistock, 188.
21. Diamond, M.A. (2017). *Discovering organizational identity: Dynamics of relational attachment.* Columbia, MO: University of Missouri Press, 3.
22. Diamond, M.A. (2017). *Discovering organizational identity: Dynamics of relational attachment.* Columbia, MO: University of Missouri Press, 5.
23. Diamond, M.A. (2017). *Discovering organizational identity: Dynamics of relational attachment.* Columbia, MO: University of Missouri Press, 19.
24. Allcorn, S. (1994). *Anger in the workplace: Understanding the causes of aggression and violence.* Westport, CT: Quorum Books.
25. Colman, A. & Bexton, W. (Eds.) (1975). *Group relations reader.* Sausalito, CA: Grex, 26.
26. Weaver, M. (2018). Burqa bans, headscarves and veils: a timeline of legislation in the west European states have moved over the years to outlaw Muslim headwear in public. *The Guardian.* https://www.theguardian.com/world/2017/mar/14/headscarves-and-muslim-veil-ban-debate-timeline.
27. Stanley, J. (2018). *How fascism works: The politics of us and them.* New York, NY: Random House.
28. Applebaum, A. (2020). *Twilight of democracy: The seductive lure of authoritarianism.* New York, NY: Doubleday.
29. Klein, E. (2012) Romney's theory of the "taker class," and why it matters. *Washington Post.* https://www.washingtonpost.com/news/wonk/wp/2012/09/17/romneys-theory-of-the-taker-class-and-why-it-matters/.
30. Colman, A. & Bexton, W. (Eds.) (1975). *Group relations reader.* Sausalito, CA: Grex, 24.
31. Colman, A. & Bexton, W. (Eds.) (1975). *Group relations reader.* Sausalito, CA: Grex, 27.

13 A Culture of Grievance

Creating Polarization
from Chosen Traumas

The political "right" in many countries, including the United States, is experiencing a resurgence especially during the Age of Trump. Trump has assembled a durable and motivated cadre of special interest groups that pursue ideologies that include the minimization of federal, state, and local governments, and taxes so low as to promote the privatization of roads, education, and public services. These groups include some elements of the military and militarized police, anti-immigrant/pro-whites, and the infamous culture wars largely based in ultra conservative religious beliefs that include opposition to birth control and abortion. These special interests have been pursued for many decades, but successes have been elusive. This has compounded the sense of grievance that can be understood as a form of continual retraumatization arising from historically political, economic, and social traumas. Understanding the historical and current aspects this *culture of grievance*, and the accompanying special interest group's feelings of marginalization, contribute insight into the causes but not likely the cures of this social dynamic in the United States in the twenty-first century.

The sweeping nature of this line of inquiry led to narrowing the documentation of these social dynamics to two recent books – Thomas Frank's *What's the Matter with Kansas? How Conservatives Won the Heart of America*[1] and Arlie Hochschild's *Strangers in Their Own Land: Anger and Mourning on the American Right.*[2] They will serve as our "case" studies and "data." The work of these two authors is complemented by additional commentary and insights drawn from other contemporary sources. A review of all this content contributes to locating organizing precepts that not only ground what is discussed here but also provide a basis to develop a theoretical understanding of what makes cultures of grievance so powerful and enduring.

The following encapsulation of the work of these two authors provides insights into the past and present depth of the culture of grievance they describe. Reading about Kansas and Louisiana gradually reveals that the people described are being victimized by their leaders – wealthy people, corporations, and conservative politicians. These leaders have located traumas that resonate with the "people," and they have exploited them to motivate them to vote for conservative causes and politicians. These traumas are "chosen traumas" in the sense that they are present in history and magnified in the present.[3] These traumas are pursued by conservative politicians in terms of getting traction with enough people to "authorize" these politicians to fulfill their ideological vision for the future. These overviews of the books are then examined using the theoretical perspectives of Vamik Volkan followed by speculations about the near-term future.

Thomas Frank – What's the Matter with Kansas?: How Conservatives Won the Heart of America

Frank asks and answers the question, why is Kansas so conservative? One contributing explanation is its trending demographics. Kansas and many relatively rural states (North and South Dakota, Maine are examples) have aging populations that are older, white, and homogeneous and are moving these states to the right. This trend has been accentuated by the departure of younger adults. The effect of street drugs (disability, early death, and inability to pass drug screening for employment) combined with fewer well-paying jobs (automation, farm mechanization, corporate farming) and lower levels of education and training and access to the internet (infrastructure) have led to a migration of younger people to cities.

These trends are reinforced by seductive ideologies such as free markets, deregulation, tax cuts, small government, and laissez-faire pro-capitalism, supported by billionaires who limit their taxes that might pay for better education, training, and infrastructure. Corporate and anti-labor interests reign supreme.

David Koch provided nearly $900,000,000 to help right-wing candidates and causes in 2016 alone. Charles Koch says: "To bring about social change… requires a strategy [that uses] vertically and horizontally integrated [planning] from idea creation to policy development to education to grassroots organizations to lobbying to litigation to political action."[4] Big money is being used to create well-organized conservative cultural and economic change. Frank also emphasizes the same two underlying elements of Kansas conservatism – culture and economics.

Cultural Policy

He frames the Kansas problem as backlash to unfulfilled political promises related to the culture wars mobilized by explosive social issues. At the same time "culture wars" that are fundamentally opposed to social change (anti-liberal change, anti-intellectualism) take the form of opposition to abortion, gay marriage, and LGBTQ issues such as bathroom privileges. They are also pro-patriot, flag, church, and traditional family values. This led in Kansas to a significant shift from moderate conservatism (conservative fiscal policy and moderate social policy) to a hard right conservative fiscal and social policy orientation. The liberal left is identified as "not us" and an enemy that evokes a sense of being looked down upon and judged as deficient ethically, morally, and in terms of depth of knowledge (dumb red necks). Conservative identity is threatened. This experience of being marginalized by the liberal, bi-coastal, and urban elites yields a lengthy list of grievances that form the foundation of a polarizing culture of grievance so prominently present today on the right. "They" not only do not understand "us," but they also look down on us for our values and beliefs. Frank notes: "...the Republicans are the party of the disrespected, the downtrodden, and the forgotten. They are always the underdog, always in rebellion against a haughty establishment, always rising up from below."[5]

Economic Policy

Frank notes that the primary contradiction of the backlash is: "it is a working-class movement that has done incalculable, historic harm to working-class people. The leaders of the backlash may talk Christ, but they walk corporate. Values may 'matter most' to voters, but they always take a backseat to the needs of money once the elections are won. This is a basic earmark of the phenomenon, absolutely consistent across its decades-long history."[6] The backlash includes imagined countless conspiracies where the wealthy, powerful, well-connected elites and the liberal media control their lives. Also, free markets and corporate interests often marginalize the economic wellbeing of rural economies creating fear, anger, and anxiety. These deeply felt emotions are displaced (redirected by rhetoric on the right) onto social change that is said to be controlled by liberal influences that must be stopped.

This polarization is further highlighted by Frank. "In the backlash imagination, America is always in a state of quasi-civil war: on one side are the unpretentious millions of authentic Americans; on the other stand the bookish, all-powerful liberals who run the country but are contemptuous of the tastes and beliefs of the people who inhabit it."[7] George W. Bush was embraced by the plain people of the heartland who see themselves as humble, guileless, and righteous. It is the "cosmopolitan" upper middle class that considers itself socially enlightened but know little of rural America. It is lattes versus the heartland and its kind, cheerful, loyal, down home working stiffs, who are tired of moral decay and the parasites taking advantage of the producers. This black and white depiction is underpinned by an array of psychological defense mechanisms such as splitting and projection, basic assumption groups, and narcissistic injuries, leading to Horney's expansive solutions and movement against the sources of the threats and anxiety.

The rural–urban split makes this sense of anger especially problematic in that rural voters have consistently voted against the interests of cities.[8,9] "In this tragic land unassuageable cultural grievances are elevated inexplicably over solid material ones, and basic economic self-interest is eclipsed by juicy myths of national authenticity and righteousness wronged."[10]

There is an overarching quality of historical grievance arising from unfilled Kansas voter expectations combined with a focus on cultural issues that eclipse economic wellbeing. Hochschild discovers much the same based on her extensive research in Louisiana in her recent book.

Arlie Hochschild – Strangers in Their Own Land: Anger and Mourning on the American Right

Hochschild is professor emeritus of sociology at the University of California, Berkeley who worked on her research which involved interviewing people in Louisiana for five years (2011–2016) becoming familiar with the culture and its people. Much of the content provided here is in the form of quotations from these interviews to ground what she learned in lived experience. She organizes what she learned around two guiding perspectives – strangers in their own land and paradoxes around zero sum tradeoffs (jobs versus pollution). These two perspectives speak to a larger psychosocial historical framing of life experience and to an almost cruel sense of personal, family, and social sacrifice of quality of life to polluting industries that provide valued jobs and a higher standard of living, albeit one that is feared may be compromised or lost at any time, leaving only sickness, death, and environmental devastation.

Those who lived in the area Louisiana Hochschild studied often expressed anxiety about the society they value. They felt they were strangers in a land where their identity, vision of America, and their valued way of life were being lost and they, as a "people," were fading out. Perceived threats from immigrants to jobs and social values, and a pervasive sense of being discounted and looked down on by educated bi-coastal elites, constitute much of the larger shared sense of becoming estranged. These perspectives are consistent with Judis who notes that that identities associated with their traditional jobs has faded and new identities have filled the void.[11] These are associated with hardline conservative politics: traditional (patriarchal) family values, church and religion, identification with flag and nation, and gun ownership. These new identities are interwoven with grievances about undocumented immigrants subsidized by their taxes who upend social values and even language and who disproportionately benefit from social programs. A distant elite in the cities disrespect them and their way of life and focus government programs on benefiting immigrants and minorities.

Alienation

Alienation speaks to a sense of being cut off from feeling connected to oneself, others, organizations, communities, and even countries ("take my country back" is a common phrase). These feelings of being isolated and alone are especially profound when they pertain to what one holds as cherished values and beliefs. This form of alienation contributes to understanding the current state of polarization in the United States and around the world. Hochschild writes: "You are a stranger in your own land. You do not recognize yourself in how others see you."[12] She continues, "They also felt culturally marginalized: their views about abortion, gay marriage, gender roles, race, guns, and the Confederate flag all were held up to ridicule in the national media as backward."[13] "I'm pro-life, pro-gun, pro-freedom to live our own lives as we see fit so long as we don't hurt others. And I'm anti–big government," Mike said. "Our government is way too big, too greedy, too incompetent, too bought, and it's not ours anymore. We need to get back to our local communities...."[14]

"Economically, culturally, demographically, politically, you are suddenly a stranger in your own land."[15] The Christian, working and middle class suffers from a sense of fading honor as a declining demographic group. Conservatives feel obliged to defend themselves from the idea that their views are, according to Hillary Clinton, "deplorable" and sexist, homophobic, old-fashioned, and backward. As one of her interviewees says: "Oh, liberals think that Bible-believing Southerners are ignorant, backward, rednecks, losers. They think we're racist, sexist, homophobic, and maybe fat."[16] Trump allows them to feel like a good moral American and superior to those who are critical of them.

Conservatives feel oppressed by liberal beliefs that are imposed on them by the PC thought police. They are seeking emotional freedom from liberal philosophy. "Liberals were asking them to feel compassion for the downtrodden in the back of the line, the 'slaves' of society. They didn't want to; they felt downtrodden themselves."[17] Massing (a journalist) says: "Maher [TV personality] portrayed evangelical Christians as a dim-witted group willing to make the most ludicrous theological leaps to advance their agenda.... As I watched, I tried to imagine how evangelicals would view this routine. I think they would see a secular elitist eager to assert what he considers his superior intelligence. They would certainly sense his contempt for the many millions of Americans who believe fervently in God, revere the Bible, and see Trump as representing their interests. Maher's diatribe reminded me of a pro-Trump acquaintance from Ohio who now lives in Manhattan and who says that New York liberals are among the most intolerant people he has ever met."[18] Massing also notes: "Many evangelicals feel themselves to be under siege. In a 2016 survey, 41% said it was becoming more difficult to be an evangelical. And many conservative Christians see the national news media as unrelievedly hostile to them."[18]

Hochschild offers the following observation which summarizes, the attachment of conservatives to Trump. Trump appeals: "to the right wing's good angels—their patience in waiting in line in scary economic times, their capacity for loyalty, sacrifice, and endurance—qualities of the deep story self."[19] Trump, Fox News, and radio personalities on the right provide validation of their identity and system of beliefs that are disrespected by liberal elites as a stereotype becoming targeted for splitting and projection projections and fighting back, led by a paranoid charismatic leader during the Age of Trump. For Hochschild's subjects white America is being edged out and white identity is being threatened by liberal elites. Alien others are also cutting in line in front of them.

Line Cutters

Line cutters are those who conservatives consider having cut in front of them to acquire government benefits when it is they who deserve them. Liberals, they assert, identify those to feel sorry for, but "we" are also victims. Many feel they are on shaky economic ground and vigorously oppose redistribution in the form of their taxes going to these needy others as defined by liberals. They feel that immigrants such as Filipinos, Mexicans, Arabs, Indians, and Chinese on special visas or green cards are ahead of them in line. Another element of this sense of victimization is that since the 1960s, white men have been being displaced by women as breadwinners. White male supremacy and patriarchy are being threatened on many fronts.

When Hochschild asked what was being given away: "It was not public waters given to dumpers, or clean air given to smokestacks. It was not health or years of life. It was not lost public sector jobs. What he [interviewee] felt was being given away was tax money to non-working, non-deserving people—and not just tax money, but honor too. If that tax money could come back to citizens—as a sort of 'raise' in the midst of a three-decade-long national economic lull, why not?"[20] Perhaps living life would be easier.

Toughing It Out

Yet another pronounced theme is the idea of remaining steadfast and resilient in the face of adversity. Many felt that being a good team player meant sacrifice, courage, bravery, toughing it out regarding pollution and property value losses. "Underlying all these other bases of honor—in work, region, state, family life, and church—was pride in the self of the deep story. The people I came to know had sacrificed a great deal and found honor in sacrifice"[21]

There is something positive about toughing it out, whether it relates to health problems or losses of financial wellbeing. Pride in this perspective is merited. However, it also creates a subtext of "We are better than you." relative to liberal "do gooders" and minorities on the public dole – "the takers" Romney referred to at a fund raiser. Also, to be noted is that "On the positive side, oil offers to restore lost honor. For if the plantation system brought shame to the South in the eyes of the nation, oil has brought pride."[22] But once again there is ambivalence. One homeowner reported when an oil company applied for permission to set up a 46-million-barrel tank farm half a football field away from his house no one could stop it and now selling it was not possible because its value sank.

But what about our tax money and that raise? Companies are lured to Louisiana using public resources. "This is the strategy Southern governors have used to lure textile firms from New England or car manufacturers from New Jersey and California, offering lower wages, anti-union legislation, low corporate taxes, and big financial incentives. For the liberal left, the best approach is to nurture new business through a world-class public infrastructure and excellent schools."[23] However, the financial incentives tended to strip communities of education resources and environmental regulators. In addition, big petrochemical plants are gradually automating production that eliminates the valued jobs leaving only devastation and despair.

The basis for feeling victimized, resentful, and immersed in a culture of grievance, is easy to identify here. Those who are toughing it out do so as somewhat passive and helpless victims of powerful corporate and political interests. Resistance seems futile (see later). Government, politicians, and corporate lobbyists are clearly a problem.

Anti-government

Conservatives and libertarians historically have been opposed to government in all its forms and at all levels. Defunding government by cutting taxes (revenue) as a means of shrinking the government (starve the beast) so it may be, as Grover Norquist advocates "drowned in a bathtub," has been pursued for decades but without success. Massive national debt has been created by this strategy. To be added to the mix is states' rights, federalism, the "neo-confederacy" and the rise of the Tea Party, libertarianism, and the Freedom Caucus. With regard to Bobby Jindal's election as governor of Louisiana, McLaughlin notes, "Like many Republican governors, Jindal came to office committed to four fiscal goals: lowering taxes, shrinking government, making government programs financially accountable, and improving the state's business climate so that the private sector could grow as the public sector shrank. Unlike some others, he meant it. Over eight years, he cut government at least as much as any American leader has done this century .... Jindal slashed state payrolls by 30,000 permanent employees (a third of the state work force), reduced the state's vehicle fleet, and privatized state hospitals, group homes, and prisons."[24]

The Tea Party movement founded in 2009 has pursued two goals: reversing progressive reform and dismantling the federal government, including getting rid of restrictive regulation – deregulation. One person interviewed "wanted to abolish state environmental agencies that he saw as "in the hip pocket of industry and couldn't give a damn whether you or I developed cancer, or our children are born with birth defects from the toxins that they allow to be spewed in our air and our water."[25] There is a profound sense of irony in defunding, deregulating, and delegitimizing government and then condemning government for not functioning as expected. In addition to defunding federal, state, and local government operations, nationwide infrastructure (roads and bridges are examples) is rapidly deteriorating with no funding in sight to maintain it. Much the same can be said for public schools and universities in conservative states that have had to drop programs and raise tuition to survive, thereby increasing student debt loads.

In sum, explored thus far are the many forms of threat and grievance resident in the Fox News audience that celebrates their news and opinion commentators, where "our deep story" is also "their" deep story. This deep story is made all the clearer by this vignette. Hochschild offers a fitting capstone to how a culture of grievance is created. She found that "The California Waste Management Board paid Cerrell Associates $500,000 to define communities that would not resist "locally undesirable land use" (LULU)."[26] The research revealed several key citizen characteristics that made them more vulnerable to being controlled and manipulated. The least resistant profile included:

- Longtime residents of small towns in the South or Midwest
- High school educated only
- Catholic
- Uninvolved in social issues
- Involved in mining, farming, ranching
- Conservative
- Republican
- Advocates of the free market

In contrast those who could be expected to be resistant to the oil industry fit a quite different profile.

- Young
- College educated
- Urban
- Liberal
- Strongly interested in social issues
- Believers in good government

There is something profound about this study being ordered and funded by a public agency. More profound are its findings that highlight the psychosocial divide that is the foundation of the nation's polarization. Through empathy readers might feel the essence of the exceptional vulnerability of those who are least resistant to being manipulated and targeted. The study also underscores how intense, unresolvable societal conflicts are created.

Conflicts

The conflict in Louisiana can be summed up as jobs versus health and environment, and the American Dream versus pelicans, frogs, and clean air and water. Incentives provided by the state to attract polluting industries (petrochemical) were funded by reallocating state funding for education and regulation that is thought to inhibit job creation. The environment and health of the workers and local communities becomes mired in the pollution as depicted by iconic pictures of pelicans helplessly covered with thick oil.

An interviewee remarked, "I remember sitting under the cypress for shade in the heat of the summer. The moss hanging on it was green then. Frogs could breathe and they could find all kinds of minnows. Then industry came in. It began to stink so bad you had to leave the windows down on hot nights. It killed the cypress and grass from here clear out to the Gulf."[27] There were for many of those interviewed a palpable sense of loss and threat.

Their faith had guided them through a painful loss of family, friends, neighbors, frogs, turtles, and trees. They felt God had blessed them with this courage to face their ordeals, and they thanked Him for that. Indeed, sitting in the shade enjoying life and nature seems like a distant memory in what is described as a post-apocalyptic reality.

> "The only one that didn't get cancer was my daddy," Harold says, "and he never worked in the plants. Everybody else—all us kids and our spouses that lived on these forty acres—come down with cancer."[28] "Janice Areno had accommodated environmental pollution through loyalty to job-providing industries and the party she identified with them. Jackie Tabor had accommodated it because it was 'the sacrifice we make for capitalism.' Donny accommodated out of respect for bravery. Each expressed a deep story self."[29] Reading these brief narratives cannot but provoke not only empathy and respect but also some deeper sense of complicity in their own demise, although the forces creating this outcome seem to be irresistible. According to *The Guardian*: "In 2015 the Pontchartrain Works facility was found to be the primary cause of some of the most toxic air in America, according to U.S. government findings. In the tract of land just behind the plant, residents in this mostly black and mostly poor town endure a risk of cancer due to air pollution that is the highest in the country and

50 times the national average."[30] But as one interviewee said, "But if I had to choose between the American Dream and a toad, hey, I'll take the American Dream."[31]

In Sum

These two authors, Frank and Hochschild, document the underlying nature of the "narrative" and polarization present today in the United States and around the world. An appreciation of the persistence of this narrative over time that is grounded in long histories, and the systemic complexity that links people in regions together that share a commonality in terms of life experience, must be acknowledged. The two books emphasized that "these good people" are being continually collectively victimized by right-wing political ideologies that work against their health, economic, and moral/religious interests. They are collectively aggrieved. They as a "people" are being diminished in number as a percentage of the population and, as the Cerrell Associates study indicates, they have been singled out as a vulnerable population of people who can be manipulated to the point that they are willing to die for a job. Their lives and livelihoods are continually at risk. The themes of fear and anger on the right clearly have a reality basis in the daily lives of the Trump and Fox News followers. Better understanding this pervasive sense of cultural grievance leads to considering the role of "chosen traumas" in creating societal and political polarization.[3]

Choosing Trauma(s) to Be Exploited

There is a three-step progression in awakening a sense of victimization, grievance, and traumatization to mobilize support for ideologically based pursuits of power and control in all cultures and forms of government. The first step is to promote *awareness of historical grievances* felt by a sufficiently large number of people to create a sense of a movement toward remediation on the part a people, culture, and nation. Step two is to promote a *shared fear and anger about the sources* of the ongoing victimization, grievances, and trauma. This is made more possible in the twenty-first century by corporate control of the media that may be exploited to create polarization for profit further enabled by social networking.[32] The objective of step two is to promote a sense of shared cultural grievance where hate, anger, and fear (emotions) are, in the third step, mobilized in the service of furthering the embrace of an ideology and support for a paranoid charismatic authoritarian leader (the chosen one) who may say, "Only I can save you."

A process such as this may be understood to *revictimize* those who share reawakened cultural grievances and trauma to mobilize their fears and anger to serve the purpose of a charismatic and paranoid leader. There is a very real sense of new and renewed victimization and persecutory anxiety accompanied by transference, furthering the reexperience in the present of past traumas transformed into a contemporary list of grievances to be acted on by members of the group (fight/flight and vindictive triumph, movement against) and exploited by a grievance leader.

During the Age of Trump this leader acts to serve the needs of the aggrieved by striving to achieve willful mastery, power, and control in political and social arenas relying on authoritarian methods. The creation of and exploitation of a culture of grievance based on selected historical (near term or distant past; real or mythologized), traumas that are reawakened, creates an intensely loyal national group of followers. This dynamic, as explained by Volkan and the second author involves a constellation of elements that are interdependent.

Historical Revisionism

Volkan makes a crucial distinction between what Donald Spence called "historical truth" and "narrative truth," that is, between what historically actually happened and the subsequent narrative elaborations, amplifications, omissions, distortions, and condensations of what happened when it is recounted.[33] The way history is used often differs from the way history happened. Past events become fused with the present, leading to a reliving of the imagined past events. Leaders who reactivate ancient "chosen traumas," raise the possibility of repairing past traumas by transferring them onto a present situation where they might be repaired.[34] "The process is less a matter of retrospective falsification, as it is a matter of retrospective mythologization."[34]

It is theoretically possible the "chosen trauma" need not have happened at all. Myth may become reality and the representation takes on a life of its own, as is becoming an abundant "reality" during the Age of Trump and its gaslighting, lying, and full embrace of conspiracy theories. Volkan makes the point that a "chosen glory" or "chosen trauma" may possess some "historical truth" – but the mythologized, elaborated, and amplified "narrative truth" may come to be experienced *as* "historical truth," and therefore real.[33,34] In sum, "Once a trauma becomes a chosen trauma (a shared mental representation), the historical truth about it is no longer consequential; the central role that the event plays in the group's [current] identity becomes more significant."[35] This outcome creates a basis for exploitation and underscores the nature of an alternate reality or facts for Trump, Fox News, and other right-wing media including social networks. "By searing historical as well as current grievances into historical memory, group members feel special, unique, and entitled by virtue of what they have endured together at the hands of their adversaries. Exclusion, disparagement, and a degree of persecution is used to justify and inflate the sense of specialness and superiority."[36]

Volkan goes on to note that, "Under normal conditions, with the passage of time, individuals mourn losses—of people, land, prestige—associated with past traumatic events and work through feelings of fear, helplessness, and humiliation. Mourning and working through the effects of an injury signify the gradual acceptance that a change has occurred."[37] However, this working through becomes compromised by a leader who chooses to exploit the trauma.

Historical revisionism – changing the past to meet a leader's needs of the present – may then be understood to be a powerful force in reshaping social memory to yield a more tolerable if not guilt-free narrative. The narrative reframing creates something a political party or society can eventually embrace, creating the basis for a mythologized chosen trauma and action based on it.

Chosen Traumas as the Bases for Political Action

A chosen trauma and its historical revision that becomes a shared mythology can be used by a paranoid, charismatic fight/flight leader who pledges to undo and reverse historical injuries and rebuild the groups identity by any means including autocratic authoritarian rule. Volkan writes, "I use the term chosen trauma to describe the collective memory of a calamity that once befell a group's ancestors. It is, of course more than a simple recollection; it is a shared mental representation of the event, which includes realistic information, fantasized expectations, intense feelings, and defenses against unacceptable thoughts."[38] He also notes, "Adopting a chosen trauma can enhance ethnic pride, reinforce a sense of victimization, and even spur a group to avenge its ancestors' hurts. The memory of the chosen trauma is used to justify ethnic aggression."[39] It is this dynamic that helps to explain how right-wing cultures of grievance can be transformed into legitimized attacks on liberal elites as well as on non-whites who represent an existential threat to white Christian identity and white nationalism. In sum, chosen traumas become a way of knowing and sensing life. "The group draws the mental representation of a traumatic event into its very identity."[40]

Political ideologies on the right, combined with packaging them with special interest groups and their various historical grievances, allows for the recasting of these groups and their members as victims of an elite, liberal, bi-coastal cabal that looks down on them for their cultural and social values. Fighting back against an identifiable enemy that has inflicted pain, suffering, and humiliation (traumas) and a threatened loss of identity becomes an imperative.[41,42] This reactivation of pain-filled life experiences that are linked to some immediate purpose of the leader can have dramatic and destructive consequences.

It is then the case during the Age of Trump that these grievance groups are continually reminded of their suffering and fear. Trump warns that there will be continued or worse suffering to come. This authorizes him to pursue any means to eliminate and punish all those who are said to be threats, to remediate the pain (lower taxes, farm bailouts) to Make America Great Again.

A Note on Transgenerational Transmission of Trauma

For historical chosen traumas (and glories) and their narrative truths to be relevant in the present they must be passed forward from one generation to the next. "Because the traumatized self-images passed down to members of the group all refer to the same calamity, they become part of the group identity, an ethnic marker on the canvas of the ethnic tent."[43] For Volkan, transgenerational transmission involves elders externalizing their sense of shared traumas to inculcate these traumas in their children. "It becomes the child's task to mourn, to reverse the humiliation and feelings of helplessness pertaining to the trauma of his forebears."[44] This passing of "narrative truths" such as a "lost cause" may take many forms – literature, theatre, movies, music, and storytelling. "For each new generation, the account is modified: what remains is the role it assumes in the overall psychology of the group's identity."[45]

This notion of a cumulative historical large group identity resonates with the content of the two books discussed earlier. Many generations may have farmed the same land, worked in the same town if not the same plant or coal mine, and stayed in the county of their birth. These psychosocial dynamics that drive twenty-first-century social polarization contain unconscious and out of awareness psychosocial dynamics that must be better understood if any type of meaningful change is to be accomplished.

Psychodynamics – The Why?

We need to understand (or attempt to do so) why "others" are targeted to receive our bad feelings, fantasies, and aggression, and why people are willing to kill for the sake of protecting and maintaining their large group identities. Volkan writes: "Individual values can give way to a collective will and the monstrous vision of a charismatic leader."[46] He continues: "When ethnic groups define and differentiate themselves, they almost invariably develop some prejudices for their own group and against the others' groups."[47] These relationships with the foreign *other* are "contaminated with shared perceptions, thoughts, fantasies, and emotions (both conscious and unconscious) pertaining to past historical glories and traumas; losses, humiliations, mourning difficulties, feeling of entitlement to revenge, and resistance to accepting changed realities."[48]

Individuals and groups that encounter distressing experiences and anxiety resort to psychological defenses first relied upon in childhood. Three of Volkan's psychodynamic insights regarding the use of psychological defenses are:

- "Externalization is a primitive mechanism by means of which the child seeks to rid himself of unpleasant self-images and their accompanying feeling states, which he has not yet learned to integrate with the rest of himself." [49]
- "Projection, which develops at a later stage, is a far more sophisticated mechanism. Externalization pertains to aspects of the self and of an internalized object representation, where the individual uses projection to attribute his unacceptable thought or impulses to someone out there in an effort to be rid of them." [49]
- "Displacement is the investment of feelings about one object in another object."[49]

These psychologically defensive dynamics make the "other" individual or group a reservoir for our own attributes. As a result, the other is familiar (us), and we with almost uncanny certainty seem to know them and what their motivations are.

When these dynamics are examined from an object relations viewpoint, we see the potential for using ethnicity and nationality as targets for splitting and projection. The externalizations and projections imposed on our enemy are repugnant to us. We disavow them within ourselves leading to our seeing important differences relative to "other" which in turn supports our sense of self and of membership in our own group. Herein resides the unconscious nature of "us versus them," where we are good and the others are bad, in part because we have attributed to them many of our disowned deplorable personal qualities and intentions. In sum, the enemy is constructed of our split off and projected bad qualities such as arrogance or incompetencies, perverse motivations, and aggression, becoming evil in mind thereby meriting hate, rage, and destruction.

Psychodynamic Origins of Cultures of Grievance

Where do cultures of grievance come from? Stein writes: "I think that, from a psychoanalytic viewpoint, the questions become: why would people emotionally invest in folklore and religious beings and practices if they did not at least in part echo or resonate with early experience with caregivers?"[50] These early developmental experiences, interacting with one's unconscious life, lead to investment in cultural beliefs and identity that must be defended at the risk of loss of self and group affiliation. "Psychological vulnerability, embedded in a sense of eternal recurrence, becomes economically and politically exploitable and mobilizable."[51] Political leaders (Trump, Governors, Mayors) seeking power mobilize these vulnerabilities in "red states" leading them to strike out at the hated liberal elites. Everyone is ready to follow a paranoid charismatic leader who promises to protect them and provide them solace for their shared sense of despair and grievance.

Exploiting Chosen Traumas and Victimization

The two overviewed books depict a large segment of American society that, for a variety of reasons, share, during the Age of Trump, a sense of chosen trauma that leads them to self-victimize, adding fuel to the anger associated with their traumatic past. This is understandable and must be respected. This idea that a political leader, supported by a political party, intensively exploits these all too human experiences to create polarization (divide and conquer) would seem to fundamentally lack any real sense of morality and humanity. The strangers in their own local communities are revictimized and retraumatized to serve the leader's need to acquire power and control. This is especially true for narcissistic leaders such as Trump who lack empathy and are autocratic and authoritarian.

This appreciation also takes into consideration the historical record that reaches back not only to slavery and colonialism but also to ancient Rome and beyond. It is not new, but it is also painful to witness. Bearing witness to these psychological and social dynamics is important but ultimately insufficient as a response given the scope of the political dysfunction during the Age of Trump.

Writing in 1977 Stein and Hill offer observations as relevant today as then.

It is probably only a matter of time until every self-defined and politically powerful minority is able to apply pressure from its lobby for a reparative and remedial quota, thereby making the American mosaic a collectivity of fragmented islands united only by a sea of discontent and animosity. We would also predict that less visible and politically influential (and exploitable) minorities will be less fortunate in the demands for proportional representation—although the bandwagon is certain to be crowded. With the prevalence of ethno-political opportunism, the gerrymandering of equality is certain to make some more equal than others on the tranquil American animal farm. At worst this should lead to open competition in the name of multicultural pluralism, and to personal, corporate, and governmental manipulation of quotas, thereby corrupting its original intent. Or if we awaken quickly enough to the prospect ahead, it may demonstrate the absurdity of the quota system and lead to its dismantling rather than proliferation.[52]

A concept like ethno-political opportunism speaks to phrases such as white nationalism and white supremacy, "wall them out" and "send them back." The dynamic of the threatened, victimized, and aggrieved far right pursuing its cause of white nationalism, has led to a broad spectrum of persistent efforts to seize control of the three levers of democratic governance – executive, legislative, judicial. The perception of victimization of those described by Frank and Hochschild has led to righteous anger. But "Are they angry and hateful for the right reason?" is the fundamental underlying question. Who exactly is being victimized?

In Conclusion

When changing direction, you must know two points – where you are now and where you want to go. The first point can be encompassed by a notion like a culture of grievance that has its origins in leader-awakened and exploited historical trauma. Life as "we" know it is or perhaps knew it is slipping away. Time, it is felt, is running out to save the mythologized past and its idealized cultural identity.

The second point to plot (Where to?) is much less demarcated, seemingly buried under an avalanche of manipulated polarizations. So long as it remains *profitable* to promote polarization; the burden on society will not likely be lifted. Developing mutual respect and understanding, however, offers a way forward. Arlie Hochschild writes: "In peacetime, too, in this political moment, the best approach is to learn about what is sometimes the alternative truth in which Fox News watchers live, the class and cultural grievances it appeals to and amplifies, and to understand, as one keeps listening, a curiously hidden moderation in substance and tone [referring to understanding the opposing side]."[53] There is then to be accepted some sense of despair where hope itself (the hope Obama spoke to) is largely unavailable. Is there a way out of this polarization? The possibility of a less exploited and polarized future that has so regrettably transformed many Americans into victims of the past in the present remains just that – a possibility. There is however value in understanding the starting point – a culture of grievance.

Chapter 14 continues this exploration of grievances in that the *exploitation* of white nationalism, white supremacy, and blatant racism by Trump motivates voters to fear the loss of their "white privilege," often requiring the suppression of black voters by every means available, which initially arose post-1865.

Notes

1. Frank, T. (2007). *What's the matter with Kansas?: How conservatives won the heart of America*. New York, NY: Picador.
2. Hochschild, A. (2018). *Strangers in their own land: Anger and mourning on the American right* [Kindle Edition]. New York, NY: The New Press.
3. Volkan, V. (1997). *Blood lines: From ethnic price to ethnic terrorism*. Boulder, CO: Westview Press.
4. Hochschild, A. (2018). *Strangers in their own land: Anger and mourning on the American right* [Kindle Edition]. New York, NY: The New Press, location 363.

5. Frank, T. (2007). *What's the matter with Kansas?: How conservatives won the heart of America.* New York, NY: Picador, 119.
6. Frank, T. (2007). *What's the matter with Kansas?: How conservatives won the heart of America.* New York, NY: Picador, 6.
7. Frank, T. (2007). *What's the matter with Kansas?: How conservatives won the heart of America.* New York, NY: Picador, 13.
8. Badger, E. (2019). How the rural–urban divide became America's political fault line. *The New York Times.* https://www.nytimes.com/2019/05/21/upshot/america-political-divide-urban-rural.html?action=click&module=Well&pgtype=Homepage&section=The%20Upshot.
9. Graham, D. (2017). Red state, blue city. *The Atlantic.* https://www.theatlantic.com/magazine/archive/2017/03/red-state-blue-city/513857/.
10. Frank, T. (2007). *What's the matter with Kansas?: How conservatives won the heart of America.* New York, NY: Picador, 239.
11. Judis, J. (2018). It's the economies, stupid. *Washington Post.* https://www.washingtonpost.com/news/magazine/wp/2018/11/29/feature/the-key-to-understanding-americas-red-blue-split-isnt-ideology-or-culture-its-economics/.
12. Hochschild, A. (2018). *Strangers in their own land: Anger and mourning on the American right* [Kindle Edition]. New York, NY: The New Press, location 2480.
13. Hochschild, A. (2018). *Strangers in their own land: Anger and mourning on the American right* [Kindle Edition]. New York, NY: The New Press, location 3690.
14. Hochschild, A. (2018). *Strangers in their own land: Anger and mourning on the American right* [Kindle Edition]. New York, NY: The New Press, location 231.
15. Hochschild, A. (2018). *Strangers in their own land: Anger and mourning on the American right* [Kindle Edition]. New York, NY: The New Press, location 3699.
16. Hochschild, A. (2018). *Strangers in their own land: Anger and mourning on the American right* [Kindle Edition]. New York, NY: The New Press, location 531.
17. Hochschild, A. (2018). *Strangers in their own land: Anger and mourning on the American right* [Kindle Edition]. New York, NY: The New Press, location 3666.
18. Hochschild, A. (2018). *Strangers in their own land: Anger and mourning on the American right* [Kindle Edition]. New York, NY: The New Press, location 2019.
19. Hochschild, A. (2018). *Strangers in their own land: Anger and mourning on the American right* [Kindle Edition]. New York, NY: The New Press, location 3910.
20. Hochschild, A. (2018). *Strangers in their own land: Anger and mourning on the American right* [Kindle Edition]. New York, NY: The New Press, location 1145.
21. Hochschild, A. (2018). *Strangers in their own land: Anger and mourning on the American right* [Kindle Edition]. New York, NY: The New Press, location 629.
22. Hochschild, A. (2018). *Strangers in their own land: Anger and mourning on the American right* [Kindle Edition]. New York, NY: The New Press, location 3512.
23. Hochschild, A. (2018). *Strangers in their own land: Anger and mourning on the American right* [Kindle Edition]. New York, NY: The New Press, location 3953.
24. McLaughlin D. (2016). Bobby Jindal's legacy. *National Review.* https://www.nationalreview.com/magazine/2016/10/10/bobby-jindals-approval-ratings-legacy-louisiana/.
25. Hochschild, A. (2018). *Strangers in their own land: Anger and mourning on the American right* [Kindle Edition]. New York, NY: The New Press, location 4156.
26. Hochschild, A. (2018). *Strangers in their own land: Anger and mourning on the American right* [Kindle Edition]. New York, NY: The New Press, location 1487.
27. Hochschild, A. (2018). *Strangers in their own land: Anger and mourning on the American right* [Kindle Edition]. New York, NY: The New Press, location 820.
28. Hochschild, A. (2018). *Strangers in their own land: Anger and mourning on the American right* [Kindle Edition]. New York, NY: The New Press, location 363.

29. Hochschild, A. (2018). *Strangers in their own land: Anger and mourning on the American right* [Kindle Edition]. New York, NY: The New Press, location 856.
30. Laughland, O. & Lartey, J. (2019). First slavery, then a chemical plant and cancer deaths: one town's brutal history. *The Guardian.* https://www.theguardian.com/us-news/2019/may/06/cancertown-louisiana-reserve-history-slavery.
31. Hochschild, A. (2018). *Strangers in their own land: Anger and mourning on the American right* [Kindle Edition]. New York, NY: The New Press, location 2138.
32. Allcorn, S. & Stein, H. (2017). The post-factual world of the 2016 American presidential election: The good, the bad, and the deplorable. *The Journal of Psychohistory*, 44(4), 310–318.
33. Spence, D. (1982). Narrative Truth and historical truth: Meaning and interpretation in psychoanalysis. New York, NY: W.W. Norton.
34. Stein, H. (2014). "Chosen trauma" and a widely shared sense of Jewish identity and history. *The Journal of Psychohistory*, 41(4), 239–240.
35. Volkan, V. (1994). The need to have enemies & allies: From clinical practice to international relationships. Northvale, NJ: Jason Aronson, xxvi.
36. Stein, H. (1994). *The dream of culture.* New York, NY: Pscyhe Press, 380.
37. Volkan, V. (1997). *Blood lines: From ethnic price to ethnic terrorism.* Boulder, CO: Westview Press, 34.
38. Volkan, V. (1997). *Blood lines: From ethnic price to ethnic terrorism.* Boulder, CO: Westview Press, 48.
39. Volkan, V. (1997). *Blood lines: From ethnic price to ethnic terrorism.* Boulder, CO: Westview Press, 78.
40. Volkan, V. (1994). *The need to have enemies & allies: From clinical practice to international relationships.* Northvale, NJ: Jason Aronson, xxv.
41. Volkan, V. (2013). *Enemies on the couch: A psychopolitical journey through ware and peace.* Durham, NC: Pitchstone Publishing.
42. Volkan, V. (1994). *The need to have enemies & allies: From clinical practice to international relationships.* Northvale, NJ: Jason Aronson, xxvii.
43. Volkan, V. (1997). *Blood lines: From ethnic price to ethnic terrorism.* Boulder, CO: Westview Press, 45.
44. Volkan, V. (1997). *Blood lines: From ethnic price to ethnic terrorism.* Boulder, CO: Westview Press, 43.
45. Volkan, V. (1994). *The need to have enemies & allies: From clinical practice to international relationships.* Northvale, NJ: Jason Aronson, xxvi.
46. Volkan, V. (1997). *Blood lines: From ethnic price to ethnic terrorism.* Boulder, CO: Westview Press, 20.
47. Volkan, V. (1997). *Blood lines: From ethnic price to ethnic terrorism.* Boulder, CO: Westview Press, 22.
48. Volkan, V. (1997). *Blood lines: From ethnic price to ethnic terrorism.* Boulder, CO: Westview Press, 117.
49. Volkan, V. (1994). *The need to have enemies & allies: From clinical practice to international relationships.* Northvale, NJ: Jason Aronson, 19.
50. Stein, H. & Hill, R. (1977). *The ethnic imperative: Examining the new white ethnic movement.* University Park, PA: The Pennsylvania State University Press, 246.
51. Stein, H. & Hill, R. (1977). *The ethnic imperative: Examining the new white ethnic movement.* University Park, PA: The Pennsylvania State University Press, 252.
52. Stein, H. & Hill, R. (1977). *The ethnic imperative: Examining the new white ethnic movement.* University Park, PA: The Pennsylvania State University Press, 264.
53. Hochschild, A. (2019). Think Republicans are disconnected from reality? It's even worse among liberals. *The Guardian.* https://www.theguardian.com/commentisfree/2019/jul/21/democrats-republicans-political-beliefs-national-survey-poll.

14 White Supremacy and the Pursuit of Power

Toward the end of a novel, all the plots, and subplots, weave together into a single fabric, or story arc, like many tributaries to form a single river. This chapter completes the arc of this book by exploring the ideology and practice of white supremacy and the pursuit of power in the Age of Trump, with the aid of the three psychoanalytic theories we have been using as interpretive and explanatory instruments. Here we will show how and why the themes and perspectives offered in this book coalesce into what are simultaneously current and recurrent American historical, cultural, ideological, political, and economic overarching themes.

This chapter also rightfully fits into a section on *Trump's followers*. It is, after all, the ideology of white supremacy and the groups of white supremacists (Unite the Right 2017 rally in Charlottesville, VA) who create and sustain a psychological and political environment where authoritarian leaders such as Trump, embodies their ambitions. We have elsewhere written of Trump's uncanny psychological fit with his ardent supporters and how they mirror each other (Chapter 7). In this chapter, we explore how his white supremacist followers, in seeking to fulfill their own ideologies and needs, give him power to respond to their desires to rescue their whiteness. Build the wall!

The pursuit of power by a paranoid charismatic leader symbolically culminated in Trump's 4th of July 2020 Mount Rushmore speech. The speech was grounded in race-based polarization and the accompanying psychological splitting and projection. He advocated that confederate statues should be revered and a movement like Black Lives Matters should be viewed as a far-left extremist and terrorist threat to "good Americans." Trump promoted fear, to create a bond between himself as a fight leader and his followers who embrace an ideology of preserving white supremacy and their social, economic, and political dominance (a movement against people of color). And to be noted Mount Rushmore and the surrounding area, the Black Hills, is sacred Lakota Sioux land dating back 12,000 years. The 1851 Treaty of Ft. Laramie acknowledged this, but the Black Hills were invaded by white gold miners with impunity in the 1850s.

Our effort in this chapter is to explore the nature of white supremacy as pervasive ideology in the pursuit of power and control in the Age of Trump. Unpacking white supremacy and its pervasive presence in American society, it must be acknowledged, is a humbling undertaking. Books such as *Grant* by Ron Chernow[1] and *The Half Has Never Been Told: Slavery and the Making of American Capitalism* by Edward Baptist[2] offer exceptionally sobering knowledge and insights into and emotional awareness of, the depravity of white supremacy and the exceptional commitment to suppress, contain, limit, subjugate, and dehumanize the human beings who were enslaved and their descendants. The effort made here is to link white supremacy as a form of racial ideology to current events and the explicit white supremacy Trump uses to split family member from family member, neighbor from neighbor, and the nation into ever-brighter colors of red and blue currently used by the media to depict the two parties.

Understanding the importance and depth of Trump's and the far-right's embrace of white supremacy and the accompanying structural and systemic racism is the subject of much discussion and debate among scholars, journalists, and opinion writers. The fact that Trump and the Republican Party have seized upon this as a viable and energizing approach to motivating voters, while new in its starkness and as an unveiled appeal, contrasts historically with what most often were veiled appeals since the 1960s. Racism is front and center and out of the closet for disquieting public inspection which, from the vantage point a decade from now, may be a "good thing" if it leads to positive change.

The use of the term "white supremacy" and related terms such as white nationalism and states' rights relative to the abolition of slavery and the Civil Rights and Voting Rights acts 100 years later must be explored to fully appreciate the siren call of white supremacy, white privilege, and white domination of society and government at all levels as critical to conserving white power.

White Supremacy – Briefly

White supremacy is the racist belief that white people are superior to people of other races, including Jews, and that they should have power over them. These beliefs are sometimes supported by pseudoscience and discredited doctrines. White supremacy is operationalized by a political ideology that relies on historical economic, social, political, and judicial power (Jim Crow laws in the United States, apartheid in South African) to perpetuate control, preferably crushing or neutralizing all resistance. On a more global scale white European colonization of much of the non-white and non-Christian world has left vast geopolitical dislocations in the wake of the gradual abandonment of this imperial occupation and control.[3]

Historically in America there is no better example of white supremacy ideology than black slavery that began in 1619, when African slaves were brought to Jamestown, Virginia to work on tobacco plantations. Throughout the seventeenth century through the nineteenth century in the Unites States, millions of African slaves were a labor force that helped to build the economy of America.[2]

A not unexpected outcome of centuries of enslavement and slave ownership in the Unites States was the development of not only a southern plantation economy based on slavery but also a pattern of social dynamics aimed at controlling and suppressing slaves who in some instances outnumbered whites. This numeric disparity created the threat of a revolt as happened when slaves successfully rebelled in an act of self-liberation against French colonial rule and enslavement in Haiti 1791–1804 ending with the colony's independence like the American Revolutionary War (1775–1783).

To be noted then is that there is then a long history in the Unites States of "policing" black slaves with white militias, law enforcement, terror in the form of hangings (the KKK), and the legal right supported by the Supreme Court to return runaway slaves who may have been transported to freedom by the underground railway. The dominating, harsh and even murderous policing of people of color in 2020 remains as a profound remnant of this history supported by twenty-first-century systemic and structural racism.

Systemic and structural racism arose as a response to the freeing of the slaves. When the secessionist Confederate states, "lost their cause" (1861–1865) the white citizens of the former confederacy were confronted with their former male slaves having the right to vote. Their large numbers presented a grave threat to white control and privilege.[4] Many social and legal structures were created to dominate and control these "freedmen," gradually culminating in the era of Jim Crow laws that were created by white Democratic-controlled state and local governments in the late 19th and early 20th centuries to limit black political influence and the economic gains made by black people during the Reconstruction period. The Jim Crow laws, and the accompanying socially institutionalized race-based discrimination were enforced until 1965 and the passage of the Civil Rights Act of 1964 and the Voting Rights Act of 1965.

Recent Historical Perspective

The Unite the Right August 2017 rally in Charlottesville Virginia's Lee Park, which was a response to efforts to remove the statue of General Robert E. Lee from the park, ended with rioting and the death of Heather Heyer and the wounding of others by James Alex Fields Jr. who drove his car into a crowd of counterdemonstrators. Fields is now serving a life sentence for first-degree murder and many other charges. These events made clear what the Alternate Right, white supremacists, neo-Nazis, and anti-immigrant, anti-Latino, and anti-Jew groups were about – "they will not replace us" was the slogan. This rally was highlighted foremost by the Nazi-like torch light parade, Nazi salutes, and armed militia.

The defeat of the Confederate armies left a festering historical wound and humiliation, a chosen trauma, passed down through generations of white southerners. The Unite the Right rally illustrates that the shame and anger about the defeat lives on as in the motto that "The South Will Rise Again." For many white Southerners "race" became a way to feel superior to African Americans/blacks/descendants of former slaves and by extension all non-European immigrants.[5] "The second-era Ku Klux Klan, which at its peak in the 1920s could boast millions of adherents and some control over public policy, had followers in the middle and even aristocratic classes."[3]

Add to this that President Trump insisted that "both sides" were to blame for the street battles in Charlottesville. White supremacists now feel that the President is on their side, not only making America great again but also white again. This coded and tacit support underscores the 2020 race-based and polarizing reelection appeal to white voters in the suburbs who are said to need protection from black encroachment. Shivani writing for Salon reports, "Certainly, white supremacy in some form continues, otherwise we wouldn't have President Donald Trump."[3]

The present context must then be appreciated to be an extension of hundreds of years of white supremacy and racism that takes contemporary forms but also harkening back to Nazi Germany and its extermination of inferior races. And certainly, there are still many remnants of the Jim Crow era race-based discrimination that still segregates blacks from "white society" that takes many forms such as influencing jury selection, home and business loans, and what have become food and healthcare deserts in segregated black communities.

Given this brief history of white supremacy ideology, slavery, and racism, it is important to briefly inspect the use of *language and symbols* relative to the discussion of white supremacy and white power.

The Language and Symbols of White Supremacy

Newkirk writes, "The language of white supremacy has become increasingly central to understanding the argument over the broad currents of Donald Trump's ascendancy." A fundamental question is, "Who are white supremacists?"[6] What is white nationalism and white power?

The use of language is seen by some as critical to understanding the Age of Trump. There is much debate on the use of these terms on the right and left. On the left some declare Trump as obviously racist, whereas on the right it is asserted the left sees racism everywhere. This raises the question as to whether the definition of white supremacy threatens to become too all-inclusive and imprecise.

Newkirk frames this debate by discussing critical race theory, which is itself controversial, by relying on Frances Lee Ansley, a legal scholar, who asserts white supremacy must have an expansive definition.

> By 'white supremacy' I do not mean to allude only to the self-conscious racism of white supremacist hate groups. I refer instead to a political, economic, and cultural system in which whites overwhelmingly control power and material resources, conscious and unconscious ideas of white superiority and entitlement are widespread, and relations of white dominance and non-white subordination are daily reenacted across a broad array of institutions and social settings.[6]

Newkirk adds context to this meaning by suggesting the latent benefits of white supremacy are still present even though white liberals, moderates, and conservatives have promoted a fiction of progress that denies their collective benefit from it.[6] Similarly, American politicians have been racist, and politics is, at times, ladened with elements of white supremacy, creating historical repetitions of fear and suppression where non-whites such as Native Americans, African Americans, and Latin Americans, and many other non-European Americans find themselves suppressed in many ways. This is to say American society is permeated by its racist history that includes the ethnic cleansing of Native Americans and the enslavement of Africans. These influences are omnipresent and a large part of the psychosocial dynamics of the present.

This discussion suggests language plays an important role in discussions of white supremacy for both sides of the debate. The protagonists each prefer their own definitions, labels and opposing points of view. This outcome, which seems inevitable, is based on underlying psychosocial elements of our historical and present culture and perhaps more accurately many subcultures. Blatant white supremacy on the right should not serve to conceal the remnants of white supremacy social effects on the left. There is also to be appreciated latent benefits that accrue to "liberal minded" white Americans. Much the same as the use of white supremacy-based language the use of symbols also are a form of communication for the core supporters of white supremacy.

The Role of Symbols in White Supremacy

The role of symbols associated with white supremacy and racism are important to understand. The white hoods and gowns worn by the KKK as well its iconic burned crosses are exceptional symbols of white supremacy. Equally attention-getting are rope nooses and swastikas as well as Confederate flags and statues and the evolving use of adapted Nazi symbols as tattoos as well as hand signals. These many symbols speak loudly using no words at all.

Also, to be considered are the growing number of cell phone and police camera videos of various forms of violence directed at black Americans, including the excessive and in appropriate use of force and deadly force by police officers who have as their presumptive mission to protect and serve. A knee on a black man's neck joins memory of nooses and massive scars on the backs of slaves from whippings. The symbols of white supremacy deserve to be attended to.

Words and symbols are important elements of white supremacy that contribute to the contemporary political and social polarization. This is underscored by the Black Lives Matter social and political movement and accompany, at times, over policing of the protests reminiscent of historical suppression.

Black Lives Matter

Erin Kaplan offers an opinion that underscores the tensions and the lack of progress in dealing with black and white polarization contributed to by psychological object relations theory and splitting and projection. Kaplan begins by recognizing "Black Lives Matter" should not be considered as progress but as a starting point to address systemic racism and white supremacy. Going from the current enthusiasm of the protests to doing what needs to be done to start correcting systemic racism will be exceptionally challenging. Kaplan writes, "The last large-scale effort aimed at improving Black lives was the war on poverty back in the '60s, and the backlash to that was swift and relentless. In some ways, we're still living it. Critics of the war on poverty didn't object just to money being spent, they objected to the notion of helping Black folks specifically because they were not worth helping, at least not to that degree."[7] Ronald Reagan's racist dog whistle "welfare queens" underscores this. Systemic racism and white supremacy that turn non-white human beings into "objects" to be managed and suppressed is underscored during the Age of Trump when immigrants and their children are locked up at the border, the SARS-Cov-2 virus is referred to as the Chinese virus or "kung-flu," and Muslims are linked to terrorism leading to their exclusion as permissible immigrants.

In sum, white supremacy and racism are deeply woven into the fabric of American society. Kaplan notes, "Racism is a form of convenience, in the sense that it's designed to make life easier for its beneficiaries. So is white privilege — the phenomenon of not having to think about the costs of oppression, or about Black people at all."[7] The consciousness raising of 2020, that may not be sustainable, may reduce the harmful use of language and the use of oppressive symbols, remove monuments to the Confederacy, and rename military bases, but the fundamental underlying question is whether a society can ultimately embrace its white supremacy past and persist in removing the systemic nature of racism and white privilege. This is likely an ongoing and even intergenerational challenge for

Americans to meet as echoed in post-Nazi Germany and post-apartheid South Africa.

Systemic and Structural Racism

Black Lives Matter as a national movement aimed at excessive use of force by police and lethal force against black communities is underpinned by a long and evolving history of systemic and structural racism.

What Is Systemic Racism?

Definitions of systemic racism generally focus on the imposition of and the pervasive presence of social norms and customs as well as systems that contain institutionalized processes (policies and procedures, rules and regulations, laws and their enforcement) that are at the minimum unsupportive of African Americans and their communities achieving social and economic wellbeing. They may also proactively inhibit, block, and discriminate against these valued social outcomes as was the case during the era of Jim Crow laws. To be noted is these considerations apply equally well to Native Americans and all non-white human beings. The difference between systemic and structural racism for some is a difference without a distinction. Systemic racism however carries a connotation of being everywhere existing throughout all aspects of society in many forms, whereas structural considerations speak more directly to the instruments of society and levers of power that are used to impose racism.

What Is Structural Racism?

Structural racism is a system in which public laws and policies, institutional practices, cultural representations (language and symbols), and other social norms work in various, often reinforcing ways to perpetuate racial group inequity. Governmental structures are present at all levels of society (systemic). The word "structure" speaks more directly to a less personal and even hygienic approach (only following the rules) to controlling and suppressing people of color. In this regard the use of the word *structure* suggests it is more mechanical in nature, running methodically and consistently as the word *bureaucracy* suggests is the case for these social institutions.

These considerations are especially relevant in 2020 regarding the spread of the SARS-CoV-2 and the associated disease COVID-19. Katherine J. Wu writes: "Regardless of the methodological drawbacks of this study, experts agree that 'the causes of disparities, whether in Covid-19 or other aspects of health, are intricately linked to structural racism,' Dr. Mitchell said. In the United States, Latino and African American residents are three times as likely to become infected by the coronavirus as white residents, and nearly twice as likely to die."[8]

Perhaps little more needs to be mentioned regarding the powerful and detrimental historical and present impact of white supremacy, white nationalism, racism, and white privilege. It is without a doubt impossible to fully illuminate this powerful seemingly everlasting social dislocation of norms and values associated with fellow human beings.

This appreciation is further underscored by inspecting this dislocation using psychodynamically informed perspectives.

Understanding White Supremacy – Psychodynamically Informed Insights

Object relations perspectives can be used to explore what has become an obvious white and black world filled with fears, anxieties that lead to individual, social, and political dysfunctions. Group relations based on Wilfred Bion's theorizing also offer a way to understand psychosocial aspects of social polarization that includes race-based divisions. Karen Horney's perspectives also contribute to understanding the relationship between a paranoid charismatic leader and dependent followers who he promises to save while eliminating all opposition his imposition to his worldview on American society.

Object Relations

The black and white world of object splitting and projection, whether in mind or interpersonally (projection and projective identification) is accompanied by transference of past affective experience onto a fantastic mindful object. These dynamics eventually leak out into the interpersonal world. For instance, the actual external "object" may come to incorporate forcefully expelled projections and become invested with thoughts, feelings, actions, and self-experiences that magnify the original projective creation.[9,10,11,12] Given these psychological dynamics, the black and white world created uncomfortably speaks to white supremacy, white nationalism, and racism, where those who are not white are viewed with suspicion, dread, fear, and anxiety. They are not like me or my group and are, via splitting and projection, invested with disowned negative qualities – we are "good," and they are "bad."

Object relations theorizing suggests that much of what happens in this black and white interpersonal and inter-group world is filled with unconscious psychological dynamics that often go unnoticed, unobserved, and when commonly shared they simply become "the way things are" – racist. This dynamic, it should also be appreciated, is not a one-way dynamic – white toward black. People of color must also come to understand the racist world that they live in is also black and white where they are not only singled out for discrimination but also are resentful and resist. They form their own splits, projections, and transference where "whitey" and "cracker" are examples of pejorative labels aimed at "bad others." They, however, based on history and the present, *reasonably* object to those who project their fears and anxieties onto them to denigrate and suppress them to secure feelings of superiority for themselves.

We are left, in the twenty-first-century America, with a split apart world based on skin pigmentation on the surface and deeply felt and unconscious dynamics that go unexamined beneath the surface. These dynamics have become commonplace and accepted as the way things are. If one is to consider changing these observable and more importantly unobservable psychosocial dynamics, they must first be surfaced in a safe enough space that can contain the many anxieties that will inevitably arise if the object relations below the surface are to be inspected and discussed. This is the challenge faced in the Unites States and around the world if meaningful and enduring change is to be created. Regrettably, this level of analysis and change seems unlikely, except in small groups and limited geographic areas.

Group Relations

Bion's ideas about group relations also contribute to understanding white supremacy.[13,14] Fear and anxiety on the part of white European Americans held toward people of color and historically their slaves who might revolt leads us to consider the fight or flight basic assumption group. This group is most suitably led by a paranoid and charismatic leader who finds threats everywhere from these "other" people. White supremacy is manifested as aggression in many ways such as discrimination in hiring, housing, and jury selection and historically in major eruptions of violence such as the burning out of black communities in Tulsa, Oklahoma, Springfield, Missouri, and Rosewood, Florida. The fight basic assumption that is led by a paranoid charismatic leader such as Trump finds plenty that white supremacists fear and want to fight back against – you will not replace us was a chant in Charlottesville, Virginia, 2017. It is then also readily under-stood that black communities in the past as well as today are in flight from white supremacy and aggressive, oppressive, and sometimes militarized policing as well as fighting back against it.

These fight/flight groups contain a flood of emotions that serve to trun-cate thoughtful reflection and analysis. The presence of fight and flight groups signals a readiness to act and having a fight or flight leader is essen-tial in terms of mobilizing the group to act. Given this powerful psy-chosocial dynamic, once again the question may be asked as to how to create change.

The presence of the paranoid charismatic fight leader makes creative social and economic change problematic in that anyone who questions the leader, what is happening, and why it is happening is quickly identified as a threat to the leader and the group that must be extinguished. The ability to stand against the leader and what is often a loyal group of unquestioning supporters (sycophants) is a task filled with a very real sense of threat. The 1965 police action at the Edmund Pettus Bridge in Selma, Alabama is an example. There is then also a fight or flight dynamic for those who oppose racism in all its forms.

Perhaps the only viable way to create change is for the fight/flight leader to be removed or replaced or a more powerful leader to emerge, an individual to whom even this leader will submit. In the longer-term within the Unites States, with an elected change in leadership, there may be opportunities to call into question what happened, reflect on white supremacy and racism, and perhaps work toward a better way to achieve "safety." Safety can promote reflection grounded in accurate reality testing accompanied by thinking that before was overwhelmed by emotion. How can we respond better in the future without fight or flight?

Karen Horney

Karen Horney's three directions of movement when excessive fear and anxiety are encountered also contribute to understanding white supremacy and the targets of its ideology.[15] Movement against to gain mastery of self, others, and the context-driven by narcissism and arrogant-vindictive triumph, offers insights into the dynamic energy invested in white supremacy to control, limit, regulate, lock up, and otherwise remove people of color from the "white world." Individuals with significant narcissism if not malignant narcissism who seek to be admired and dominate over others are enhanced immeasurably by acquiring positions of power and control (social, corporate, political). This perspective helps to understand Trump and the Age of Trump where the appeals to white supremacy, white nationalism, and racism are observable. Trump's followers, who assume a role of moving toward him as a charismatic leader (dependency and submission), are a psychosocial match in that the leader seeks these followers and the followers seek this leader (Chapter 7).

Equally observable on the part of Trump is moving against others in the form of arrogant-vindictive triumph, where at an extreme almost any level of interpersonal social and self-harm will be embraced to get even many times over. All those who oppose, question, or do not submit to becoming sycophants must be punished, neutralized, or fired – a dynamic entirely consistent it appears with who Trump is and his starring role in his TV program *The Apprentice* where he held court in Trump Tower.

The third direction of movement – away (the appeal to freedom) provides insight into those who are subjected to the power and control of white supremacy. Slaves did flee to freedom in the North. However, resistance to white supremacy thus far over hundreds of years has been largely futile. Segregation, destruction of black communities, locking up immigrants and children at the southern border all indicate that any real sense of freedom is only achievable by avoiding the power and control of white supremacy and white nationalism.

In sum, Horney's perspectives once again raise the question and problem of how these psychosocial dynamics might change, especially within basic assumption groups that contain a considerable amount of individual and group unconscious process that includes splitting and projection. The likely solution to these psychological, social, and political dynamics is, much the same as the solutions offered for the object relations and group relations perspectives. The solution begins with the ability to create a safe enough time and interpersonal and intergroup space to surface these dynamics for inspection – in a metaphoric psychotherapeutic consulting room.

Yet as noted, holding up individual and group psychodynamics for inspection increases anxiety on the part of leaders of opposing groups as well as their followers. Inspection can readily reinforce the selected ideological solutions to anxiety further mobilizing the leader who pursues an expansive solution to anxiety moving against others. The increased anxiety may also increase the neediness of a group that seeks dependency on and care-taking by the leader even if the leader is abusive. Creating the safety and willingness to become reflective is a truly demanding task for anyone to undertake, perhaps best approached not so much in the moment when it appears worst – although leadership failures can present an opportunity – but more likely during a period of less threat, fear and anxiety arises.

In Conclusion

In this chapter white supremacy and the pursuit of power in the Age of Trump has been explored in terms of how power is used to create, enforce, and maintain systemic and structural racism that flows from 1619, through the Civil war that freed the slaves, the Civil Rights and Voter Rights acts of the 1960s, to the present filled with grossly aggravated racial and social polarization in the service of electing and reelecting a Republican as President. These historical and current psychosocial dynamics are perhaps without hyperbole horrific. We have described and suggested how these psychosocial dynamics can be better understood using the three psychodynamically informed perspective relied upon in this book. These perspectives, however, and unfortunately, also suggest that the complex nature of the psychological, social, and political polarization may be self-sustaining and not readily changed for many decades to come. We the authors are saddened to suggest this likely outcome.

Chapter 15 concludes this book by looking back upon the learning curve it represents for us the authors and you the reader. What has been learned? What can be hoped to be learn in the future? How might white, Christian, patricidal, white supremacy-oriented culture and values evolve to embrace diversity in all its forms in a meaningful way? How does a psychodynamically informed approach contribute to understanding the Age of Trump?

Notes

1. Chernow, R. (2017). *Grant*. London: Head of Zeus.
2. Baptiste, E. (2014). *The Half Has Never Been Told: Slavery and the Making of American Capitalism*. New York, NY: Basic Books.
3. Shivani, A. (2017). What is "white supremacy"? A brief history of a term, and a movement, that continues to haunt America. *Salon*. https://www.salon.com/2017/04/23/what-is-white-supremacy-a-brief-history-of-a-term-and-a-movement-that-continues-to-haunt-america/.
4. Meacham, J. (2020). The south's fight for white supremacy. *The New York Times*. https://www.nytimes.com/2020/08/23/books/review/lost-cause-meacham.html.
5. Stein., H. (2017). The Charlottesville turning point. *Tulsa World*. https://www.tulsaworld.com/opinion/opinionfeatured/howard-f-stein-the-charlottesville-turning-point/article_78bc500c-972d-5b8e-82c2-6c02576d3488.html.
6. Newkirk, V. (2017). The Language of white supremacy. *The Atlantic*. https://www.theatlantic.com/politics/archive/2017/10/the-language-of-white-supremacy/542148/.
7. Kaplan, E. (2020). Everyone's an antiracist. Now what? *The New York Times*. https://www.nytimes.com/2020/07/06/opinion/antiracism-what-comes-next.html?action=click&module=Opinion&pgtype=Homepage.
8. Wu, K. (2020). Study of 17 million identifies crucial risk factors for coronavirus deaths. *The New York Times*. https://www.nytimes.com/2020/07/08/health/coronavirus-risk-factors.html.
9. Greenberg, J. & Mitchell, S. (1983). *Object relations in psychoanalytic theory*. Cambridge, MA: Harvard University Press.
10. Grotstein, J. (1985). *Splitting and projective identification*. Northvale, NJ: Jason Aronson.
11. Scharff, J. (1992). *Projective and introjective identification and the use of the therapist's self*. Northvale, NJ: Jason Aronson.
12. Segal, H. (1973). *Introduction to the work of Melanie Klein*. London: Karnac.
13. Bion, W. (1961). *Experience in groups*. London: Tavistock.
14. Rioch, M. (1975). Group relations: Rationale and technique. In *Group relations reader*, Colman, A. and Bexton, W. (Eds.). Washington, DC: A.K. Rice Institute Series, 11–33.
15. Horney, K. (1950). *Neurosis and human growth*. New York, NY: Norton.

15 The Learning Curve

This book has been about a learning curve to understand the Age of Trump. Learning curves are a conceptual visualization of a mapping of data points over time that promote understanding a complex phenomenon such as dynamic events and history. Learning curves as a metaphor speak to an ever-growing understanding, but one that is asymptotic, never reaching a complete understanding as is the case here. Learning curves also speak to what amounts to a lot of work on the part of those learning. This includes mental striving to confront and overcome resistances, ambiguity, and simply the challenge of comprehending branching complexity of a systemic nature. The subject matter of this book underscores all these considerations.

This book began with another metaphor, that of *triangulation* and a triangle within a triangle that suggests that Trump himself, Trump as a leader, Trump as having followers are an interlinked, reinforcing complex system of relationships. Trump and his followers identify as Republican and conservative, and his followers highly approve of him and his performance (supreme court and judicial appointments, immigration, deregulation, and law and order). These elements of the triangulation represent an intertwined social, political, and psychodynamic context. This complexity, when fused with the chaos of the Age of Trump, requires an equally insightful way to understand it – our triangulation is one way. This concluding chapter has the advantage of looking backward over the learning to be gained from of the chapter analyses and what was and continues to be an ongoing learning curve in terms of our understanding human behavior in large organizations – with the United States being the ultimate large organization.

The learning curve that has been provided in this book involves both learning about and explaining the Age of Trump as it unfolded and as explored by a series of published papers (2017–2020). Our learning curve can be viewed as a historical story arc. An example of such an arc is an unlikely leader, Trump, rising to power and gradually failing and ending with being "kicked to the curb" having lost the 2020 election after one term as president with his brand (himself and the name) disparaged and removed from buildings, with legal investigations underway by the New York Attorney General, and most recently Steve Bannon's arrest by the postal service. It is also the case that the brand, which is identified with wealth and opulence, conflicts with the demographics of his followers who are aggrieved about being left behind economically and fear of losing their white cultural identity. We learned as we progressed along this long path.

A parallel concept to the learning curve is the *longitudinal case study* where researchers follow leaders, followers, and events across a period of time documenting, bearing witness to and trying to comprehend events as they unfold by most often sampling (usually by interviewing people) at discrete intervals to capture the experience of those being studied.[1] The learning curve shares many of these elements in that the individual papers written that form the basis of this book were created in relation to a flow of events across a number of years.

The learning curve has also involved learning to apply three different but complementary psychodynamically informed perspectives to analyze and gain insight into the many aspects of Trump, leadership, ideology, and followership discussed throughout the book. These three perspectives (Chapter 2) have and do shed light upon and insight into the interpersonal, group, and organizational world that is our lives. Appreciating how unconscious, often out of awareness psychological defenses continually influence what we think and feel provides deeper insight into what goes on around us. These perspectives help us to make more sense of ourselves, others, and group and organizational dynamics including the political area.

The use of triangulation (Figure 1.1) combined with a conceptual learning curve and a longitudinal perspective, together with these triangulated psychodynamic perspectives provides a methodology that can help citizens, politicians, leaders, and researchers to better understand, change, and otherwise adapt to what is the complexity of daily life. We have learned over time that an approach like this helps people, organizations, and political systems to heal by learning reflectively from experience and overcoming resistance to change.

What Has Been Learned from the Learning Curve?

The weaving together of a number of "data points" ranging from Trump's business record, his narcissism and his autocratic and authoritarian tendencies that are embraced by the far right, including the religious right, have been explored. Trump's TV screen persona of a paranoid and charismatic leader who spots threats everywhere, along with an endless grievance list of narcissistic injuries that echo his follower's social and political grievances have created a strong unwavering bond. This bond is accentuated by many who are willing to submit to his control, some of the time out of fear, as supporters and sycophants and who identify with ideologies such as deregulation, America first, and white supremacy. The outcome of these interactive data points is a steadfastly loyal voter base of followers who identify with him and what he represents to them.

The learning curve that connects these data points across time has yielded insights and promoted reflection that led the authors from one sense-making effort to another that, when taken together, create new insights and perspectives. A few of the of the efforts are worth revisiting.

The Autistic Cocoon

What does it matter to those millions who follow a paranoid charismatic leader that the leader's actions, supported by a cadre of sycophants, gradually turn a nation's governmental powers against those who are opposed, in the service of fulfilling ideologies? The events of the past four years underscore that nations and organizations contain many irrational elements that produce less than logical public policies and their implementation that fall far short of intentionally designed processes. The imagery of immigrants and children confined within overcrowded inhumane chain-link enclosures is a product of irrational fears of "alien" others. Nations and organizations may not always act logically to optimize their contribution to society.

Concepts such as the autistic "cocoon" or imprisoning "third" highlight that many people many times prefers not to know and understand how systems that produce meat for the table and pursue toxic and dysfunctional ideological beliefs work.[2,3,4] They do not want to know what they know at a deeper level. This is what Christopher Bollas calls the "unthought known," a repetition compulsion in which censorship, conscious and unconscious, and denial create an unreflective dynamic where what is known becomes unconsciously suppressed and unknown.[5]

Despised "others" are created as an object in mind that can be manipulated individually as well as shared in a group or even nationally. After all, liberals, socialists, if not hated communists, and immigrants are, from the perspective of white supremacists, drug smugglers, murders, and rapists, although there may be a few good people mixed in. Part of this mental manipulation is the splitting off of less than desirable aspects of self and locating them in this "other" as an object held in fantasy. This leaves people feeling better about themselves. They no longer have these attributes themselves and magically become "all good." These images in mind direct our thoughts, feelings, and actions relative to the despised "other," allowing for the exclusion and imprisonment of "evil" immigrants and protestors are transformed into rioters and terrorists, all of whom must be guarded against and even eliminated. The fact that these others are human beings becomes wrapped in an autistic cocoon. Their humanity is lost and replaced by a shared fantastic construction.

Qualitative Research and Analysis

We relied upon three complementary psychoanalytic theoretical perspectives to make sense of and "unpack" some of the aspects of recent political life in the United States, and to ground this pursuit of insight in qualitative methods as compared with empirical positivistically rooted research. Relying on conventional empirical research methods where complex psychosocial realities exist falls short of providing insightful and in-depth understanding of the lived experience of the citizens of the United States and the world relative to the United States and its right-wing leadership. Positivist-based empirical research methods do not access the heart of this experience and what it means. The vast range of complexities and chaos resident in the Age of Trump and the country arise most fundamentally from human nature and all of its variability. A paranoid and charismatic leader (the chosen one) may be willingly followed by many people, some of whom prostrate themselves before the leader as sycophants. This appreciation necessitates understanding the underlying psychodynamics of social and political life.

We hope the careful application of theory to interpret the psycho-social-political lived experience of the Age of Trump, the Republican party, the far-right, as well as the Never Trumpers organized to oppose him, together with the devastating events around the pandemic, provide some measure of insight that helps to make sense of (validating) our individual and shared experience of these dynamics.

Consensual Validation and Resonance

A sub-element of using psychoanalytically informed analysis is whether this work yields to consensual validation between the authors and the readers. Does the selection of topics for the chapters and the accompanying analyses generate resonance? Are we somewhat on the same page with you the reader? Consensual validation, as an element in psychotherapy and psychoanalysis, involves the therapist offering an interpretation for the patient, and the patient possibly immediately but equally as often eventually, acknowledging that the interpretation holds real meaning for the individual – however painful and distressing the interpretation. Interpretations often trigger psychological resistance to reading, hearing, and knowing this truth.

Consensual validation is then a factor in this book in that not all the topics and interpretations are meaningful to all readers. They may even be distressing calling into question strongly held and comforting ideological perspectives that must be protected. In these instances, a willingness to at least *consider* them offers the possibility of developing insights, reflectivity, and learning. However, in other instances it may be felt and thought that the topics and interpretation are "exactly what I was thinking." In these cases, while the interpretations inform and reinforce these thoughts and feelings, attention should also be directed to a self-reflective stance so that "I" might wonder why they echo my own thoughts and feelings. In sum, do these in-depth understandings using psychoanalytically informed theoretical perspectives provide further understanding of current events and life in general?

We hope the chapters and analyses have promoted reflection and a greater awareness of the many psychosocial perspectives that we have explored. We emphasize here that this reflective process is essential if the nation is to move forward to a fairer and more just society.

Words Matter

Politicians fill the air with words – some meaningful, some factual, some providing important direction, and some that are lies, distortions, obfuscations, racist dog whistles, and misrepresentations. At other times there are no words in response to reasonable questions, only words of avoidance, changing the topic, stonewalling, distraction, and counterattacks including arrest and murder in some countries directed at those who question the powerful autocratic leader. Words then are perhaps not merely self-evident but rather symbols where that which is symbolized is more powerfully communicative than the words or Twitter character limits on the internet. Symbols much like pictures that substitute for a thousand words give voice to lived experiences that are socially detonative and condemned (Chapter 14). How horrible to many people on the right is the word image of a "welfare queen" or Romney's 47% of takers? These word symbols become a form of shorthand that communicates at a more basic emotional visceral level. They embody positions and experience that is officially denied.

The appreciation that words are often packed with symbolic and unconscious meaning is critically important to understanding the lived experience of the political realm where up can become down, and what you think you know is not known and becomes "gaslighting," where someone is manipulated by psychological means into questioning their own sanity. It turns out that what you see and hear is not what you saw or heard.

Certainly, words can become euphemisms that serve to displace and conceal the real meaning of events. What exactly is acceptable collateral damage when a target in an urban setting is bombed (Oklahoma City) or employees are turned into "organizational fat" who must be cut from the organization via downsizing? "Euphemisms are not strange, exotic, rare creatures from foreign lands. They are not the private property of literature and national politics. They are garden variety national and organizational features and part of everyday life."[6] Euphemisms are symbolic in nature and can be used to cunningly negate understanding, including changing up to down and black to white. Much the same as gaslighting, the perceiver of the words enters an alternate reality of alternate facts set forth by the writer or speaker. When embraced and internalized by loyal followers it becomes the new reality where separating small children from aspiring immigrant parents protects citizens from rapists, murders, and drug dealers. The new "normal" becomes normal where this form of anti-social behavior is magically transformed into a deterrent to discourage immigration and preserve white nationalism.

The Dark Side of Human Nature

This book has explored aspects of three social and political dynamics – leader (individual), leader-follower (group), and the public political sphere. In doing so we have explored the ebb and flow of deviance and normality, good and evil, and dark and light side behaviors in public and private life.[7] It is this shift in thinking that permits us to more fully appreciate the nature of the psycho–social–political dynamics that have been discussed.

These considerations direct attention to the problematic nature of creating sustainable change when resistance to change is deeply embedded in ideologies and those who embrace them. However, positive change cannot be achieved by denying the negative aspects of underlying psychosocial dynamics of the Age of Trump, the Republican Party, Trump, and his followers. The Age of Trump has transformed the former Republican Party alienating many conservative thought leaders and advocates (the Lincoln Project). What it was for it is now often against.[8] These "bad" elements should be acknowledged.[9] Understanding these elements requires a theoretical framework that provides insight into the dark and light sides of human nature.

The psychodynamic perspectives relied on here have shed light on the unconscious dimensions, and intersubjective structures, of relationships.[10] Actions by leaders and their followers may, on the surface, appear to contain rational and logical elements that are supported by words spun to promote this understanding. However, upon closer inspection, it is often easy to reveal there are irrational and illogical elements to these ideologically informed decisions, directions, and actions. And to be noted, dark side behaviors can be hard to spot, and the harm created may only unfold across an extended time. This is especially the case where the charismatic leader is highly invested in self-promotion to create and maintain idealization that serves to create devoted and loyal followers. We are left to wonder, "Is change possible?"

Navigating the Future

The triangulations that are the dynamic geometry this book have offered insights into the problem of placing an "X" on a cognitive map marking "You are here." The remaining profoundly important question is where to from here? How can a divided and polarized nation with leaders on the right committed to maintaining power by exploiting the social splits and the underlying polarization be healed? Is some sense of national unity and reconciliation possible? Are armed demonstrations and riots on the far right going to continue expanding to many state capitols and offer major security threats to the U.S. capitol post-January 6, 2021? This is the question President Biden faces.

Regrettably, it would seem there are no easy, viable, sustainable ways to create change to heal the splits. Human nature "is what it is" echoing what Trump had to say in an interview regarding deaths from Covid-19. There exists a dark side to human nature that has created horrific outcomes across millennia. However, and sense of healing the splits begins with step one – *acknowledging this and embracing the presence of the dark side of human nature*. Not paying attention to its omnipresence (selective inattention, denial, rationalization) simply assures its indelible presence and influence in the future. However, if there is no HOPE, there is then only sadness, despair, and depression. How might "we" begin to heal the splits, reduce the polarization, and promote a greater sense of a communal good?

A psychodynamically informed perspective is helpful in conceiving how this critically important work might unfold. Leaders are a critical element of realizing this healing process. Locating a leader who can *embrace* the pain, suffering, and chaos initially without becoming personally disorganized in the process is perhaps the first step.[11] Biden's personal history and experience suggest he may well be able to embrace the pain, suffering, and chaos. Those who follow and rely on the leader must sense and know the leader knows and feels much as they do. Listening is a critically important element of this step.[12] During the summer of 2020 this is what Joe Bidden said he can and will do encouraging his followers to have some sense of hope for a better national future "together."

This sense of mutual inter-subjective awareness, understanding, and appreciation empowers the leader to formulate plans to respond to the political and economic issues at hand. This planning should be done as near as possible in an open, inclusive, and collaborative manner where the opposition is respectfully listened to, but where ideology on both sides of the aisle, while acknowledged is not allowed to become a blocking factor. Instead, the goal is to rise above ideologies. There is no "black box" of secrecy that promotes fear, anxiety, and demoralization. Compassion and empathy, rather than autocratic and authoritarian top-down command-and-control, further serves to minimize resistance to change. The current extreme level of polarization, however, offers any leader seeking to span the splits in society an exceptional challenge. To be acknowledged, there will be inevitably compromised boundary spanning efforts to minimize the polarization, so long as the dark side of human nature is manifest, and politicians promote the polarization for self-serving purposes. Even so, these basic principles can be effective if the leader is sufficiently well

integrated and not prone to becoming personally injured and psychologically defensive.

It is less about the taboo "C"-word, *compromise,* and more about several
even more important "C"-words: compassion, conversation, and creativity. When two people, or two groups of people, who regard the other as
foes, sit down and engage in dialogue, they often discover that they fear
the same things, that they feel vulnerable and afraid beneath the façade of
bravado and rage. Often, too, they become capable of thinking creatively
about mutual problems, and together arriving at solutions that neither one
could have come up with by themselves.

The Learning Curve: In Conclusion

The many elements of our triangulation combined with the triangulation of the three psychodynamic theories ideally should promote critical thinking and learning. There is hope that a big country with many
diverse subcultures and identities can locate a converging distant point
where much greater unity and mutual respect exists. Striving toward this
distant point is the **HOPE** of and for future generations. Fear, anger, and
grievance are not so much to be left behind but successfully managed.

Notes

1. Allcorn, S., Stein, H. & Duncan, C. (2018). Organisational change: A longitudinal perspective. *Organisational and Social Dynamics,* 18(2), 273–296.
2. Modell, A. (1984). *Psychoanalysis in a new context.* New York, NY: International
Universities Press.
3. Ogden, T.H. (1992). *The primitive edge of experience.* Northvale, NJ: Jason
Aronson.
4. Stein, H. & Allcorn, S. (2015). To look or not to look: The backward engineering of atrocity. *The Journal of Psychohistory,* 43(2), 78–88.
5. Bollas, Christopher. (1989). *The shadow of the object: Psychoanalysis of the unthought
known.* New York, NY: Columbia University Press.
6. Stein, H. (1998). *Euphemism, spin, and the crisis in organizational life.* Westport,
CT: Quorum Books, 1.
7. Diamond, M, and Allcorn S. (2009). *Private selves in public organizations: The
psychodynamics of organizational diagnosis and change.* New York, NY: Palgrave
MacMillan.
8. Stevens, S. (2020). *It was all a lie: How the Republican Party became Donald Trump.*
New York, NY: Knopf.
9. Allcorn, S. (1994). *Anger in the workplace: Understanding the causes of aggression and
violence.* Westport, CT: Quorum Books.
10. Diamond, M. (2017). *Discovering organizational identity: The dynamics of relational
attachment.* Columbia, MO: University of Missouri Press.
11. Stein, H. & Allcorn, S. (2014). Good enough leadership. *Organisational & Social
Dynamics,* 14(2), 342–366.
12. Stein, H. (2017). *Listening deeply.* Columbia, MO: University of Missouri Press.

Index

218   *Index*

autistic cocoon 211
autocracy 8–9, 60, 62, 67, 124–5;
    defined 62–4
autocrat(s) 1, 9, 62–3, 75, 89, 107; loyal
    followers 66; Trump 1, 67; who seized
    power 106; would-be 5
autocratic 6, 64; behavior 1, 7; com-
    mand and control 23; delegation to
    expendable others 79; leader/leader-
    ship 6, 9, 33, 64–7, 79, 104, 107, 127;
    lives by the sword 62; noun 62–3;
    powerful 88, 213; rule 64, 190; ten-
    dencies 62, 210
axis of evil 134

backlash 180–1, 202
ban on Muslims 105
bankruptcies, Trump's 8, 35–8; profited
    from 37; Trump Plaza casinos 37
Bannon, Steve 66, 210
Baptist, Edward 198
Barr, William 54
basic assumption groups 22, 25,
    127, 167, 206–7; defensive
    enactment 149; dependency 23,
    83, 172, 175; fight or flight 22,
    46, 59, 83, 96, 107, 150, 169–71;
    pairing 24, 83, 172, 175–6; psy-
    chological regression 22; regres-
    sion to 59, 150; sentience based
    11; unconscious group dynamic
    127; work group 24
Behind the Looking Glass 149–51
Benghazi 137–8
Bennis, Warren 147
Bexton, W. Harold 168
bias: biased 18, 69, 77, 131; against
    Trump 91, 106; confirmation 59, 77,
    93, 96–7; liberal 94; social 93
Biden, Joseph 106, 215; Sleepy Joe 108
Bion, Wilfred 8, 11, 22, 83, 127, 167–76,
    204–5; fight or flight group 107
birtherism 8, 39, 42–5, 58, 84; Obama's
    birth certificate 39
black and white world 16, 46, 58, 85,
    94, 126, 134; creation of 116, 130,
    143, 204; depiction 181; far-right,
    consistent with 153; polarization
    results 150, 202; simplistic 113; world
    not bland and white 83
Black Lives Matter 9, 19, 40, 106, 197,
    202–3
black versus white 3, 58, 113, 143

Blau, Peter 120
Boehner, John 4, 43; hell no 3, 43, 67
Bollas, Christopher 115, 211; unthought
    known 211
Bolsheviks 117
Bolton, John 64, 108
Boot, Max 4, 164
born again: ideologically 116; the
    individual 116; in him (Trump) 70;
    Republican Party 12
boundary warping 147
brand 1, 38–9, 96–100, 209–10; empty
    vessel 99; identification 3; loy-
    alty 3; Obamacare 42; political 96;
    Republican rebranding 2, 10, 89,
    135–6; Trump as brand 4, 39, 54–5,
    96, 209–10
branding 39; of people as worthless 59;
    Trump's 4, 35–8
Breitbart News 65, 90
Brooks, David 163–4
Buettner, Russ, 37, 105
bureaucracy 10, 80, 115–128, 203; alien-
    ation 124; as hierarchy 122; federal 17;
    in modern society 120; irrationality
    of 123; operated by people 123; per-
    vasive 117; social costs of 117
bureaucratic leader(s) 126
Bureaucratization of the World 117
Burn, Shawn 64–5
Burr, Richard 139
Bush family 165
Bush, George H.W. 91
Bush, George W. 3, 10, 108, 116, 135,
    152–5, 181
Bush, Jeb 104
Butler, Eamon 166

C-word 42, 67
California Waste Management Board
    186
capitalism 105, 120, 131, 135, 158, 187;
    free market 132; pro- 180; unfettered
    105
Cantor, Eric 4
Carlson, Tucker 41
Carroll, Lewis 149
Carter, Jimmy 152
celebrity 39; self-branding 39; TV 44
Central Intelligence Agency (CIA)
    138–9
centralized power 63–4
Cerrell Associates: study 186, 188

influence on bureaucracies 128; introduction to 10, 115; left-wing 86; racial 198; relation to human nature 10; Republican 146; right-wing 3, 10–11, 57, 106, 130, 136, 146; rigid adherence to xiii, 3, 47; simplifies psychic landscape 116, 130; shameless pursuit of 144; Trump lacks 45; unreality of 150; white supremacist 45–6, 95, 197, 200, 206
imagining the future 71
images of mirrors 94–6
immigrants 27, 149, 166, 173, 182, 200, 202; anti-immigrant 97; characterization of 98; criminal 24; dangerous 77, 83; excluding 4; evil 211; Hispanic 142; illegal 39, 91; locking up 206; loss of jobs to 149; not welcome 39; opposition to 131; subsidized by taxes 182; undocumented 84
inconvenient truths 140
individualism 57, 104, 131, 153, 165
infotainment 92
Inside Bureaucracy 119
intersubjective 79, 165; structure 168, 214
intersubjective experience 68, 165, 168
introduction to: ideology 115; psychoanalytic theory 7, 14
invention of facts 68
Iran 29, 80, 107, 152
irrational 68, 122–7, 146, 211; attachments 150; decision-making 53; exuberance 146, 154; fears 211; hatred 83, 110; human factors 148; in hierarchical organizations 125; side of groups 168; side of human nature 123; side of organizations 126; unreality 146
ISIS 91, 141

Jacoby, Henry 117–8, 123
Jamestown, VA, slavery 199
Jefferson, Thomas 58. 165, 174
Jim Crow laws 12, 198–200, 203
Jindal, Bobby 105, 185
Jobs, Steve 52
John Birch Society 131
Justice Department 139

Kafka, Franz 149
Kansas 11, 179–82
Kasich, Jeff 164

Kelly, John (General) 41
Former White House Chief of Staff 41
Kernberg, Otto 125
key year for media 1996 93
Khashoggi, Jamal 55
Kim Jong-un 84; Little Rocket Man 84
Kirk, Russel 165
Kleinknecht, William 153
kleptocracy 38
Know-Nothing: nativism 39
Koch brothers 40, 44; Charles 180; David 180
Krauthammer, Charles 165
Kristol, Bill 4, 44
Krugman, Paul 40, 105, 153
Ku Klux Klan (KKK) 44, 140, 199–201

laissez-faire pro-capitalism 135, 180
Lawrence, Gordon 148
leader(s) 53, 88, 94, 109, 152–3, 169; aggression of 98, 105; all-powerful 80, 97; authoritarian 24, 62, 65–6, 76, 188, 197; autocratic 6, 9, 33, 64–5,72, 79, 104, 127, 213; avenging 70, 97; becomes disorganized 80; caretaking of by followers 79; chaotic: chaos 2–3, 9, 39, 70–1, 75, 100, 103–12, 209; charismatic 59, 66–72, 75–82, 88–90, 110, 158, 161, 171,191, 204–6; constructed in mind 77; idealization of 27, 99, 176; identification with 23, 54, 153; in mind 81, 90, 100; fantasized 98; fight/flight leader 25, 46, 83, 106–7, 111, 150–2, 156–7, 171, 190, 205–6; followership 83, 111, 163, 170, 210; legal authority of 78; loyalty to leader 78, 64–8, 86–9, 125; narcissistic 28, 193; of thought development 3–4, 36, 117, 147, 163–5, 214; other in mind 133; paranoid 46, 66, 78, 82, 107, 111, 158, 173, 184; rage 98–9, 111; routinized 121–2, 126; self-presentation 77; style 33, 63, 107; toxic 72; vacuum 104; victimize the people 179, 207
learning curve xii–xiv, 7, 12, 207, 209–11, 216; as metaphor 209
Lee, Bandy 53, 57
Lee, Robert E., park 199
Levinson, Harry 124–5
Levitsky, Steven 5, 65
LGBTQ 83, 140, 166, 174, 180; anti-4, 41; community 56; rights 75

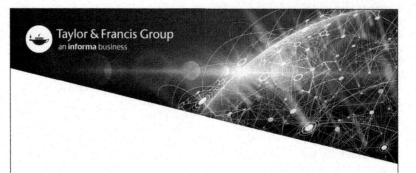